OXFORD

Essential
Office Handbook

THE OXFORD

Essential
Office Handbook

BERKLEY BOOKS, NEW YORK

THE OXFORD ESSENTIAL OFFICE HANDBOOK

A Berkley Book / published by arrangement with
Oxford University Press, Inc.

PRINTING HISTORY
Berkley edition / July 2004

ISBN: 0-425-19703-4

A BERKLEY BOOK®
Berkley Books are published by The Berkley Publishing Group,
a division of Penguin Group (USA) Inc.
375 Hudson Street, New York, New York 10014.
BERKLEY and the "B" design
are trademarks belonging to Penguin Group (USA) Inc.

PRINTED IN THE UNITED STATES OF AMERICA

10 9 8 7 6 5 4 3 2 1

Contents

Staff

Senior Editor: Erin McKean

Managing Editor: Constance Baboukis

Staff Editor: Christine A. Lindberg

Manuscript Editor: Julia Penelope

Special Consultant: Evan Schnittman

Contributing Editors: Joseph Gerharz, Orin Hargraves, Sandra Ban, Linda Costa, Beth Ann Koelsch, Joseph Patwell, Marina Padakis

Preface

The Oxford Essential Office Handbook is intended as a comprehensive, easy-to-use guide to modern office life and procedures for working professionals, students, and anyone who works nine to five. This handbook covers all aspects of basic office work, including proper telephone, fax, and e-mail etiquette, using common filing systems, understanding important business and financial concepts (P&L, ROI, price to earnings ratio), mail and e-mail safety, giving presentations (with PowerPoint), making meeting arrangements, and much more.

Two comprehensive sections outline business writing and correspondence, explaining not only how to go about writing in a business context, but also proper capitalization and punctuation, commonly misspelled and confused words, and common letter formats. A glossary of commonly used business terms is also included.

This handy "essential" guide is an excellent yet economical choice for those who need a quick reference for standard office practices, and is a helpful and comprehensive guide for those just entering the world of work.

CHAPTER 1

Your Office Environment

The office of the twenty-first century is vastly different from that of the twentieth century. Most of the obvious differences have been introduced by rapidly changing technologies that have altered the way office records are updated and maintained and how office space is utilized. In the offices of large and small businesses, medical establishments, and institutions, virtually all of the information required for efficiently running and maintaining the organization is now processed and stored in computer memory, eliminating the need for rows of file cabinets and the time involved in handling paper documents. Branches and divisions of organizations are connected by large area networks (LANs), eliminating the time and expense of exchanging information using postal services. Keyboards have replaced manual typewriters and adding machines. Every aspect of conducting any kind of business or institution is now done electronically, and familiarity with the software required for working successfully in any office is a necessity.

BASIC TECHNOLOGIES

In the twentieth century, the telephone was the technological breakthrough in the workplace. It connected the outside world to the business world, giving salespeople a running start. That same technology plays another role in today's business world. Telephone lines give our computers extra "connecting" power through the use of e-mail, voice mail, faxes, scanners, modems, printers, and the Internet, making business transactions more convenient and cost-effective. Where once, not so long ago, business meetings required sometimes lengthy and expensive travel plans, business can be conducted via e-mail, fax, teleconferencing, and even videoconferencing, connecting businesspeople and their prospective clients all over the globe.

Computer chips are finding their way into everything from cash registers, calculators, and cameras to stoves and refrigerators, medical equipment, and airplane cockpits. Increased memory in computers offers the office professional greater diversification in the workplace through a variety of software programs. Through the use of sophisticated computer programs and printers, offices can save money by creating printed brochures and other materials with offset printing quality in-house.

Computers

The computer, a device that processes information through **input** and **output** of data, has become the central feature of the workplace. Computers in all shapes, sizes, and capacities are now available. An organization can choose an industrial-size mainframe computer, or one or more personal computers (PCs), depending on the size of the company. The larger PC that sits on a desk and has multiple components is called a **desktop**. Individuals may also have the more compact and portable **laptop** PC available to them. Laptops (or notebooks) are especially useful for businesspeople who travel frequently and need to be able to connect to their home office or to clients or to work while they travel. Business travelers also may use **PDAs** (personal digital assistants) or

tablet PCs when they travel. These are smaller than laptops and used mostly for quick access to information rather than for serious work. A laptop or desktop computer that is not connected to other computers is called a **stand-alone**. A **network** can link together several computers for the purpose of sharing information, and printers and communicating with other computers. The main computer in such a network is called a **server**.

MEMORY.

The computer's **memory** stores data. There are two types of memory: **RAM** and **ROM**. RAM (random-access memory) is the temporary storage of memory. When the computer is turned off, temporarily stored data is lost unless it is stored on floppy disks or on the hard drive. ROM (read-only memory) is unalterable, permanent memory, encompassing such information as the internal instructions for the computer's operation.

Computers have varying amounts of RAM and ROM, depending on the model or make of the computer—the more the better. Eight binary digits (**bits**) equal a **byte**, which can represent a single character, digit, or letter. The amount of information a computer can store is expressed in bytes:

1 kilobyte (KB)   = 1 thousand bytes
1 megabyte (MB) = 1 million bytes
1 gigabyte (GB)   = 1 billion bytes
1 terabyte (TB)   = 1 trillion bytes

Printers

The three most common types of printers are ink-jet, dot matrix, and laser. Cost and the particular needs of an office must be considered when deciding which type of printer to buy. Is a printer that uses only a black ink cartridge all you need?

Color printers provide eye-catching graphics when making presentations to prospective clients or colleagues, but is the extra cost of such a printer warranted? Is speed or appearance a factor? If not, a dot matrix printer may suffice. If quality or speed is important, then the expense of a laser printer is justified. These are all factors to be considered before buying a printer.

Here's a brief overview of what each type of printer can do:

laser: A laser printer operates by electrostatically charging a photosensitive drum that attracts toner particles. These particles are heat fused onto paper in the form of the image being copied. These printers offer fast, attractive print images.

ink-jet: An ink-jet printer sprays tiny droplets of ink onto the paper to form the type or graphics being printed. While not as fast as the laser printer, it offers good quality print images. Because of its compact size, it can be easily transported for laptop users.

dot matrix: A dot matrix printer has pins that strike the paper through a ribbon, making dots on the paper that form the type or graphics. These printers work well with multipage forms such as invoices and purchase orders. They also use continuous-feed paper with holes on the sides that fit into tracks to help the feeding process. After the page is printed, the form can be separated at the perforations at the bottom and the sides. The dot matrix printer is not a high-quality printer, but it's economical and useful in the workplace.

Copiers

The copier, like the telephone and computer, has become an essential item in the workplace. The kind of copier to buy is

Do You Need a PDA?

You've seen them and they look seductive, those tiny electronic devices that are half appointment book and half *Star Trek* tricorder. But do you really need one?

1. Do you already have an organizer that works? If you're committed to your paper planner or to a calendar function on your desktop computer, it may be more trouble than it's worth to switch to a PDA.
2. Do you travel often? Travelers often find PDAs attractive for two reasons: their small size and the automatic backup of data to a computer at home or work. Losing a paper planner while traveling can be traumatic. Losing a PDA is a little less so, since at least you know that you haven't lost the information, just the information container.
3. Are you happy with gadgets? If your VCR is unprogrammed and you regularly swear at your desktop computer, a PDA might be more than you want to wrestle with. However, most PDAs have good interfaces and can be learned quickly, even by the most tech-averse of users.
4. What kind of information do you need to access? If you only need a basic calendar, names and phone numbers, and a calculator, there are smaller and cheaper devices that might meet your needs at any office supply store. Check them out before springing for a larger PDA.
5. Will your desktop computer support a PDA? Many older computers may not have the USB (universal serial bus) connectors that modern PDAs require. Adapters are available but are an extra expense and may add to your setup and troubleshooting time. You don't want to have to upgrade your entire system just to use a PDA.
6. Will your desktop software support a PDA? One of the main advantages to using a PDA is being able to synchronize data from your desktop applications to the

(continued)

PDA. If your company mandates a particular e-mail, meeting coordination, or calendar software, make sure that it will 'sync' with your PDA. Otherwise, you'll spend a lot of time manually entering information, or wishing you had.

7. Do you already carry another electronic device? If you carry a cell phone or digital camera for work, you might want to look into multipurpose PDAs. However, make the switch only if the multipurpose device fulfills all your requirements for both devices.

8. Do you lose things? If you go through a dozen pens a week, two pairs of reading glasses a month, and replace your keys twice a year, you may not be the best candidate for a PDA.

9. Do you need specialized information regularly? There are many add-on software titles for PDAs that deliver everything from prescription drug interaction information to the location of the closest Chinese restaurant to stock portfolio management. If having such information on-the-go would be useful to you, consider a PDA.

10. Will it improve your life? If a PDA is just one more thing to keep track of and worry about, stick to your paper planner or current system. However, if you think you would use a PDA to the fullest—including reading e-books or playing games or keeping track of your personal finances—there are many Web sites that will guide you through buying the one that's right for you.

determined by the volume it will handle, along with the speed at which it produces copies. Other decisions regarding the capabilities needed in the office include:

- color copies or black-and-white?
- collating?
- stapling?

- enlarging/reducing?
- automatic feed?
- ability to handle pages larger than 8½" x 11" (11" x 17", blue prints, etc.)?

The number of special features usually determines the cost and size of the copier.

Scanners

The central function of a scanner is similar to that of a fax machine or copier: it reproduces an image. The difference is that the scanner can duplicate a photo that can then be transferred to a computer document, making it more polished, professional, informative, and visually appealing. A scanner can also take a typeset text and place it into a word-processing document, eliminating the need to rekey and reformat. Scanners are capable of handling black-and-white text, color, or gray for photographs, depending on the model.

Not long ago dismissed as superfluous equipment, the scanner has increasingly become a standard fixture in the modern office. If its value had to be expressed in three words, they would be *time, space,* and *aesthetics*.

Time. Scanning a document of prepared text and/or graphics is an electronic imaging process that replicates the document into, for instance, a word-processing program, making it directly accessible for review or revision. Eliminating the need for rekeying and reformatting not only saves time, but assures the exactitude of the copy as well.

Space. After only a few years of operation, the typical office has any number of file cabinets, boxes, and shelves brimming with inactive printed material. Although many accumulated documents could probably be discarded, this is certainly not a task to be done carelessly, as "inactive" is by no means synonymous with "unnecessary" or "disposable."

The electronic storage facilitated by the technology of scanning provides an efficient alternative to the often unwieldy physical storage of documents.

Aesthetics. Until recently, it was a matter of simple discernment to recognize the difference between expensive farmed-out "professional" graphics and economical in-house "do-it-yourself" graphics. The distinction is becoming less dramatic with the rising availability of affordable high-performance scanners. From brochures to newsletters to portfolios to major presentations, the impact of artwork is a worthy consideration.

SCANNER FEATURES.

For the best results in the reproduction of photographic material, choose a scanner that fits your needs, inquiring into such features as:

- high resolution
- automatic sheet feeder
- speed
- software
- correction

SCANNING TIPS.

Once a document has been scanned into the computer, it should always be backed up (for example, on a diskette). Before disposing of the paper pages, it is wise to confirm that they were scanned successfully and that they are electronically retrievable.

Fax Machines

The fax machine has given the workplace a tremendous boost, enabling businesses to cut expenses and save time by faxing documents rather than using postal services ("snail mail") or overnight delivery services. The fax machine scans an image of a document, transmits it via telephone lines, and duplicates it at the recipient's fax machine in a matter of seconds. The unit may be a stand-alone version or one that operates through the computer or via the Internet. When choosing a fax machine, print quality and speed are important factors to consider. Checking into special features that may be available, along with monthly telephone or provider fees, is important as well.

Multifunction Machines

Some machines are capable of handling more than one function, such as a telephone/answering machine/fax/copier unit. In an office where space is limited, the multifunction machine offers compactness and cost-effectiveness while delivering useful and necessary technology. A desktop PC can come equipped with an internal modem that connects the user to the Internet, enables the user to make and receive phone calls, and provides faxing capabilities.

THE INTERNET

The Internet, created by the U.S. Department of Defense in the 1960s, consists of thousands of connected networks of computers that share information. Businesses, schools, libraries, organizations, governments, and individuals use it worldwide for innumerable purposes, especially to send and receive e-mail, to access and retrieve stored documents, information, games, and music, and to conduct such transactions as banking and shopping. **Cyberspace** refers to the environment through which all this information is processed and transferred.

Internet Connections

The computer connects to the Internet through telephone lines via a piece of hardware in the computer called a **modem**. The modem converts the computer information from digital to analog form so that it can be carried by the telephone lines. It is the most common and least expensive form of "dialing up" the Internet. An Internet service provider (ISP), such as AOL, Earthlink, or AT&T, provides such a service for a monthly fee, though there are a few free Internet services available. When Internet use is completed, there is a disconnect feature to click on, which is the equivalent of hanging up the receiver of a telephone. A digital subscriber line (DSL) is more costly but is very fast because the telephone line is always open, much the same as leaving a telephone off the hook after connecting to another party. It requires, however, a different type of modem. Another option is having a television cable hooked to the personal computer, rather than going through the telephone lines. This requires extra hardware. Monthly fees are similar to that of DSL, and the connection is also faster than the dial-up option.

The software required to use the Internet is called a **browser**. This provides the PC user with a means to connect to information stored on the Web in places called **Web sites**. Microsoft Internet Explorer or Netscape is sometimes already installed in newer computers; e-mail capability is usually part of the browser package. Common e-mail programs include Microsoft Outlook and Eudora.

THE WORLD WIDE WEB

The "World Wide Web," or "the Web," is the most used aspect of the Internet. It contains an unlimited source of information that is accessed by keying in a uniform (or universal) resource locator (URL), the unique domain name assigned to each site. The URL is also called the "address" of a Web site. The domain name identifies where the site can be found on the Internet. A typical URL contains several different elements, each of which provides specific information, and might look like this:

http://www.sdsu.edu

Many URLs begin with http://, which stands for hypertext transfer (or transport) protocol and identifies the address as a Web site; www. indicates that the site will be found on the World Wide Web. Some URLs begin with ftp:// (file transfer protocol) or gopher:// (individuals and organizations around the world have set up several thousand Gopher computers, or servers, that provide Internet users with a wide variety of information presented as menus, or lists, written in plain language). The address ends with one of the following, which identifies the kind of site:

.com (commercial)
.net   (network)
.org   (non-profit)
.gov   (government)
.edu   (educational)

These elements of URLs are read "dot-com," "dot-net," "dot-org," and so on. In the example provided, "sdsu" tells users that this is the address for San Diego State University, and ".edu" identifies it as an educational institution.

Occasionally the core of an address is shared by two different domains. The United States Postal Service is at www.usps.com, but the United States Power Squadrons is at www.usps.org. The computer will display a prompt requiring the user to choose the proper domain.

Setting Favorites (Internet Explorer) or Bookmarks (Netscape)

The modern office relies on the Internet in numerous ways, not the least of which are for the gathering and dissemination of information. The Internet has become essential in business research: for observing competition, for profiling clients, for accessing industry news, for following worldwide trends, and so on. With so many sources to track, an online bookmark system can be a useful tool. Here are some tips to setting up and organizing a directory of Web site favorites:

1. Bookmark (that is, save a link to) every Web site that may be of use to you at a later time. This insures simple retrieval of an address that may otherwise become lost or forgotten. For sites that are visited daily, bookmarking is especially convenient.

2. To save a link to the page you are viewing in Internet Explorer, click "Favorites" on the toolbar at the top of the screen. Within the Favorites menu, click on "Add to Favorites." You may click "OK" to add the link to a running list, or you may assign it to an appropriate folder. You can manage the content of your Favorites folders at any time by clicking "Organize Favorites."

3. To save a link to the page you are viewing in Netscape, click "Bookmarks" on the toolbar and then "Add to Bookmarks." If you want to move it to a folder, open the Bookmarks menu and click on "Organize Bookmarks."

4. Create a logical taxonomy for your Favorites/ Bookmarks. Broad subjects can be organized by primary folders with titles like "Marketing" and "Competition." As relevant Web sites are added, subfolders may be created. For example, if your Marketing folder has 20 bookmarks, you may want to organize them further in subfolders such as "Online," "Direct Mail," and "Outdoor Advertising."

—*Evan Schnittman*

If the user does not know a specific Web site address, a search can be made using a **search engine**. When a key phrase or word is keyed in, the search engine is activated to locate any sites that may be linked to that topic. For example, if the user is looking for publishers, keying in "publishers" will result in millions of Web matches. If the user wants to narrow the search, the phrase "publishers in New York" will result in a more specific listing. (Using quotation marks around the request tells the search engine to restrict its search only to those words in that order, although the protocols for different search engines may differ.) Many Web pages have their own search engine, but users can choose from dozens of others, including AltaVista, Excite, Google, Lycos, Yahoo!, and Dogpile. Because of the volume of information stored on the Internet, not every keyword or Web site has been indexed by a search engine, resulting in incomplete listings, and search engines frequently turn up unrelated, therefore useless, information. The more specific the request to a search engine, the fewer the irrelevant Web sites listed.

Web Page Formats

Hypertext Markup Language (HTML) is a coding system that produces readable text but also contains hidden text that tells the browser where to display bold text or where to put graphics. Also, HTML lets the user know where to find more information on certain subjects within the text by highlighting words or phrases, often by underlining them. By clicking on the underlined word or phrase, the browser sends the user to another Web page or **link**. The first page of a Web site is called the **home page**. Web sites consisting of more than one page to browse through usually provide a link that will take the reader back to the **home page**.

CHAPTER 2

You and Your Career Development

CAREER DEVELOPMENT

Computers and the Internet have made business more efficient, but the new technologies have also speeded up ordinary business processes and made them more complicated. The business of any typical company requires support for its computers, telephone system, and e-mail, fax, and Internet capabilities. The modern office professional can choose from among several different career paths, from specializing in technical support, data management, or telecommunications to being a generalist and doing a little bit of everything. Even in specialized fields like information management, you can learn a lot on the job, but you will first need formal education to acquire systematic, expert knowledge.

As a beginner, you may choose to be a generalist. Because the generic duties of an office are easier to grasp than those requiring specialized training and knowledge, you can be immediately productive, while learning new skills along the way. Establishing your usefulness will open doors to expanding your responsibilities. By so doing, you may discover that you have an aptitude for research or data management. Perhaps you'll find that you like and are good at keeping track of times, events, people, and places—in short, managing. Duties and responsibilities vary from business to business, but the fundamental duties typically include:

- answering and routing telephone calls;
- receiving, distributing, and answering mail;
- scheduling meetings and appointments;
- attending meetings and conferences;
- preparing the minutes of meetings;
- making travel arrangements and planning itineraries and schedules;
- operating computers and other equipment;
- doing word processing.

As you acquire experience, your duties may come to include:

- using the Internet for research and purchasing;
- coordinating business and office functions with telecommuters, other departments, and other businesses;
- processing contracts and leases;
- maintaining company books and records;
- managing desktop publishing of business documents;
- managing in-house or outside publishing of business documents;
- purchasing office supplies, equipment, and furniture;
- preparing budgets and financial statements.

At the senior level, your duties probably will include:

- setting work and office standards and being in charge of quality control;
- interviewing, hiring, training, and supervising temporary workers and assistants;
- performing job evaluations;

- setting up and maintaining electronic and traditional filing systems;
- setting up online databases;
- designing, developing, and managing projects.

PREPARING YOUR RÉSUMÉ

Before you begin work on your résumé, take the time to do a thorough, honest self-evaluation. It will be beneficial to assess your marketable skills before applying for a job. Begin by making a simple list, writing down your strengths and weaknesses. Outline your skills and abilities and your work experience as well as your hobbies and other interests. Having such information helps narrow the job-search field and indicates which positions you can realistically apply for with the expectation of being perceived as a serious candidate. (If you're having trouble evaluating yourself, a placement agency has staff qualified to help in this assessment.) Now you're ready to prepare a résumé that will present your skills and experience in the best light.

A résumé is a one- or two-page summary (no more) of your education, skills, accomplishments, and work experience. If you think that the purpose of a résumé is to land you a job, you're wrong. A résumé's purpose is to get you in the door. If you're called for that first interview, your résumé has successfully served its purpose.

Form and Design

Your résumé (along with a cover letter) is your first contact with prospective employers, so keep it simple and keep it clean. The following suggestions will make your résumé easy to scan into a company's database.

- Use white or off-white paper (no colored paper).
- Use 8 1/2" x 11" paper.

- Print on one side of the paper only.
- Use a font size of 10 to 14 points.
- Use a large, clear (nondecorative) typeface.
- Choose one typeface and stick to it.
- Avoid italics, bold print, script, and underlined words.
- Do not use graphics, horizontal or vertical lines, or shading.
- Do not use lines or borders.
- Do not fold or staple your résumé.
- Use a large manila envelope if you must mail your résumé.

The preceding suggestions are designed to make a résumé scannable, which is often a necessity. However, you may wish to create a separate version of your résumé, especially if you know for certain that your prospective employer does not scan submitted résumés. In this version you can be more flexible about formatting and aesthetics, but the final product should still have a clean look to it.

All of your contact information—name, address, telephone, e-mail address, Web-site address—should be centered at the top of the first page:

Elaine Bertolli
1234 Grosse Point Court
Hartford, CT 06655
203-925-0032
ebertolli@yahoo.com

Here are some additional dos and don'ts to help you present yourself professionally:

- Avoid nicknames.
- Use a permanent address. If you don't have one yet, use your parents' or a friend's address.

- Use a permanent telephone number and include the area code. (If you have an answering machine, record a neutral greeting.)
- Choose an e-mail address that sounds professional.
- Include your Web site only if it reflects your professional goals.

Content

Businesspeople say that your résumé is a critical tool in evaluating potential candidates' qualifications. They look for key phrases and words, they review accomplishments, and they are critical in assessing the quality of your written document. Your résumé must be perfect in its visual presentation and the quality of the written word.

OBJECTIVE/SUMMARY.

Your objective (or summary) tells potential employers the kind of work you hope to do. Be specific about the job you want, and tailor your objective to each employer you target and every job you seek. This will take some time, but it will be worth your effort.

EDUCATION.

If you're a recent graduate without much work experience, then list your education first. (If you have significant work experience, list that first, followed by your education.) Begin with your most recent educational information and go back in time. Include your degree(s) (A.S., B.S., B.A., M.A., M.S., etc.), your major, the institution(s) attended, and any minor or concentration. If your grade-point average (GPA) is higher than 3.0, include it. Remember to list any academic honors you may have received.

WORK EXPERIENCE.

Give the employer an overview of work that has taught you skills, and use action words (*achieved, acquired, composed, formed, founded, set up, supervised,* etc.) to describe your job duties. List your work experience in reverse chronological order, as you did with your education: put your last job first and go backward to your first relevant job. Include the following information for each job you list: title of position, name of the organization/business, location of work (town, state), dates of employment, and a description of your work responsibilities emphasizing specific skills and achievements.

OTHER INFORMATION.

If you think it is relevant to the job you're applying for, you may want to include additional information, such as special skills or competencies, leadership experience in volunteer organizations, and sports participation. If you have access to a career services office, someone there can advise you on the kinds of information that might be important enough to mention.

REFERENCES.

Before you give anyone's name as a reference to a potential employer, ask that person if he or she is willing to give you a reference. Do not include your references on your résumé. At the end of your résumé add: References furnished on request. Or, if your references are available from a career placement office, provide that information.

Reviewing Your Work

You've written your résumé, but you aren't finished yet. It's important to check it for spelling and grammatical errors.

A Sample Résumé

LI-YANG MAI
4446 River Ridge Road
Topeka, KS 66600
785-272-0102
LIYM0016@mindspan.com

OBJECTIVE
An entry-level position in the U.S. Department of
Agriculture, especially one related to genetics research

EDUCATION
Bachelor of Science in Agriculture, 2002
Texas A&M University, College Station, TX

RELATED EXPERIENCE
• Collected samples of insects found in Central Mexican
  cornfields (summer, 1998)
• Identified and catalogued Central Mexican insects
  (Carney Research Lab, 1998–1999)
• Gained thorough knowledge of insect identification
  during summer studies at Central Kansas State
  Agricultural Station (1999)

Before anyone looks at your résumé, run it through a spell-
check on your computer. Next, ask someone whose opinion
you respect to read it over and comment on it. Ask another
friend to proofread your work. The more people who read
your résumé, the more likely it is that misspelled words and
awkward phrases will be noticed (and corrected).

JOB TITLES AND JOB DESCRIPTIONS

As companies, organizations, and institutions evolve, job
titles change, as do the job descriptions associated with

- Worked as undergraduate research assistant
  (Carney Research Lab, 1999–2001)

ORGANIZATION/COORDINATION
- Coordinated and wrote research reports for Carney
  Research Lab
- Designed a study of corn fungi in a research project
- Coordinated research projects for beginning agriculture
  students

PROFESSIONAL PROFILE
- Highly organized and motivated
- Excited about genetics research in agricultural science
- Able to work carefully and attend to minute details
- Accustomed to long hours in the lab

EMPLOYMENT HISTORY
Library Assistant, Texas A&M University, College
   Station, TX (1999–Present)
Night Manager, Patch Convenience Store, College
   Station, TX (1997–1998)
Cashier, Bright Days Discount Store, Topeka, KS
   (summers, 1996–1998)

---

them. For example, the old job title "secretary" was used in such a broad and generic sense for so long that the title eventually took on a demeaning connotation, especially for secretaries who had reached a high level of responsibility. Today, those with specific secretarial skills and various levels of experience can enjoy more appropriate titles, such as "administrative assistant" and "executive secretary."

As traditional secretarial duties have become more and more dependent on electronic resources, the once clear line between secretarial jobs and non-secretarial jobs has become less distinct. In the past, for instance, good typing

Sample Cover Letter

Employers expect a résumé to be accompanied by a cover letter, which should be written in a formal style, but without sounding stuffy or awkward. A conventional cover letter is also part of selling yourself to a potential employer. It should identify the position for which you're applying, contain a brief outline of your skills and experience, indicate that you know something about the organization, and inform the employer when you'll be available. (For additional information on writing conventional business letters, see Chapter 8.)

José Hernández-Hidalgo
603 Ventura Court
Santa Barbara, CA 94512
June 17, 2002

Ms. Elizabeth Corning
Personnel Manager
Artemis Publishing
1601 Avenue of the Americas
New York, NY 10011

Dear Ms. Corning:

I am applying for the position of editorial assistant advertised in the Career Services Center at New York University. The position seems to fit well with my education, experience, and career interests.

According to the advertisement, the position requires excellent communication skills, computer literacy, and a

skills were hardly a concern for someone with no interest in secretarial work. Today, most office employees rely daily on their computers; hence, reliable keying is now a skill required at virtually all levels of office work. Conversely, those whose responsibilities are primarily secretarial may find themselves dealing with such diverse issues as elec-

B.A. degree in the sciences or humanities. I have just graduated from New York University this month with a B.A. degree in English, with a concentration in technical and scientific writing, and with minors in biology and chemistry. My studies have included courses in computer science, vertebrate and invertebrate biology, organic chemistry, and modern literature. I understand that the position also requires a candidate who works well with people, is attentive to detail, works well under the pressure of deadlines, and is able to deal with many different kinds of people. These are skills I developed both in my coursework and in my summer work at Goldentree Books, Inc., in Garden City, New York.

My background and career goals match your requirements well, and I am confident that I can perform the job effectively. I am excited about the possibility of working for a high-profile publishing house well-known for the quality of its publications. If you would like to schedule an interview with me, please call me at 914-997-1642. I am available at your convenience.

Thank you for your consideration.

Sincerely,

[Signature]

José Hernández-Hidalgo
Encl: Résumé

tronic communications and compliance with state and federal regulations.

Certain job titles include words that specify ranks within the company hierarchy. The most common are "assistant," "associate," "senior," and "executive" (in order from lowest to highest in the hierarchy). In job postings, more general designations are often used, usually "entry-level," "intermediate," and "advanced."

Entry-level positions typically require basic skills in keyboarding and communication (written and verbal). The work is closely supervised and is usually repetitive. Many office professionals begin at the entry level as a way of "paying their dues" and adapting the general skills learned in school to the style of a particular company. An intermediate position is offered to an individual who is able not only to fulfill the obligations of an entry-level position, but who is ready to take on more responsibilities, presumably with the intention of working toward a promotion to an advanced position.

An advanced position requires an excellent command of English, speed and accuracy in keyboarding, computer literacy, and knowledge of the company's standard operating procedures. Workers in advanced positions have much more autonomy and responsibility; they work with minimal supervision and are expected to be able to supervise others, especially those in entry-level and intermediate positions.

Advanced positions also require specific traits of character or temperament in addition to technical proficiency, depending on the nature of the business or the function of a department within a company. For instance, a publishing house that publishes textbooks or other hardcover books needs assistants with proven experience in copyediting and proofreading. These tasks, which can be exacting and tedious, are well-suited to a detail-oriented individual with a high threshold for concentration and tedium. In a magazine publishing house, however, or at a newspaper, there are nonstop deadlines, so an attention to detail must be balanced with the ability to work well under pressure.

There are advanced positions in specialized fields such as medicine and law (the "learned professions") that require knowledge and understanding of the technical vocabulary and language usage of the profession, knowledge of the professional ethics of the learned profession, knowledge of federal and state laws, regulations, and guidelines affecting these professions, and knowing how to work with and process the numerous medical, legal, and insurance documents and forms. Such knowledge can be acquired either by formal schooling or by long experience working in one of the learned professions. In addition to mastery of these very demanding intellectual technical skills, which must be performed with perfect accuracy and great speed, an advanced office professional in a learned profession may also be expected to manage the office as well, a position that requires great organizational skill, efficiency, tact, and discretion.

In sum, the proper matching of job to individual is vital to any company's success. When on a job search, make the effort to match yourself to appropriate job opportunities. Honest self-evaluation and clear career objectives will help both you and those from whom you seek employment.

CAREER PATHS

As an example of how complicated office work has become and how fast an advanced professional career in a learned field has grown, consider that the career of a paralegal and one in the field of information technology (IT) did not exist thirty years ago and probably could not have been predicted. The work that paralegals now do was done by lawyers, which was very expensive for their clients, or by office staff who often did not have the necessary skill or experience. The position of the paralegal was created in order to keep lawyers' fees affordable for clients. The work that a paralegal does in a law office can be learned on the job, but an advanced office professional in another field (say, in insurance), might find it advisable to earn a paralegal certificate or degree in order to begin work at a law office at the same level of responsibility and salary as in the insurance industry. Many community and four-year colleges offer paralegal courses that can be taken full-time during the day (usually for one full academic year), on an accelerated basis (two semesters of courses taught in one semester), at nights, or on weekends. Such flexibility allows the aspiring paralegal to select a schedule of courses that fits in with his or her business, personal, and financial requirements. In addition, the schools and colleges provide professional contacts for their graduates with employment agencies and law firms.

Information technology (IT) is already of vital importance to all businesses and will become even more critical in the future; IT is, therefore, an excellent choice for a career path. By definition, "information technology" is the study or use of systems—especially of computers and telecommunications systems—for storing, retrieving, and sending data, sound, and video. Every business function nowadays has physical tasks and corresponding IT functions: computers and telecommunications are used to perform routine tasks such as accounting, record keeping, payroll preparation, and the processing and fulfillment of orders. In addition, IT allows companies to collect and analyze more data than ever before, which results in streamlining production, marketing, and distribution within a company and between a company and its customers or suppliers. Using IT, a company can develop new products and services or modify existing products and services more rapidly for its customers, thereby gaining a competitive advantage.

The most common business uses for computers are: (1) word processing, (2) communications, (3) developing and maintaining databases, (4) accounting, (5) spreadsheets, and (6) graphics. All companies will use the first three applications and, depending on the size and nature of the business, most companies will use some or all of the others.

Word processing is a facility that enables users to compose, edit, reformat, store, and print documents.

Communications using computers is the sending and receiving of data from computer to computer; it also includes Internet research, videoconferencing, and person-to-person communication via e-mail.

Databases are organized, structured sets of data in a computer, accessed by a database management system (DBMS). A database consolidates and stores information from many separate files so that a common pool of information serves as a central file for data processing.

Accounting procedures (that is, bookkeeping, maintaining and auditing a company's books, analyzing the financial position of a business) can be done either within a business or by an outside firm, depending on the size of a company.

Spreadsheets are computer programs used especially for budgets and general accounting. A spreadsheet consists of horizontal rows and vertical columns, with the boxes (called "cells") containing numerical information and formulae or text. Each time the value within a cell is changed, the values of all the other cells whose values depend on it are changed.

Graphics (in full, **computer graphics**) are visual elements of text made, displayed, and manipulated using a special computer program. Graphics applications include:

- *paint programs,* which allow the user to make rough freehand drawings that can be stored and edited;
- *illustration/design programs,* also called "draw programs," which are more advanced than paint programs and allow the user to draw precise curved lines;

- *presentation graphics software,* which allows the user to make bar charts, pie charts, and other images for printed reports and slideshow presentations;
- *desktop publishing* (DTP), which is the use of a computer and a page printer to perform many of the functions of a print shop, including page layout and design, choice of fonts and type size, and the inclusion of diagrams and pictures. Many companies will use outside printers for full-size books or magazines, but will use in-house DTP for advertisements, brochures, or newsletters.
- *computer-aided design* (CAD), which allows the user to design a product or manipulate a specific kind of design, especially in architecture, in electronics, and in electrical, mechanical, and aeronautical engineering.

Within IT there are many different careers to choose from, depending on one's aptitude and interest. The word-processing and communications functions are nearly universal at home, school, and business; they are relatively simple and easy to learn. Other functions can be learned, at least in part, on the job, but in order to gain proficiency to learn a new career or advance your current one, formal study is necessary.

If, for instance, you have good organizing skills, database management is a possible career choice. A database is somewhat like a library's card catalog or a filing system in that the books, papers, or data are organized into a system for easy access and retrieval. A database is made up of fields, records, and files. A **field** is a space set aside for a piece of information. In a phone book entry, for example, there are three fields: one for the name, one for the address, and one for the phone number. The **record** consists of all the fields in the phone book entry. All the records in the phone book, from AAA Auto to Zyza, are, in computing terms, the **file**. The data in a database are accessed by a DBMS, a collection of programs for the retrieval, modification, and storage of data.

You can learn some aspects of database management on the job—for example, by helping a technical expert set up an electronic filing system or by sorting and updating files. Eventually, however, you will need to know something about programming languages, for which you will have to go to school. Nearly all community and four-year colleges offer certificate or degree programs in database management.

If you are creative and have visual skills, then computer graphics may interest you. Skills in the various applications of computer graphics are valuable for marketing and advertising, and for using desktop publishing to produce employee handbooks, instruction manuals, house organs, and magazines. Word-processing skill is essential, and you can also acquire some on-the-job experience in setting up columns and charts, creating graphs, drawing pictures, and using shade and colors. Many of the applications of computer graphics, however, need computers with a powerful central processing unit (CPU) and a very large memory. Moreover, the software for computer graphics requires a graphics monitor and support for the graphics standards. Many, or most, companies will not have computer graphics because of the special requirements and will have such work done by outside contractors.

Many computer graphics professionals prefer Apple computers ("Macs") rather than the PCs used in nearly all businesses and at home. If a career in computer graphics, appeals to you, you may have to become proficient on both types of computer. In any case, it will be necessary to take courses in computer art and graphics, and it would also be helpful to study public relations, advertising, and marketing principles.

EDUCATION

Physicians, lawyers, scientists, and professors continue their professional education throughout their working lives by conducting their own research and writing up the results for publication and by reading journals in their fields. So, too, businesspeople will—and must—continue their education for the rest of their careers. For most, frequent or daily reading of the business and other sections of newspapers such as the *New York Times*, the *Washington Post*, and the *Wall Street Journal* will keep them abreast of recent developments in business, politics, and computer technology.

The daily reading of well-written material has the added advantage of providing a model for writing good, clear English. Indeed, all the courses you can take—computer science, accounting, paralegal studies, computer graphics, finance, database management, advertising, marketing— will not advance your career unless you can write clear, simple English. The effectiveness of an expensive, glossy, well-researched, four-color brochure will be undone if it contains such howlers as "It's application to our system ...," "There expectations were not met," or "Please join Lee and I for lunch." Many law firms require writing samples from paralegals applying to their firms, and many publishing houses administer tests in copyediting for even relatively senior positions, not to determine whether or not the applicants know legal terminology or usage or how to edit a manuscript, but to ascertain how well the applicants can read, write, and edit Standard English.

For those interested in accounting, business administration, database management, or computer systems theory, courses in mathematics above introductory calculus are necessary.

THE JOB SEARCH

In the ups and downs of the job market, it is imperative that job seekers know what is available in order to avoid the pitfalls of wasted time and energy in their search for the perfect job. After assessing what skills you can offer, check various sources to see if the occupation you are interested in is viable. Oftentimes certain career choices become saturated in the marketplace while there are insufficient qualified applicants for other positions. Here are some sources for finding out which positions are most in demand:

- employment agencies
- the Internet
- newspapers
- trade journals
- libraries
- word-of-mouth
- cold calls to area businesses

OPPORTUNITIES IN OTHER COUNTRIES.

Don't overlook the possibility of working in another country. The Internet offers many listings for foreign job opportunities. Multinational companies will also list overseas jobs in newspapers and trade journals. Be aware that certain criteria must be met, and a background check is usually done before an applicant is seriously considered for a position.

PROFESSIONAL ASSISTANCE.

The professional with lofty goals has a much greater chance at success and climbing the corporate ladder through a mentor or a good working relationship with another successful professional. Sound advice from someone who has "been there" is invaluable, whether it is in regard to deciding whether to make a career change or to accept new responsibilities or promotions. The "who you know" game may have been around a very long time, but it is still extremely valid.

YOUR FIRST JOB

Taking on that first job out of school is very exciting but can also bring uncertainty and insecurity. It's the true test of how much was absorbed in class and can now be applied in the workplace, in addition to the problem of fitting in with a whole new environment. Finding that perfect job, however, will take some planning. Unfortunately, if the job market is slow, there may be few choices. On the other hand, a booming economy will open the field in such a way that a job prospect can be identified by answering a few questions:

- Am I willing to relocate? How far?
- What size company would I like to work in?
- Do I want a job that deals with the public?
- What kind of job will highlight my strengths?
- What are my salary requirements?
- What kind of work schedule will fit my lifestyle?

If the answers to any of these questions aren't immediately obvious, perhaps an employment agency can help find the perfect job fit. Being uncertain about the perfect career may also warrant a look at a temporary employment agency. Some companies require extra help at busy times of the year, don't want the expense of hiring a full-time employee, or just want to evaluate whether a position is necessary on a regular or more permanent basis later on. Whatever the reason, working at a job as a "temp" has great advantages for people unable to decide on the type of job they are best suited for. Also, new skills are developed with each temporary position, which adds to your résumé. Trying several temporary jobs

Returning to the Workforce after an Absence

Looking for a job is always challenging. It can feel especially daunting for people who have not been getting a paycheck for a while, whether by choice or not. If this is your situation, here are some tips to help you with the job hunt:

1. Take time to think about what you want to do. You are a different person now than you used to be. Are you interested in the same things you were the last time you were in the job force? Consider attending workshops or talking to a career counselor.

2. Find out what is new in your job field. Read professional journals. Learn about the current issues being discussed by your peers. Pick up on the latest jargon. Talk to people who are currently working in the field you are interested in.

3. Evaluate your skills. The work world has changed while you've been gone. You probably need to update your skills, especially technology and computer skills. Take courses at community colleges or job centers.

4. Call up your former employers and colleagues and all of your friends and let them know you are looking for work again. Network!

5. Build a support system. You don't have to do this alone. Attend workshops for job seekers or form a support group with others.

6. Consider doing temporary work, freelancing, or even volunteering to get your foot back in the door.

7. Be prepared to explain the time gap in your résumé. Prospective employers will want to know what you have been doing in your "time off." Be honest, but emphasize your desire to return to the workforce.

8. Consider doing a "functional" instead of a chronological résumé. Highlight your skills rather than simply list

(continued)

each job you have held. What have you learned in your
time away? Many experiences and skills learned at
home, in school, through volunteer activities, or even in
the pursuit of hobbies are transferable to the workplace.
9. Act confident even if you don't feel that way. Many
people returning to the workforce are stymied by their
fears. A positive attitude is essential. Apply for jobs even
if you don't feel you have all of the necessary credentials
for a particular position.
10. Don't be discouraged by job leads and opportunities that
don't pan out. Finding the right job takes time. Be
persistent and expect a favorable outcome.

also provides you with a firsthand look at the types of jobs
available and the skills required to perform them. Sometimes
a company that hires a temp decides to fill that position permanently, especially if the temp handles the job efficiently
and works well with others.

Whether the first job is temporary, part-time, or full-time,
new skills can be acquired and honed, and confidence can
be boosted. It's a stepping-stone for greater opportunities, as
long as the individual is willing to be open to new challenges
and thought processes.

PROFESSIONAL ORGANIZATIONS
AND ASSOCIATIONS

American Society of Corporate Secretaries (ASCS)
521 Fifth Avenue
New York, NY 10175
Phone: 212-681-2000
Fax: 212-681-2005
E-mail: webmaster@ascs.org
Web: www.ascs.org

Finding Free or Inexpensive Career Advice

Job got you down? Hate what you're doing but you don't know what else to do? Laid off and sick and tired of your industry? Try finding some free or inexpensive career advice online, at the library, and/or in bookstores. A great way to jump-start this process is to take a career assessment test. There are several legitimate career assessments out there, such as the Strong Interest Inventory, the Birkman Career Assessment, and the Myers-Briggs Interest Inventory. Each has its own unique methods and outcomes. Avail yourself of a free assessment, and from there get a few books on the career type you are leaning toward. For starters, check out these resources:

1. http://www.jobhuntersbible.com/counseling/ctests.shtml
   Read this article before you take any test.
2. http://www.quintcareers.com/online_assessment_review.html A helpful review of online career assessments that rates them and lists prices.
3. http://www.allthetests.com/career.php3?katb=0640
   An alternative review of career assessments.
4. http://discovery.skillsone.com/strong/Default.asp
   A free Strong Interest Inventory with a report.
5. http://www.advisorteam.com/user/ktsintro1.asp
   A Myers-Briggs type of test.
6. http://www.princetonreview.com/cte/quiz/default.asp
   A Birkman style quiz.
7. http://www.tenspeedpress.com/catalog/all/item.php3?id=1260 Order the bible of the career hunt, What Color Is Your Parachute? by Richard N. Bolles.
8. http://www.monster.com
   Post your résumé and search for jobs.

—Evan Schnittman

Home Office Association of America (HOAA)
PO Box 51
Sagaponack, NY 11962-0051
Phone: 212-588-9097 / 800-809-4622
Fax: 212-286-4646
E-mail: hoaa@aol.com
Web: www.hoaa.com

International Association of Administrative Professionals
    (IAAP)
10502 NW Ambassador Drive
PO Box 20404
Kansas City, MO 64195-0404
Phone: 816-891-6600
Fax: 816-891-9118
E-mail: service@iaap-hq.org
Web: www.iaap-hq.org

National Association of Executive Secretaries &
    Administrative Assistants (NAESAA)
900 S Washington Street, Suite G-13
Falls Church, VA 22046
Phone: 703-237-8616
Fax: 703-533-1153
Web: www.naesaa.com

National Association of Home Based Businesses, Inc.
    (NABB)
10451 Mill Run Circle, Suite 400
Owings Mills, MD 21117
Phone: 410-363-3698
E-mail: nahbb@msn.com
Web: www.usahomebusiness.com

National Association of Legal Secretaries (NALS)
Resource Center
314 East 3rd Street, Suite 210
Tulsa, OK 74120
Phone: 918-582-5188
Fax: 918-582-5907
E-mail: info@nals.org
Web: www.nals.org

National Association of Working Women (9to5)
1430 W Peachtree Street, #610
Atlanta, GA 30309
Phone: 800-522-0925
Web: www.9to5.org

National Business Association (NBA)
5151 Beltline Road, Suite 1150
Dallas, TX 75254
Phone: 800-456-0440 / 972-458-0900
Web: www.nationalbusiness.org

Office & Professional Employees International Union
    (OPEIU), AFL-CIO, CLC
265 West 14th Street, 6th Floor
New York, NY 10011
Phone: 212-675-3210 / 800-346-7348
E-mail: opeiu@opeiu.org
Web: www.opeiu.org

Professional Secretaries International World Headquarters
10502 NW Ambassador Drive
PO Box 20404
Kansas City, MO 64195-0404
Phone: 816-891-6600
Fax: 816-891-9118

CHAPTER 3

You and Your Colleagues

BUSINESS ETHICS

Many companies specify in their company or employee handbooks the mutual obligations between employer and employee and minimal standards of behavior and procedure. The "learned professions" (medicine, law) have their own standards of professional ethics founded on centuries-old custom and nowadays enforced by federal and state law. In addition, businesses such as banks and brokerage houses are regulated by various federal and state agencies. Some of the rules to be followed are common sense; others must be learned either on the job or by outside reading or classes or by in-house classes and lectures. In general, business ethics require employees:

1. to keep confidential their employer's private business matters and information regarding customers and clients;
2. not to slander or damage the reputation of another or engage in unfair competition with others;
3. to acknowledge a colleague's accomplishments and not claim them for themselves;
4. to take responsibility or blame for their own mistakes and not pass the blame to another;

5. not to use company equipment such as telephones, copiers, and computers for personal matters without permission and to be aware that personal e-mails sent and received on company equipment are not private or protected by the First Amendment;
6. not to take business supplies for personal use;
7. not to leave private or confidential materials on their desks or other unsecured areas;
8. to lock or secure desk drawers, filing cabinets, computers, storage areas, and offices overnight;
9. to ensure that confidential documents are disposed of or destroyed properly and in accordance with state and federal regulations on burning and shredding;
10. to observe copyrights when reproducing paper or electronic documents.

WORKING WITH AND FOR OTHERS

Working in an office or a business means that you will work with people from many different backgrounds with different skills, educations, and limitations. There may, for instance, be someone in the "back room" who does remarkably good and thorough technical analysis and can write clear, succinct reports, but is uncomfortable at company parties and functions. Good sales representatives typically like to be their own boss and set their own schedules; they enjoy traveling and meeting strangers, as part of their sales routine. Neither the retiring analyst nor the extroverted sales representative is likely, usually, to be a good manager. Neither the analyst nor the sales representative needs or wants to be supervised or to supervise others. The analyst's reserved temperament may make interaction with employees strained and artificial; the sales rep, because of a free-and-easy style, is likely to be unsuited to the daily procedures of office work. Yet, both the technical analyst and the sales representative are essential for the success of a business.

At the beginning of your career as an office professional, you can expect—even welcome—training and supervision so that you can learn standard procedures as quickly and efficiently as possible. As you acquire experience and seniority, you will work more and more on your own without direction and, finally, probably train and supervise new employees yourself.

The willingness to contribute to a cooperative work environment is something you should demonstrate at all levels of your career. As a matter of custom, you should:

1. know exactly, from your supervisor, what the standards for your work or a project are;
2. make clear to those you supervise what the standards are, and be eager to help them understand what is expected;
3. maintain close contact with others working on a project so that everyone knows what parts of the project are ahead of schedule, on schedule, or behind schedule;
4. maintain good humor and morale, especially over a long or complex project;
5. use the first person plural pronouns (we, our, us) and not the singular (I, my, me) to reinforce the fact that everyone is included;
6. compliment others publicly for good work;
7. never criticize the work of someone else in public;
8. acknowledge your own mistakes;
9. know your strengths and weaknesses and those of your colleagues, and exploit the strengths and help to improve the weaknesses;

10. pitch in when extra help is needed, and ask for extra help if you need it.

Working for an executive is an acknowledgment of and compliment to your professionalism and competence, but it has its own peculiar difficulty in that your personality and the executive's personality must mesh almost as a single unit. If you and the executive get along, your job will be exciting and personally and professionally rewarding; if not, you will be personally miserable and your career stymied or even ruined.

The executive may be a hands-on manager, closely directing everything and demanding constant feedback, or may prefer to delegate responsibility and keep a watchful eye on long-term developments. The executive may be easy-going and patient or hard-driving and explosive.

Assuming that you and the executive you work for get along, you will become privy to a great deal of important business and personal information. Some of the information may be open and public or may be rumor in the office, but in all cases you must be scrupulously discreet and loyal to your boss. The well-being, even the survival, of the company, the executive's career, and your career, may well depend on your discretion and tact.

The higher up the ladder you go, the less you are told; this applies to men and women, young and old. If you enjoy socializing with your colleagues, you may find that you and they have less occasion to socialize with each other and they may not be so willing as before to talk shop. You will have to make compromises between your career and life outside work.

If you work for several executives, managing your time among them will probably be your most important problem. If it should turn out that you simply do not have enough time

to arrange or manage all your executives' affairs, you owe it
to them and to yourself to tell them exactly what the problems are and to suggest solutions. Perhaps the executives
will arrange among themselves how much of your time each
of them will use; perhaps they will decide to hire more assistants or an assistant for you.

Telecommuting

You may work for someone who travels a lot at regular or irregular intervals or is away at another office or branch for
considerable periods. He or she will not be present for many
routine managerial or executive matters, which will then be
your responsibility. If you find yourself in such a position of
greater responsibility and authority, and work unsupervised
for much or most of the time, you and your supervisor or
executive should be certain that several aspects of the situation are clear to both of you. At the very least, you should:

1. establish clear limits of your responsibilities and
   authority—for example, in signing letters,
   documents, and checks;
2. set up a system of communication, with a backup,
   by telephone (landline, cell phone, and voice mail),
   faxing, and e-mail;
3. determine whom you should contact in
   emergencies or for matters beyond your authority
   when your superior is unavailable.

There should already be in place standard operating procedures for routine office tasks.

Working with Temporary Assistants

Many companies outsource their work in order to save
money. Companies may hire full-time or part-time assistants
or temporaries to work in-house for, say, keyboarding, or

freelancers to work off the business premises. Your company may hire its outside help through an employment contractor such as Kelly Services or Manpower, or it may have its own roster of temps for seasonal work, such as extra sales staff for a large retail store from Thanksgiving till Christmas or extra clerical help during tax season for an accounting firm. If your company has a standard procedure for hiring temps through an agency or a list or roster of temps, all you need do is contact the agency or the temps and fill them in on the latest developments since their last employment.

If your company has no procedure for hiring temps, you may be responsible for interviewing, recommending for hiring, or even hiring temps or assistants. You may also be responsible for training and breaking in assistants and temps, from showing them where to hang their coats and where to find restrooms and the cafeteria to explaining the nature of the project and what they'll be doing. You may even be obliged to relinquish some of your routine duties in order to orient and train temporary assistants.

Training Assistants or Temporary Workers

If you are dealing with skilled temporary workers or assistants, you need only give them specific instructions because they will be familiar with typical office routines and the equipment they will be using. Be sure, however, to show them where your office or work station is and give them your phone extension in case a problem should arise.

If your company is hiring an assistant who has just graduated from school or who is new to the business world, the human resources department will select a list of suitable candidates from which you or your supervisor can choose for further consideration. If your company does not have a human resources department, you or your supervisor will have to make your own selection.

The first test is a negative one: read the applicants' cover letters carefully for spelling, grammar, punctuation, and coherent syntax; if the cover letter has incorrect spelling, grammar, or punctuation or is confusing, consider the candidate no further. If the letter is correct in spelling, grammar, and syntax, then consider whether the letter is a "shotgun blast" with no particular target or whether the letter is directed to your type of business or even to your firm. Obviously, the closer the cover letter comes to the "bull's-eye" of your company's requirements, the more suitable the candidate is.

Next consider the candidate's résumé. If the candidate has prior work experience, check the kinds of businesses for compatibility with your firm. Also take note of the lengths of employment; is there a pattern of reliability? Check references; if none are listed, contact the applicant's former employers. A recent graduate entering the workforce for the first time will likely have little or no work experience; therefore, check the courses the applicant has taken to see if they are relevant to the needs of your business. If the applicant has done any internships, check with the organization for references.

Training experienced temporary workers or assistants is relatively easy; they will need relatively little supervision and have enough experience to recognize an unusual or special problem with which they need help. Recent graduates, however, may be nervous and unsure of themselves no matter what their technical strengths are; everything and everyone is new to them. Your job is to help them settle in and do productive work as quickly as possible. In order to accomplish this, you must:

- be friendly, helpful and patient;
- be aware that many procedures in a business office are simple and logical but not obvious and that what

is second nature to you must be learned by new
employees;

- introduce new assistants to their coworkers and make
  them welcome;
- show the new worker the physical layout of the office;
- instruct the new worker regarding the standard
  business procedures of the office and of office
  etiquette (make sure the new worker has a copy of
  the employee manual or office handbook);
- make sure all pertinent equipment is hooked up and
  operating (computer, telephone and voice mail,
  Internet and e-mail), and that the new worker has
  appropriate supplies (pencils, paper, etc.), and
  explain the company policy on personal calls and
  e-mails (remind the person that e-mail is not private
  and is not protected by the First Amendment);
- set up brief, regular sessions with the new worker—
  such as one session at the end of the workday for
  review of the day's work, and one in the morning for
  instruction about that day's work;
- use positive language in critiquing the new
  employee's work;
- encourage the new employee to ask questions and
  show initiative;
- watch for the new employee's strong and weak points
  and concentrate on improving the latter.

BUSINESS ETIQUETTE

You should treat others the way you would like to be treated.
Courtesy is a two-way street: treat others well and expect to
be treated well yourself. Courtesy reflects favorably on you
personally and on your company. It will be welcomed by

Managing Telecommunications and Telecommuting

Experience shows that teleworkers generally enjoy greater productivity, reduced stress, and improved quality of life over their workplace counterparts. The following ten tips will help you make your teleworking arrangement a success:

1. **Create your work environment:** It's still a job, even if you're doing it in your pajamas. The home workplace has a different set of distractions than the traditional one, and it is not unusual for the teleworker to find the distractions of home far more compelling and attractive, even demanding, than those of the office. Make a place for yourself at home that is reserved for work, and set aside the time that you are going to be there. If necessary, establish a protocol for others in the household who may be tempted to take you away from your work. Get a separate telephone line to take your work calls, put it in your office, and get the household telephone out of there.

2. **Be clear on what your job is:** If your employer already has a teleworking policy and agreement, familiarize yourself with them. If you're starting from scratch, check out some of the agreements and policies published on the Internet in order to formulate your rules. Be sure that you understand your responsibilities and your employer's expectations. Take special care over any part of your teleworking job that is going to create an expense, and be sure that you know who is paying for what.

3. **Make a schedule and keep it:** You need to be available for your colleagues when they expect you to be working, and they need to know if you're not going to be available at a time when you normally would be. Rumors about your activities may start very easily if you're not in the office to set matters straight, so it's important to signal any deviations from your routine in advance via e-mail. Don't forget to build into your daily schedule the breaks that you need from work, especially breaks from sitting at your computer.

4. **Maintain your voice links:** Working at home enables you to streamline communication with your colleagues, cutting out a lot of what is unnecessary and focusing on conveying significant information. But don't let the principle of "out of sight, out of mind" apply to you. Friendly chats with your boss and colleagues are necessary for maintaining your good relations with them, in addition to dealing with matters that are strictly business. When you are not physically present in the office, you need to ensure by the way you communicate that you remain a vivid and positive presence in the minds of those you work with. This is especially important when you need to thank or encourage someone; your phone voice has to do all the work. Remember that the best way to combat the isolation of teleworking some people feel is to maintain close relationships with your workmates.

5. **Maintain your data links:** The data link from your computer to your employer's computer or server is as vital as your voice link. Get the fastest and most reliable data link available for your home, and invest the time to understand how it works and how to troubleshoot it. Make sure that you have a backup link, such as a dial-up modem, to connect you in case the main link fails. Educate yourself as much as you can about your e-mail client software and any other electronic link between you and your employer; you will be a star in the eyes of technical personnel if you can meet them halfway in ironing out any problems that occur.

6. **Respond in real time:** Timely communication with all of your colleagues is the key to assuring them of your competence and effectiveness. You cannot easily dismiss someone inquiring at your office door, and you should not easily dismiss the inquiring e-mail from one of your colleagues or your boss if this is the only way they have of getting in touch with you. Make it a point to respond as quickly as possible to all of those who legitimately require your attention, even if all you can do for the moment is to acknowledge that you

(continued)

hear them. Solicit feedback from your key communication contacts about their contact with you; it is better for you to hear it from the horse's mouth than for it to arrive on your desk weeks later or indirectly in the form of a complaint.

7. **Demonstrate your effectiveness:** In the minds of many employers, the jury is still out on the benefits of teleworking. If you like the home setup, it is up to you to show that your effectiveness is not compromised by not working at the office. Even if your most effective contributions are made quietly and behind the scenes, there should be no doubt in anyone's mind that you are doing your job, and you should have at hand the means of proving it. Make sure that your being at home is not going to make more work for someone in the office, or more expense for your employer, and be ready to document it. When you are not physically present in the office, your employer knows your effectiveness only by your results.

8. **Monitor your effectiveness:** If your work at home isn't at least as productive as your work at the office would be, your employer is not getting a good deal. Keep track of your productivity; if necessary, identify and eliminate the distractions that are keeping you from meeting your production goals or deadlines. You need to look at the technical side of things, as well as your time-management habits, your workload, and the real-time demands that others make on you. Don't hesitate to propose changes in your way of working if you think they will lead to an improvement, and don't hesitate to ask the big question, whether teleworking is really the best solution for you in this job.

9. **Exploit technology:** Constantly advancing developments in electronics and telecommunications are what make teleworking possible. Now that you are teleworking, be sure that you're using all the conveniences and devices that allow you to be virtually present in the workplace. Keep abreast of new developments that will make you even more effective,

and don't hesitate to ask for the technology you need to do your job. Check the Internet for forums, sites, and software for and about teleworking; there's a lot more out there than you might think!

10. **Provide your own safety net:** All the elements in the infrastructure of an office need to be duplicated in the home workplace, and you need to feel confident that these are in place and reliable. Make sure that you give attention to how your work will be backed up; think about the kind of reception a caller gets when you're not there; consider a power source backup if your house is subject to electrical outages. Familiarize yourself with the occupational safety aspects of your employer's workplace and ask yourself whether your home office is completely in compliance with them.

those of good nature and may mollify those who are angry or difficult. Courtesy need not be, nor should it be, elaborate or forced, but simple and unaffected; with practice it becomes almost second nature.

Many people want to be courteous but simply do not know the rules of courtesy in the business world, where young and old, superiors and inferiors, familiar faces and strangers are mixed in all sorts of combinations. The rules for courtesy at the workplace are simple, logical, and flexible.

Doors and Elevators

The opening of a door for another is no longer a matter of a gentleman's proper gesture to a woman. Everyone, male or female, is grateful for this small courtesy, regardless of who has extended the kindness. Men and women hold doors for each other; whoever gets to the door first holds the door open. It is only common sense, and therefore common courtesy, to hold doors open especially for someone carrying packages, using a cane or crutches, or otherwise encumbered.

Elevators are usually crowded at the beginning and the end of the business day. Since there are so many women working in business, the traditional "ladies first" rule no longer applies in getting on and getting off elevators; whoever is closest to the elevator doors gets on or off first. It is courteous to hold the door for others coming toward the elevator and to thank those who hold the door for you.

Introductions

It is important to you in social functions and in business to project friendliness, interest, and self-confidence when introducing yourself or when you are being introduced. For all introductions, whether social or business, shake hands firmly, look into the eyes of the person you are being introduced to, and smile. Do not turn your face away or look down: that implies shyness or diffidence and may upset or annoy the person you are being introduced to. After being introduced, repeat the name of the person you were introduced to and say something like, "I'm very pleased to meet you, Ms. Jewett."

There is a protocol for making introductions. The person to whom someone is introduced will be older or more senior in rank than the person being introduced—for example, "Professor Barnes, I'd like you to meet my daughter Mary." In social situations, introduce a man to a woman: "Ms. Andersen, I would like you to meet Martin Parwell." Introduce a younger person to an older one: "Mom, I'd like you to meet Johnny Culhane." In business situations, introduce a junior employee to a senior employee or manager or executive regardless of gender—for example, "Mr. Prokop, I would like you to meet Pauline Abbas." Introduce a fellow employee or colleague to a customer or client: "Mr. Hanrahan, this is John Kernahan, the head of our legal department. John, this is Michael Hanley, the publisher of the Lynn *Daily News*." Do not presume to use first names; wait till the person to whom you are being introduced suggests it or asks you to: "I'm pleased to meet you, Mr. Kernahan; call me 'Mike.'"

Always use the names of both (or all) people in an introduction, for example, "Ms. Jewett, I'd like you to meet Mr. Seki." It is common, but no longer necessary, except in very formal situations, to repeat the introduction in reverse order: "Ms. Jewett, I'd like you to meet Mr. Seki; Mr. Seki, this is Ms. Jewett." "Mr." is the usual courtesy title for a man, and "Ms." for a woman unless she specifies "Miss" or "Mrs." Professional titles such as "Doctor" or "Professor" are used for both sexes. If you are introducing people of equal rank, titles are unnecessary.

In informal situations, names alone are sufficient, but more formal occasions and many business situations require using a person's title or rank to identify him or her. If a person is a former public official, he or she is introduced by that title, for example, "former senator Jacob Mandrel"; if the person is retired from the military, use that person's title or rank: "Colonel O'Brien." It is helpful, too, if the person making the introductions gives some information about each person to make small talk easier: "Mr. Contarini, this is Francis Jones, professor of French and German at Regis. Professor Jones, Mr. Contarini's son James is a freshman at Regis."

If a man is sitting, he always stands up for introductions. If a woman is sitting, she usually sits for introductions unless she is meeting a government official or other important person, and then she should stand up. A young woman should always stand up when meeting an older man or woman. Men always shake hands with other men. Formerly it was the custom that a man did not shake hands with a woman unless she extended her hand first. Some older men still follow that custom, which may cause them to hesitate slightly. Nowadays, however, it is nearly universal that a woman extend her hand to be shaken.

Do not hesitate to reintroduce yourself or repeat your name if someone seems to have forgotten it: "Hello again, I'm Catherine Bellantonio—Kate." Likewise, be frank if you have forgotten a name, and simply say, "I'm sorry—I've forgotten your name."

SPECIFIC SITUATIONS.

When introducing yourself to a receptionist, say hello, state your name and the purpose of your visit, and offer the receptionist your business card if you have one—for example, "Hello, I'm Myrna Jacobson, and I'm here to meet Mr. Canavan." If you are the first person to greet a visitor, introduce yourself, "Hello, I'm Kevin Carpenter, Ms. Costello's assistant. Can I help you?"

If you are introducing a person to a group, address the new person unless those in the group outrank him or her, allowing the individual enough time to shake hands with each member of the group—for example, "Bob, I'd like you to meet some of my colleagues: Peter Wang, Joyce Zorara, and Jim Griffith. This is Bob Winkin, the owner of Winkin Musical Instruments." If you are being introduced to several people at the same time, repeat each person's name as you shake her or his hand unless you feel there isn't sufficient time for this nicety. (Repeating someone's name as you shake hands is one way of ensuring that you remember it.) If you are introducing a group of people to a group of people, make the introductions in descending order of seniority and use titles.

Introduce your spouse to a superior, regardless of gender: "Mr. Lattimore, I'd like you to meet my husband, Chu."

Answering Invitations

Most invitations for business functions are sent by e-mail or photocopy to the entire company, division, or department, and not to individuals. Such invitations are not meant to be answered. A formal invitation, whether for a business function, a social function, or a combination of the two, addressed and sent to you personally, must be answered as a matter of courtesy and for the practical task of planning and seating. If the invitation has a reply card enclosed, send it with your acceptance or regrets. If the invitation does not have a reply card but has an RSVP printed on it, send a handwritten note for a social function (typed notes are acceptable for business functions) with your acceptance or regrets. If a telephone number or an e-mail address is printed with the RSVP, you may reply by telephone or e-mail.

In your reply you should use the same third-person style of the invitation. Do not wonder whether you may take a guest with you, let alone assume that you may; the invitation will specify whether you may take a guest with you. If you have accepted an invitation and something happens that prevents your attendance, notify your host immediately.

Business Lunches

Business lunches, where everyone can relax away from the workplace, are good venues for becoming acquainted with new or potential employees or clients. Some common sense considerations will help make the lunch successful:

1. Let the guest choose the time for lunch (he or she may have deadlines, travel reservations, or other appointments).
2. Ask the guest for culinary preferences (Italian, Indian, vegetarian, seafood) or dietary restrictions (for example, due to allergies or diabetes).

3. If necessary, arrange to pay for the guest's parking fees and coat check.
4. If the host and guest arrive separately, the host should arrive first.
5. In many states, counties, or cities, smoking is not permitted in restaurants. If, however, smoking is allowed, ask the guest to decide where to sit.
6. The guest should have the seat of honor or the best seat, and the host should sit opposite for good eye contact and ease of conversation.
7. If someone orders an alcoholic drink, you may order an alcoholic drink for yourself, but only if you want to. Otherwise, ask the other diners whether anyone cares if you have a drink.
8. A 15-percent tip is the minimum at most restaurants; a 20-percent tip is usual at expensive restaurants. Many restaurants automatically add a minimum tip onto a check for a party of six or more people.

Business Cards

Business cards are essential whether you are a self-employed stenotypist or an employee of a multinational corporation. The business card identifies you, your company, and your position within the company. You can attach your card when sending a newspaper article or an article from a technical journal to a client (clip it onto the upper left-hand corner of the reading material) or when sending a colleague a gift or flowers (write a short message on the back of the card, and sign it with your first name). Business cards may also be exchanged at social occasions, especially for networking. Your card should contain:

- the company logo
- the full legal name of the company

- the business address of the company (post office box numbers should follow the street address)
- the company's phone number and your extension number (also include any toll-free numbers)
- fax numbers
- your office e-mail address
- the company's Web-site address
- your name and job title
- your business days and hours, if they are unusual (that is, your regular hours are not Monday through Friday, 9:00–5:00)

The business card should be of heavy paper and be about 3½ by 2 inches. Engraved cards are expensive and usually unnecessary unless you are an executive; offset or letterpress printing is attractive and is used for most business cards. The fonts used on the card must be clear and easy to read so that the card does not look cluttered. If your company uses color on its letterhead, then use that color on your card; otherwise, use black or blue type on white stock. If you are responsible for ordering business cards, you must be sure to proofread the order before it goes to the printer and after it comes back.

Domestic Partners

A "domestic partner" is a live-in lover of either sex. This is no longer shocking at the social level, at least in big cities, but there has been much agitation in recent years for state and federal legal recognition of such partnerships for medical, social security, and survivor benefits, all of which is controversial and may generate a lot of heat in a casual conversation. Therefore, to avoid embarrassment and the possibility of misunderstanding, use "guest" instead of "spouse" in sending out invitations to a company function or party, and treat the domestic partner as you would a spouse.

Cards and Gifts

The basic rules of etiquette for business and social introductions are clear, simple, and universal throughout North America. There are, however, no standard rules for sending cards and giving gifts, and many companies have their own policies regarding such. The most sensible thing is to follow the procedures or customs of your workplace.

Many executives give cards and/or gifts to their assistants or take them out to lunch on birthdays and holidays. In such cases, all the assistants need do is thank the executive; it is inappropriate to reciprocate. Many managers will give nominal gifts (candies, calendars) to their subordinates in December. Again, all the subordinates need do is say "thank you." It is not necessary for them to send cards or give gifts to their managers or executive officers.

Many companies send cards and/or gifts to customers and clients in December. The cards should be secular, not religious, in order to be appropriate for recipients of all beliefs. Likewise, the inside of the card should proffer a neutral greeting such as "Happy Holidays" or "Season's Greetings." Gifts may also be sent to long-term or valuable clients and customers. An up-to-date list must be kept of those to whom cards and gifts are sent. Cards should be ordered well in advance (two months) and contain a personal message from the sender (CEO, president, branch manager) or personally signed.

DIVERSITY IN THE WORKPLACE

Today's workplace reflects the diversity of today's society. You work with and socialize at lunch and after work with people from all over the country and all around the world. In addition there is federal and state legislation protecting the rights of people based on their race, gender, age, national origin, ethnicity, language, religion, physical disability, and sexual orientation. The important thing for you to remember is to treat others as you would like to be treated; be friendly, open-minded, and willing to learn, and you will avoid friction at the office, not to mention inadvertently violating someone's civil rights.

Different cultures have different norms of greeting, casual conversation, body language, facial expression, and eye contact. For a man from a culture where men and women are more or less segregated and a man does not look at or talk to a woman who is not his relative, it will be a real and constant effort for him, at least initially, to associate with women in a friendly, professional, business setting. Someone from a very hierarchic culture may find it very difficult to begin a conversation with his or her boss and would prefer to speak only after being spoken to.

People like talking about how things are done back home or in the "old country." Friendly curiosity about another culture and friendly explanations of how things are done in the United States will break the ice and avoid mutual misunderstanding, and you will learn how other people look at things. In addition, you can attend workshops devoted to teaching diversity in the workplace and pick up reading material about diversity from these workshops.

UNBIASED LANGUAGE

Everyone is aware of the changes in vocabulary and usage in English with regard to gender, race, and disability over the past 30 years or so, and everyone has different reactions to these changes, from automatic acceptance of the most extreme proposals to scorn or bewilderment. People who express their distaste for such simple linguistic courtesies often try to pass off their lack of concern for others' feelings by referring to such changes in terminology scornfully as "political correctness." This dodge, however, reveals only that the individual intends to harbor her or his delusions of superiority to other people. The issue is not about what is "correct" or "incorrect," but about acknowledging the diversity of our society and our individual differences with respect.

It is very easy to write good Standard English and offend no one without lapsing into euphemisms or awkward constructions. Just remember that language changes constantly, and no one can predict whether a new form or usage will become part of the standard language, be uneasily accepted, or simply die. Nevertheless, there are some commonly accepted usages that will demonstrate courtesy and consideration for the various groups with which people identify. When in doubt, ask, if you can, how individuals prefer to be described.

Both *African American* and *black* (sometimes, but not usually, capitalized) are standard. *People of color*, but not *colored*, is also acceptable, and acknowledges that people of ethnic identities come in many shades and colors, including those who lack distinctive pigmentation.

Hispanic (always capitalized) is the usual, generic term for those of Spanish or Spanish-American ancestry. If possible, however, use the specific national term, such as *Cuban* or *Cuban American* or *Peruvian. Latino* or *Latina* is also standard in English as an adjective (as in "Latino culture"), but is a little problematic as a noun referring to a person since *Latino* (plural *Latinos*) is specifically masculine (with corresponding *Latina* and *Latinas* for women), a distinction not usually made in English. The same distinctions apply to *Chicano* and *Chicana*, but the terms properly refer only to Mexican Americans and are, therefore, inaccurate when used to refer to someone of Nicaraguan or Bolivian heritage.

Do not use *oriental*, which has connotations of inscrutability or deviousness. Also, because it means 'eastern,' in contrast to *western*, it is descriptively inaccurate because our world is a sphere. What is "west" or "east" from one position on the planet is also "east" or "west" from another position, so the outdated putative distinction is not only false but potentially confusing. Alternatively, *Asian*, which is the most generic term, refers to the continent of origin, and can be qualified by *East Asian* for Koreans, Chinese, and Japanese; by *South Asian* for Indians, Pakistanis, and Afghanis; and by *Southeast Asian* for Thais, Laotians, Cambodians, and Vietnamese. Of course, as with *Hispanic*, it is preferable to use the specific national term.

Indian, American Indian, and *Native American* are all acceptable, although individuals may have a personal preference. In Canada, it is common to speak of the people who first dwelled in North America as *First Peoples*, a term that acknowledges their claim to precedence. Again, as with *Hispanic*, use the specific term (*Cheyenne, Inuit, Mohawk*) if you know the person's group of origin.

"Ms." is now standard when referring to women. If a woman prefers "Miss" or "Mrs.," she will tell you so.

The most common difficulty in writing is with *he, his,* and *him* when used generically to refer to an unspecified individual, as in "Every employee must show *his* ID card to the guard at the gate." Many older people in the United States were taught that it is correct to refer to an indefinite person using the masculine pronoun forms, but this supposed grammatical "rule" originated, not in the English language itself, but in an 1850 Act of Parliament. Its continued use as though it included women as well as men is, therefore, sexist. One solution, common in spoken and informal varieties of English is "singular *they*," "Every employee must show *their* ID card to the guard at the gate." This familiar usage can be found in Chaucer, Shakespeare, and many other writers, yet pundits continue to discourage its use in formal contexts. Others reject the use of both pronouns, "Every employee must show *his or her* ID card to the guard at the gate," because it's "awkward," but this argument, too, is disingenuous. The simplest solution, however, is using plural nouns: "All employees must show their ID cards to the guard at the gate," which will put you beyond the reach of critics of any stripe.

The use of nouns ending in -*man* (for example, *policeman*, *fireman*, and *mailman*) is also discouraged, and for the same reasons that the pseudogeneric use of the masculine pronoun forms were criticized: such nouns position males alone as agents, exclude women from specific careers, and, as well, make women in those careers invisible. Objections to gender-neutral forms merely exposes a lack of creativity on the part of the speaker because English makes so many options available—for example, *police officer*, *firefighter*, and *letter carrier*. Instead of *salesman* or *saleswoman*, *salesperson* and *sales representative* are commonly used; in fact, *sales representative* has become so well established that *sales rep* is now common in informal usage. *Spokesperson* for *spokesman*, may sound "awkward" to some, but it is becoming more common and may become standard. (Of course, there is absolutely nothing wrong with sex-specific terms like *spokesman* and *spokeswoman* when the sex of the individual is known.)

Occupations that once had two forms, one for women with an identifying suffix (-*ess* or -*ette*) and one for men (without a suffix)—for example, *steward* and *stewardess*, have either been replaced entirely (*flight attendant*), or the specifically female forms have been abandoned; thus *poet* and *author* are used for both men and women, and *poetess* and *authoress* are obsolescent. Sometimes, however, the specifically feminine form can be used for economy, as in, "There are relatively few jobs for middle-aged and older actresses," when the alternative, "There are relatively few jobs for middle-aged and older women actors," requires an extra word. In fact, some writers prefer to use forms that make women more visible as agents in the world. Using *actor* or *poet* to refer to women, they argue, implicitly accepts the idea that men are properly at the center of the universe because the neutralization has shifted to the formerly male-only term. Avoid the female nouns with the suffixes *-ess* and *-ette*, however, because they suggest that women are inferior to men, a trivialization explicit in pairs of terms like *major* and *majorette*, where the female-specific term is clearly applied to a vocation perceived as less significant.

Do not make irrelevant references to race, gender, religion, or ethnicity, as in, "Mr. James McPherson, the new CFO, is an African American from King of Prussia, Pennsylvania, and a graduate of the Wharton School of Business." Mr. McPherson's being an African American is no more relevant to his new position than, say, Mr. Michael Canavan's being a red-haired Irishman is to his.

There simply are no terms with positive connotations for referring to people with physical, mental, or emotional handicaps, and the euphemisms that have been suggested (for example, *physically challenged* and *differently abled*) are demeaning. *Disabled* and *disability* remain the most widely accepted terms, but do not make tactless distinctions that treat nondisabled people as "normal" and disabled people as freaks or "abnormal" as in, "The automatic doors are only for the disabled; the 'normals' are supposed to use the revolving doors." Instead, say something like, "The automatic doors are only for the disabled; others should use the revolving doors."

Try to avoid specifically religious terms. The traditional

"Christmas holiday" has been changed to "the holidays." Yet many businesses are closed for Rosh Hashana and Yom Kippur, which are Jewish observances, and for Good Friday, which is Protestant and Roman Catholic, but not usually for other holy days. As Eastern Orthodox Christians, Muslims, and Hindus become more prominent in the United States, ways of recognizing religious holidays on the office calendar will have to change because it is inappropriate to acknowledge only the observations of Protestants, Catholics, and Jews. It is an unfortunate habit, for example, for salespeople and receptionists to end a transaction in December by saying "Merry Christmas," but saying "Have a happy holiday" or "Happy holidays" is neutral yet still conveys the speaker's good wishes, which is the intent.

OFFICE POLITICS

Many people believe that human beings were born in order to gossip, and wherever there are three or more people, there will be politics. People are usually interested in other people and their lives—spouses, families, friends, neighbors, colleagues. Not to be interested in at least some people and curious about them is unusual. Success at work and promotion depend not only on how well you do your job but also on how well you get along with your colleagues. Nevertheless, you must be discreet and avoid the extremes of the loner and gossipmonger. A little common sense and consideration for the feelings of others, as with other office mores, will enable you to be genuinely interested in and caring of other people without being nosy or unduly prying .

- Realize that anything you say can become public knowledge in the office.
- Do not lose your temper in public.

- Keep confidential what was told to you in confidence, whether of a business or a personal nature.
- Correct gossip or a rumor that you *know* to be false.
- Do not criticize a subordinate in public.
- Do not inquire about the private lives of colleagues who are ordinarily reticent about their lives outside work.

HARASSMENT

All businesses have a fundamental responsibility, enforced by federal and state laws (through the U.S. Equal Employment Opportunity Commission [EEOC]), to treat employees with dignity and respect and to ensure that employees are not harassed because of their race, ethnic origin, sex, sexual orientation, age, religion, or disability. Should such harassment occur, it must result in immediate and effective disciplinary action. Managers in particular have the explicit responsibility to forbid and prevent the occurrence of harassment and to take immediate action when harassment is brought to their attention. Any complaints or instances of harassment should be immediately reported to management. The following guidelines identify the nature of harassment:

1. Harassment is written material, speech, or conduct that belittles or shows hostility or aversion to a person because of his or her race, ethnic origin, religion, sex, national origin, sexual orientation, age, or disability or that of his or her friends, relatives, or associates.
2. Harassment has the purpose or effect of creating a hostile, intimidating, or offensive working environment.

3. Harassment has the purpose or effect of unreasonably interfering with a person's performance at work or with a person's employment opportunities.
4. Harassment includes, but is not limited to, epithets, slurs, and negative stereotyping, as well as threatening, intimidating, or hostile acts relating to race, ethnic origin, religion, sex, national origin, sexual orientation, age, or disability.
5. Harassment also includes displayed or circulated graphic material such as photographs, pictures, or cartoons that belittles or shows hostility or aversion to a person because of race, ethnic origin, religion, sex, national origin, sexual orientation, age, or disability.

Someone who has been harassed, should:

- tell the harasser to stop the behavior (otherwise the harasser may think that the harassment will be tolerated);
- document the harassment, recording dates, times, places, circumstances, the kinds of behavior, and the attempts made to discourage or stop the harassment;
- keep evidence of harassment, such as offensive jokes or cartoons posted on a bulletin board;
- if the harassment persists, write to the harasser, complaining against the offensive behavior and demanding that it stop (and keep a copy of the letter or e-mail);
- if the harassment continues even after the letter, report the harassment to a supervisor (or to the person specified in the company handbook);
- if the harassment continues even after it has been reported to the company, file a complaint with the

local EEOC office (employees who report
harassment cannot be demoted or fired);
* if all else fails, consult an attorney about bringing a
  suit against the harasser.

SUBSTANCE ABUSE

Substance abuse includes excessive or illegal use of alcohol,
prescription medications, and street drugs. Substance abuse
is widespread throughout the United States and, therefore,
in the workplace, and it results in millions of hours of lost
productivity, inferior performance, absenteeism, and decline
in office morale. The treatment of substance abuse is properly reserved for physicians, psychologists, and other health-
care professionals, and, often, for legal authorities as well.
There is very little, therefore, that a professional office
worker can or should do except to suggest that individuals
who seem to have a substance abuse problem seek help. The
human resources departments of many companies have
brochures listing various health-care professionals who spe-
cialize in helping people with substance abuse problems.

ILLNESS AND INJURY

Illness and injury at work can range from fingers smashed in
a door or a sprained ankle to a heart attack or diabetic coma.
Many companies have instructions in their employee handbook for dealing with medical emergencies. If your company
has an in-house nurse, either take the victim to the nurse or,
if the condition is serious enough, have the nurse treat the
victim and arrange for ambulance or other services. If your
company has no nurse on staff and the sick or injured person
is able to report to a medical facility on his or her own, notify
the manager or supervisor of the absence and arrange to

have the individual's work duties covered by someone else. If the sickness or injury is serious, notify the manager or supervisor and call paramedics or a hospital emergency room or EMTs (emergency medical technicians). The manager will then notify the next of kin or human resources or legal departments in the company for possible insurance claims, workman's compensation, or negligence lawsuits.

DIFFICULT PEOPLE

Some employees and coworkers are difficult to work with or unpleasant to be around. As a result, morale, efficiency, and productivity suffer. The best thing, though not always possible, is to ignore chronic complainers and troublemakers and concentrate on your own work. If, however, the complainer is complaining to you and ignoring him or her is impossible, try to deflect the individual, not by agreeing, but by suggesting a positive alternative. If that doesn't work, politely say that you must concentrate on your work and cannot be distracted.

Do not become antagonistic or try to argue with complainers: that gives them the attention they want and the audience they need for further sounding off. If the person keeps directing his or her complaints to you to the point that you can no longer stand it or your work is adversely affected, report the problem to your supervisor or human resources department; a reprimand may stop the complaints. Under no circumstances should you lose your temper; that would only create a second problem. If a coworker or colleague is so disaffected by everything in the office or business, he or she will eventually quit or be fired.

Many businesses have public access. This means that you may at some time encounter someone who is mentally disturbed or irrationally angry with your company and who focuses attention on you because you are accessible. If you

Coping With Difficult People

Every company has them. They come in every size and
shape and age. Their behavior is marked by such unwelcome
characteristics as brutishness, laziness, fearfulness, and pet-
tiness. They make your job more difficult and less pleasant.
The following are some personality types you will encounter,
and some tips for coping with them:

1. **The Bear:** The bear has a vicious roar and roams the
   office trying to intimidate. To deal with the bear, use
   caution and a steady voice. Avoid office bears as much
   as possible, but when forced to deal with them,
   approach with firm resolve and an unflappable
   expression. If they know you aren't scared by them,
   they are less likely to use you as a target for their
   intimidation.
2. **The Slacker:** The slacker has somehow managed to
   work an unofficial three-day week for years and avoids
   all possible responsibility for anything. When you must
   depend on the slacker, firm consistency is the ticket to
   success. The sooner slackers realize that you won't stop
   your sweet but dogged pursuit of what you need, the
   sooner they react. CC'ing your boss or theirs in
   appropriate correspondence can be an effective tool,
   as slackers live to be perceived as useful in
   management's eyes.
3. **The Keeper:** To get anything done right, you have to
   work through the keeper. The keeper will never tell you
   how to do something. The keeper will never explain.
   Keepers think their jobs are protected because they
   keep what they know to themselves. Friendliness and a
   sympathetic ear are usually the best way to deal with
   keepers. They need to know that you are not a threat to
   their livelihood.

(continued)

4. **The Credit Thief:** In the movie Working Woman, Sigourney Weaver takes credit for the ideas of her assistant, Melanie Griffith. In the end, Griffith winds up with Harrison Ford and a better job. Why? Because she could explain how she came up with the ideas. Sure, that's a Hollywood ending, but there is some wisdom there. Credit thieves indeed exist in the real world, but if you have a creative nature and you enjoy crafting solutions to problems, keep plugging away and you will be recognized. Don't worry about Sigourney Weaver . . . she will eventually shave her head and get impregnated by the Alien . . .

5. **The Harasser:** This may be the worst kind of creature in the office world. The harasser often preys on those of lower rank and can be inappropriate in every way. Harassment can come in the form of racial or religious baiting or in sexual innuendos and advances. Do not let harassers go past the first step. Cut them off at the knees. If they make one single comment that you feel is inappropriate, immediately ask to speak with them in private and tell them that you took what they just said as offensive. More than likely, they will claim they never meant things that way, and perhaps you both can smile and shake hands before walking away. Chances are they will never bother you again. However, it is important that you detail this experience in writing and send a copy to yourself at home. Never open the envelope. Should the harassment be repeated at a later date, this sealed, postmarked letter is your proof that harassment occurred before and that you attempted to address it by confronting the person.

—*Evan Schnittman*

cannot reason with a distracted or angry person and feel likely to be overwhelmed or even threatened, call for assistance from a coworker, a supervisor, or security.

MANAGING YOUR TIME

Professional success depends on your personality—how well you cooperate, take orders, follow instructions, and instruct others—and on your technical efficiency—how well you do your work and how quickly.

Experienced office professionals have built-in schedules. They know how much time to devote to daily or weekly tasks and short- or long-term projects; yet even they will feel the need to set up a work schedule when there is a major reorganization within the company, a change in supervisors, or a new project to begin.

Office professionals who have less experience or who are new to the company should set up a schedule of tasks. The schedule should be a grid made on graph paper or a legal pad and cover two or three weeks of tasks. Make a separate page for each working day (10 or 15 for two or three weeks). In a vertical column running down the left-hand side, list the times of your workday in 15-minute segments. Do not forget to put on your list your two 15-minute breaks (they follow federal guidelines, and, besides, you'll need them). Across the top of the page, list your daily tasks in a horizontal row (mail processing, correspondence, staff meetings, scheduling appointments, etc.). Put an "x" or a check mark under each task in the corresponding time-column. If you are new on the job, give yourself plenty of time for each task.

You may find a daily, weekly, or even monthly pattern in your work. Monday mornings, for example, may be especially busy for incoming mail, and therefore you may need more time on Monday morning to process mail than on any other day of the week. Friday afternoons may be relatively slow, and you can then allot several blocks of uninterrupted time for tasks requiring long periods of concentration (preparing budget reports, annual reports, etc.).

Time Wasters

Even the most dedicated employees will find themselves wasting time during working hours. At times, a brief diversion from the demands of the job can be just what you need to stay fresh and focused throughout the day. However, it is important to keep those diversions in check and never to lose sight of the fact that you're being paid to work, not to kill time. Familiarize yourself with the specific policies that your company may have regarding time-management issues and be compliant. Some of the most common time-wasting activities are listed below. It's not the occasional indulgence in any of these that is problematic. It is the cumulative effect of "a little time here, a little time there" that can eat into an otherwise productive day. So think about what the company is expecting from you when you engage in any of the following:

1. Talking to friends and family on the phone.
2. Exchanging "instant messages" with friends and family.
3. E-mailing friends and family.
4. Playing Internet games or participating in Internet chat rooms or bulletin boards.
5. Customizing your desktop background and screensaver.
6. Taking extended breaks and wandering around the office.
7. Visiting with co-workers. (Remember: positive, friendly interactions with colleagues should be encouraged, but should never turn into lengthy or frequent gabfests.)
8. Running errands.
9. Conducting personal business.
10. Daydreaming at your desk.

—*Evan Schnittman*

You may be able to combine similar tasks, such as sorting incoming mail and writing correspondence, into the same time periods or spread out similar routine tasks that are too numerous or boring to do at one stretch over several different periods in one day or over several days. Eventually, as you acquire experience and proficiency, you will require less time to perform your tasks and you will be able to set aside blocks of time. You can either volunteer for extra work or study some aspect of your business, such as how the computer network operates or the history and development of the business and its accounts. Either option will benefit you personally and help your career.

Realize, too, that you are not locked into an established schedule no matter how efficient it makes your work. Flexibility is necessary to accommodate routine occurrences such as the illness of a coworker or an unexpected business development.

Do not ignore your break times. Walking around the block, enjoying a solitary cup of coffee, or joking and chatting with coworkers will refresh you physically and mentally, and you will work more smoothly and efficiently.

CHAPTER 4

Telecommunications

After more than a century of use, the telephone has undergone remarkable advances in technology that provide the workplace with more options and conveniences than could have been imagined even a generation ago. Much of today's business is conducted over telephone lines, from push-button systems, to computers, to cell phones. It is important to know the kind of system that will best accommodate your business's rate of growth. Depending on the size of your business, you may want to consider, for example, whether you need an automated operator or attendant, or a receptionist to handle incoming calls.

TELEPHONE TECHNOLOGY

There are several telephone systems available that will meet the needs of most businesses, depending on several factors:

• *Intercom:* This system works best in a company that has fewer than ten people working in the same vicinity. A receptionist answers a call and announces who it is for over the intercom: "Christine, you have a call on line 1." Each employee has an extension at his or her desk for taking calls. This system is very limited and doesn't allow for growth, such as the addition of voice mail, call waiting, and so forth.

• *Single or multiline:* This system incorporates the push-button system, which allows anyone to place or receive calls from his or her extension. It works well for small- to medium-sized businesses.

• *Exchange:* This is an advanced system. Incoming calls are handled through a receptionist or an automated attendant. A private branch exchange (PBX) offers features such as automatic call distribution, call forwarding, call waiting, conference call capabilities, and voice mail. It requires extensive wiring and equipment. A central office exchange service (CENTREX) is a more costly option, with a price-per-minute charge, but existing phones can be used and no rewiring is necessary. It also handles such features as call forwarding, call transferring, conference calls, and voice mail.

TELEPHONE FEATURES

Telephones and telephone systems offer many convenient features for the workplace. Reviewing the benefits of each feature with a telephone company representative before incorporating any of them into your system will help you to avoid wasting money on unnecessary features.

• *Answering machines:* Answering machines offer you the ability to record messages when you are not available to answer the phone, and to play them back at your convenience. Messages can be digitally recorded or recorded onto cassette tapes. Many models offer extra features such as caller ID, remote access, call waiting, and message protection.

• *Automatic attendant:* Automatic attendant plays a recorded message to handle incoming phone calls, replacing a live operator. It is especially useful during nonbusiness hours. It can be frustrating to callers, though, if the outgoing messages are long and the options are numerous. Be sure your options do not lead to dead ends. During business hours, callers should be able to speak to someone, so be sure that that option is available if at all possible.

• *Automatic call distribution:* Companies dealing with numerous incoming calls often have a central location or server that handles them initially and then transfers each call to the first available person who can handle it, usually with an automated message such as "Please hold for the next available representative."

• *Automatic speed dialing:* This feature lets you program frequently called numbers for quick access. It may be accessed by entering a code or by pushing a button, depending on your system.

• *Beepers and pagers:* Beepers and pagers offer the ability to be available to receive calls even when you are not in the office. The beeper chirps or beeps when someone is calling you. The signal goes first to the beeper service, and the message is transmitted to the beeper, which signals you to call in. The more advanced units, often called pagers, can also vibrate to let you know you have a message, a signal that is less intrusive in public than the beeping sound. Pagers can also display a number to call or a short message. As cell phones became more common and multifunctional, beepers and pagers may eventually be phased out.

• *Buzzer:* This telephone feature, with the push of a button, signals the recipient of a call to pick up the receiver.

• *Call accounting:* Call accounting allows you to monitor outgoing calls, usually to safeguard against the misuse of business phones for personal use. Outside providers offer a feature called station message detail recording (SMDR) for such telephone traffic analysis.

• *Call blocking:* This option allows you to specify phone numbers you'd like to prevent from coming through. You can also prevent your name and telephone number from appearing on others' caller-ID displays when you call them, although some companies require that you unblock this feature before they will accept your call.

• *Call forwarding:* Call forwarding allows you to forward all your calls to another number. This feature is especially helpful if you will be away from your desk for a long period of time. You can forward your call to another extension or phone number.

• *Call sequencing:* For businesses with a high volume of incoming calls, this feature is useful for monitoring the sequence of calls and lets you know which one should be taken next.

• *Call transferring:* This feature allows you to transfer a call to another number.

• *Call waiting:* Call waiting alerts you when someone is trying to call you while you're talking to someone else. The recipient has the option of placing the first call on hold to answer the second, ending the first call to take the second, or ignoring the second call.

• *Caller ID:* With caller ID, you know when important calls are coming through, even if you're on another call. Caller ID identifies the number or name of the person trying to get through, providing that caller does not have call blocking.

• *Conference calls:* This feature allows you to communicate with two or more people at the same time, with just one call, no matter where they are located.

• *Continuous redial:* If you reach a busy signal, the continuous redial feature will continue to dial the number until it becomes available.

• *Cordless phones:* A cordless phone offers the convenience of being able to talk into a receiver and walk around without the hindrance of wires or cords, but you are often limited in how far you can be from the base unit that recharges the battery.

• *Dial safeguards:* A device can be added to your telephone system to prevent unauthorized long-distance calls or access to restricted numbers.

• *Direct inward dialing (DID):* Direct inward dialing provides direct access to incoming calls to individual phones, eliminating the need for an attendant to connect every call.

• *Direct inward system access:* This feature allows employees to access long-distance company lines, even when they are not in the building, by using an authorization code.

• *Headsets:* Headsets offer hands-free communication, a useful feature for offices handling many phone calls that require the keying of information into computer databases or the handling of paperwork.

• *Hold:* Putting a caller on hold by pushing a button gives the recipient the opportunity to notify other people that they have calls or to find information for the caller. Callers often listen to preprogrammed music, a message, or a signal while they wait.

• *Last-call return:* This feature allows you to redial the last number you called by pressing a button.

• *LCD display:* Many telephones feature this display window. It may show the number you have dialed, the name or number of an incoming call, or the date and time.

• *Least-cost routing:* An outside provider can offer this feature, which finds the most cost-effective route for long-distance calls.

• *Line-status indicator:* Many telephones feature a button that lights up to indicate if a particular line is busy (often a solid light) or on hold (often a blinking light). When a call is on hold, often there is an intermittent beeping as a reminder to the recipient.

• *Message waiting:* Some telephones have a light or signal to alert you that the receptionist or attendant has a message for you.

- *Messaging:* This feature allows you to leave brief messages on someone's telephone display. A sophisticated line of PC messaging devices is also now available.
- *Music on hold:* This feature provides music, on tape or through a radio station, for callers to listen to while on hold.
- *Paging:* This feature allows you to announce a call or relay a message for a particular person through speakerphones if that person is away from his or her desk.
- *PC cordless phones:* With this feature, your cordless phone is connected to your personal computer to manage incoming calls, and offer voice mail, caller ID, call blocking, and so forth.
- *Picturephones:* If both caller and recipient have this feature, you can see the person to whom you are speaking through a small screen on your telephone.
- *Priority calls:* This feature enables you to assign a distinctive ring to selected numbers.
- *Remote-station answering:* This feature allows you to answer someone else's telephone from your own.
- *Speakerphones:* This feature allows you to speak and listen to a caller without lifting the receiver.
- *Speed calling:* With this feature, you can program frequently dialed telephone numbers and access them quickly, often with a two-digit code number of your choice.
- *Toll restriction:* This feature allows you to restrict the types of long-distance calls being made to specific kinds of telephone numbers, such as 900 numbers, international calls, Operator, Caribbean area codes, and so on.
- *Voice mail:* Voice mail acts as a personal answering machine on your telephone. It records incoming calls and plays them back at your discretion. It may be part of your telephone system or be provided by an outside source.

TELEPHONE COST CONTROL

Every company, whether large or small, is concerned with cost-effectiveness. Cutting costs significantly can often help ward off downsizing. One way to do this is to actively and consistently monitor outgoing long-distance telephone calls. It may even be advantageous to advise, in the employee handbook, that personal use of the company telephone for long-distance calls is forbidden and may result in unpleasant consequences.

Companies should also check their phone bills regularly to be sure they are not being charged for features or services they do not have. Cost control can also include keeping employees informed as to what services are more costly than others, or the most inexpensive way to place certain calls.

TELEPHONE COMPANY SERVICES

Check with your local telephone company for the services they provide. Those services usually include some of the following:

* *Calling cards:* Some companies provide calling cards to their employees, enabling them to place calls away from the office and charge them to the company. Long-distance providers offer international calling cards as well. For infrequent travelers, prepaid phone cards is a solution that avoids monthly invoicing. A specific number of minutes is purchased in advance, to be used as needed.
* *Cell phones:* Cell phones have become a popular and valuable means of communication, providing a mobile connection to the working world through strategically located transmission towers. The signal is routed from one tower to another as the cell phone user travels from one area to another. It is important to check competing cellular services

before signing up, because each has different requirements, options, and geographic limitations, and higher fees may be charged when a call is placed outside the service area. Buy a digital cell phone. It offers less interference, high-quality sound, and greater privacy than the analog type. If you use a cell phone while driving, be knowledgeable about applicable state laws. In some states, for example, it is illegal to hold a cell phone while driving. Many cell phones can be equipped with a voice recognition feature for hands-free communication. Some units also have the capacity for hookups to e-mail, fax machines, and the Internet.

• *Teletypewriter (TTY):* A TTY device (sometimes referred to as a TDD—telecommunication device for the deaf) enables people who are deaf, hard of hearing, or speech impaired, to communicate by typing their messages back and forth. A TTY device is required at both ends of the conversation. If only one person has such a device, a call can still be made by using a telecommunications relay service.

• *Telecommunications relay service (TRS):* A TTY user types a message that is then intercepted by an operator provided by a TRS. The operator then reads the message to the recipient, who answers by voice, and types the return message to the TTY user.

• *Wide area telephone service (WATS):* This service allows a company to make an unlimited number of long-distance telephone calls within a specific service area for a monthly fee, or to receive calls from specific areas at no charge to the caller.

TELEPHONE TECHNIQUES

As soon as you pick up a telephone, you are setting the tone for your company. Being pleasant to those on the other end of the line can mean the difference between bringing in a new client or turning someone away.

Using the telephone effectively in a business context is the equal responsibility of the caller and the recipient of the call. In business, as in any other area of daily life, people expect and deserve courtesy in their dealings with others, and the golden rule still applies: treat other people as well as you expect (and deserve) to be treated.

TELEPHONE ETIQUETTE

Answering the Phone

Never walk past a ringing telephone; an unanswered phone call is an opportunity lost. Take a message or transfer the call to someone who can help. The caller could be a new customer who has never done business with your company or could be your oldest and best customer. People will judge your competence and the quality of your service and product by how promptly the phone is answered and how their calls are handled. A few simple rules of courtesy will keep everyone happy.

1. Try to answer the phone by the third ring.
2. Put a smile in your voice when you answer the phone (no matter how you feel) and speak clearly, identifying the company, the department, and yourself: "Good morning/afternoon, Westville Widgets Customer Service. This is Howard Stein. How can I help you?"
3. Avoid using jargon or slang. Speak simply and in complete sentences.
4. Sound interested in what the caller has to say and listen carefully. If you have to take a message, write down the caller's name, company, telephone number, and reason for calling, and repeat the information to the caller to be sure you have written

everything correctly. Record your name and the date and time of the call, and be sure that the message gets to the person for whom it is intended or to someone who can respond appropriately.

5. If you must put the caller on hold, ask for permission. If you know that you'll be away from the phone for more than five minutes, be honest and tell the person that. This gives him or her the option of calling back.

6. If you have to transfer the call, tell the caller so and provide the correct telephone number or extension for his or her future use. Be sure that you know how to transfer calls correctly. Nothing is worse than inadvertently disconnecting callers or sending them to the wrong individual or department.

7. Be especially patient and courteous when handling customer who is upset. Let the person say whatever is bothering him or her before you respond. When the person has finished, acknowledge his or her dissatisfaction and offer to do what you can to help. Be honest and realistic with the customer about what you can or cannot do, and ask the customer if he or she is satisfied with your proposed solution.

8. Never say "I don't know" to a customer. If you don't have an answer or know what to do, ask the customer to wait, put him or her on hold, and quickly find someone who can help or resolve the problem.

Making a Call

In business, how you make a call is just as important as how you receive calls, and similar rules apply.

1. Sound cheerful and confident. Speak clearly, and identify yourself, the company you represent, the

department (if appropriate), and your reason for calling.

2. If the person you are calling is out of the office or unable to take your call, leave a message with your name, your company, and your reason for calling. Be sure that the person taking the message has written everything down correctly.

3. Don't use jargon or slang, and speak in simple, clear sentences.

4. If the person answering your call says that he or she has to put you on hold, ask how long you can expect to be on hold. If you don't want to be on hold, say so, and either ask to leave a message or tell the person that you'll call again later.

5. If the person who has answered your call has to transfer the call, ask for the correct telephone number or extension so that you can call the appropriate individual directly in the future.

6. Never call anyone when you're angry. Wait until you have calmed down and are able to speak calmly and coherently. If you have a problem or complaint but cannot describe it clearly, the person who takes your call will be unable to understand what has happened and, as a result, may be ineffective in responding to the situation. Describe the situation or occurrence that has upset you, and ask to speak to someone who can help resolve the problem.

7. Be gracious and patient, and most people will respond in kind.

CELL PHONES

A cell phone, like a noncellular telephone, has tremendous interruptive potential: we cannot control its use at the caller's end. It is aggravating enough to be constantly interrupted by your own ringing telephone. It is even more aggravating when it is someone else's phone. Many people regard cell phones as handy devices for staying in touch, while others, especially businesspeople whose work requires them to be out of the office frequently, have come to think of them as indispensable adjuncts. But there are also people who consider cell phones to be nuisances that increase the noise pollution in public places. More than 100 million people in the United States use cell phones regularly, and that number increases daily by 46,000. As the number of cell phones increases, so does the potential for unwanted noise in public spaces and aggravation on the part of those imposed on by their discourteous use. As a result, a lack of courtesy on the part of cell phone users has created a backlash, and demands for legal restrictions on cell phone use continue to escalate.

Observing a few common-sense rules will make the people around you much happier and you can still get that critical call you're waiting for.

1. Turn off your cell phone in public places—theaters, restaurants, schools, concert halls, churches, and so forth—or use the phone's silent or vibration options. No matter how important that call may be, a ringing phone in the middle of a meal, during the playing of a symphony, or at the most intense moment in a movie is rude and intrusive. Either leave your phone at home or, if you're expecting an important call while you're in a public place, set the phone to vibrate. Should the call come through, leave your seat, and take the call where no one else can hear your conversation. Otherwise, let voice mail take the message.
2. Never accept a call during a business meeting or while you're involved in a face-to-face conversation with a client or customer. To do so tells other

people that they are less important than the individual who called you, and you risk alienating your colleagues and losing customers. If you expect to receive a call that you must take during a meeting with other people, tell them in advance that you're expecting an important call and will excuse yourself in order to take it. Better, tell the person who is going to call you that you'll be unable to take the call for a specific period and arrange a time for the conversation when you are not otherwise occupied. Or, let your voice mail take the message.

3. Never conduct business in a public social setting. If you take your work with you to a movie or a concert, you won't enjoy yourself and neither will those around you. Leave your phone at home or in your car.

4. Do not turn your back on a colleague or client in order to accept a call. If it's a call that you absolutely must take, set your phone to vibrate, explain to the individual(s) that you're expecting an urgent call, and excuse yourself in order to take it. And make it brief!

5. If your work requires you to spend a great deal of time in your car and away from your office, and you need your cell phone in order to stay connected, do not use it while you're driving. If you're talking on the phone, your mind is not fully focused on your driving or the conversation. If you must make or receive a call while driving, pull off to the side of the highway. If you're driving in town, find a parking lot and have your conversation. No phone call is worth endangering your life or the lives of other people.

6. If you use your phone while in a public conveyance
(a cab, bus, train, etc.), speak at a normal level. Do
not shout or yell when using your phone. Forcing
other people to endure your noise is inconsiderate.
Most cell phones are equipped with sensitive
microphones. If there's interference or static,
yelling won't help anyway.

ANSWERING MACHINES AND VOICE MAIL

When putting messages for incoming calls on an answering
machine or voice mail, keep your greeting brief. Ask callers
to leave their name, a phone number, the date and time, and
the reason for the call. When your call is answered by an
answering machine or voice mail, speak slowly and leave
your name, phone number, the date and time, and a brief
message. In any case, don't waste time with clichés like
"Have a nice day."

SPEAKER PHONES

If you use a speaker phone, inform callers of that fact and ask
whether they mind if you use it. If other people are nearby
and will be forced to overhear your conversation, ask their
permission as well before turning it on.

PAGERS

Although there are fewer pagers (beepers) in service than
cell phones (approximately 40 million), their use still
requires courtesy and respect for other people. For recipients of messages, the same rules apply that have been
described for cell phones. For callers, however, a couple of
additional considerations will improve your calling manners.

First, keep your message very brief. Most pagers can only receive numeric messages anyway. Second, some companies will refuse to transmit any words they regard as obscene or offensive. Therefore, you should avoid potentially offensive language when addressing a client or a colleague as a matter of principle.

FAXES

Fax machines have made it possible to send and receive text quickly, a plus for businesspeople who often need information faster than any delivery service can manage. As with other kinds of electronic communications, the ability to transmit information through telephone lines requires sensitivity to what is and is not appropriate behavior. Above all, be respectful of the people to whom you send faxes and considerate of their time. Readability and brevity are essential. A few dos and don'ts will keep your recipients happy and make you look good.

1. Never send a fax without first contacting the recipient. Make sure that your recipient wants to receive the document and is prepared for its transmission. Sending an unsolicited fax is annoying. Sending one to a machine that isn't turned on is futile.
2. Use a cover sheet that includes: the recipient's name and both the telephone and fax numbers; your name and telephone and fax numbers; the date of the transmittal; the total number of pages (including the cover sheet) that you're transmitting. Indicate which number is the telephone number and which is the fax number—for example, Phone: 212-555-1212, Fax: 212-555-1213.

3. Start your text with a clear sentence that informs the recipient(s) of your purpose for sending the fax, the topic to be discussed, and the response you're expecting.

4. If the document is more than one page, provide headings. Headings make your text look more professional and, in addition, make it easier for the recipients to read (and respond to) the text quickly.

5. Simplify the text you're sending as much as possible. Keeping it simple saves time and money for everyone involved. Always remove graphics that aren't essential to your text, including cartoons, clever sayings, and any shading. Limit your use of dark colors in particular. Because such material takes a lot of time to transmit, it runs up your telephone bill and ties up your recipient's fax machine. Also, the recipients will not appreciate the unnecessary depletion of ink from their fax cartridges.

6. Keep your text as brief as possible. As a general rule, don't fax any document that is longer than five pages. If it runs more than five pages and it's really important, fax only the crucial information your recipient must have immediately and send the entire text by overnight delivery. If you send a very long document, say 30 pages, the recipient's fax machine may run out of paper and the entire text will not be received, which defeats your purpose.

7. Use a large font size, at least 12-point, and avoid fancy or italic typefaces because their delicacy makes them difficult to read in a fax. Clear, simple typefaces, such as Times Roman, will make your document much easier to read. In addition, leaving

sufficient white space around the text improves its
readability.

8. Make it easy for your recipient to respond,
especially to international faxes. For example, in an
overseas fax number, a 0 (zero) may appear in front
of the city code (for example, 046). When dialing
from the United States, the 0 is unnecessary.

CHAPTER 5

The Mail

POSTAL MAIL: THE UNITED STATES POSTAL SERVICE

For up-to-date postal rates and guidelines on size and weight restrictions, visit www.usps.com, the Web site of the United States Postal Service (USPS). This informative site also provides a calculator for both domestic and international shipments. One simply keys in weight and measurements and the calculator figures the postage required. Pickup service is available for a flat rate (regardless of number of pieces being shipped) on certain postal categories, such as Priority Mail and Express Mail. The Web site offers a toll-free number to call for details about pickup options.

First-Class Mail

First-Class Mail is used for personal correspondence, bills and statements of account, items sealed or otherwise closed against inspection, and items wholly or partly in writing or typewriting. A piece of first-class mail may not measure less than 5 inches long, 3.5 inches high, and 0.007 inch thick, and its weight must not exceed 13 ounces.

Priority Mail

Priority Mail offers two-day service to most domestic destinations but is not intended for overnight service. The item being sent cannot weigh more than 70 pounds and must be clearly marked "Priority Mail." Priority Mail envelopes and boxes, as well as "Priority Mail" stickers, are available through the USPS.

Express Mail

Express Mail offers next-day delivery by noon to most destinations in the United States and is delivered 365 days a year. Express Mail envelopes, labels, and boxes are available, free of charge, from the USPS. Items must weigh 70 pounds or less.

Parcel Post

Books, circulars, and catalogs may be sent Parcel Post, provided they weigh no more than 70 pounds. Each package must be marked "Parcel Post" in the postage area.

Bound Printed Matter

According to the USPS, Bound Printed Matter must meet certain criteria. It must:

- consist of advertising, promotional, directory, or editorial material (or any combination thereof);
- be securely bound with permanent fastenings such as glue, staples, or stitching (loose-leaf binders and similar fastenings are not considered permanent);
  not be personal correspondence of any kind;
  not be stationery, such as pads of blank forms;
  not exceed 15 pounds.

Rates vary according to weight and destination. Check the USPS Web site for dimension restrictions and other criteria.

Media Mail (Book Rate)

This category of mail includes books, film, printed music or test materials, sound recordings, scripts, educational charts, loose-leaf pages and binders consisting of medical information, and computer-readable media. Be sure to check the Web site for restrictions on advertising. Mark each package "Media Mail" in the postage area.

Standard Mail (A)

Formerly known as third-class mail, this category is used for circulars, catalogs, booklets, printed matter, and photographs. It can be used for items weighing less than one pound each, 200 pieces or 50 pounds per mailing, and is available to businesses and nonprofit organizations. USPS personnel can inspect this type of mail, whether sealed or unsealed. Individuals can also use it for mailing parcels weighing less than one pound. There are certain restrictions for sorting, bundling, or labeling, so check with the USPS in your area.

Standard Mail (B)

Formerly known as fourth-class mail, this category is used for mailing packages weighing more than one pound. There is no guaranteed delivery time and USPS personnel can inspect this type of mail also. Check with the USPS for size and weight restrictions. Rates vary depending on weight and destination.

Special Services

CERTIFICATE OF MAILING.

A Certificate of Mailing is purchased at the time of mailing and is used as proof of mailing, not delivery. No receipts are involved.

CERTIFIED MAIL.

This service provides the sender with a receipt. The USPS keeps a record of this transaction, but no insurance coverage is provided. It can be used with first-class mail and priority mail.

COLLECT ON DELIVERY (COD).

COD allows senders to collect the price of goods and/or postage on merchandise ordered by the recipient when it is delivered. It can be used for items shipped first-class mail, express mail, priority mail, parcel post, bound printed matter, and media mail. A record of this service is kept by the USPS, and it can be combined with other services but cannot be used for international mail, APO, or FPO addresses.

INSURED MAIL.

This service provides coverage against loss or damage of shipped goods. Insurance coverage must not exceed the value of the item(s) being shipped.

RETURN RECEIPT AND RETURN RECEIPT FOR MERCHANDISE.

Return receipt can be requested before or after mailing and provides proof that the item was delivered, and it indicates to whom it was delivered and when it was delivered. It can be used for express mail, certified mail, COD, registered mail, and mail insured for over $50. It can also be combined with other restricted mail options, as documented on the USPS Web site.

Return receipt for merchandise provides the sender with a mailing receipt and a return receipt. A record is kept by the USPS and provides the sender with the correct address information, if different from the address originally used by the sender.

REGISTERED MAIL.

Registered Mail offers the maximum protection and security for valuables, providing a mailing receipt and delivery record maintained by the USPS. Postal insurance is provided for items with a declared value up to a maximum of $25,000. Items over $25,000 are subject to a handling charge.

RESTRICTED DELIVERY.

Restricted Delivery gives the sender the ability to mail an item directly to a specified individual. It may be used for first-class mail, priority mail, parcel post, bound printed matter, media mail that is sent certified mail, COD, registered mail, and mail insured for more than $50.

SPECIAL HANDLING.

This service provides preferential care and handling of items requiring delicate treatment. It does not provide preferential delivery.

Postage Meters

Many businesses choose to use postage meters because they offer convenience and expediency in handling mail. You can print postage for first-class, priority, express, parcels, and international mail. Once the item to be mailed is weighed on an authorized postage scale, the proper postage rate can be found by logging onto the USPS Web site [www.usps.com]. A business envelope may be scanned through the postage meter for the proper postage amount, or a label may be fed through and affixed onto the envelope or package.

Service and leasing fees for postage meters are set by the manufacturers. The USPS has four authorized providers:

Ascom Hasler Mailing Systems, Inc.
19 Forest Parkway
Shelton, CT 06484-6140
800-243-6275
www.ascom-usa.com

Francotyp-Postalia, Inc.
140 N. Mitchell Court, Suite 200
Addison, IL 60101-5629
800-341-6052
www.fp-usa.com

Neopost
30955 Huntwood Avenue
Hayward, CA 94544-7084
800-624-7892
www.neopostinc.com

Pitney Bowes, Inc.
1 Elmcroft Road
Stamford, CT 06926-0700
800-322-8000
www.pitneybowes.com

International Mail

International Mail should be addressed in English as follows:

    Line 1: name of addressee
    Line 2: street address or post office box number
    Line 3: city or town name, other principal subdivision
              (i.e., province, state, country, etc.), and postal code
              (Note: In some countries, the postal code may
              precede the city or town name, as in Canada.)
    Line 4: country

Be sure to print in uppercase letters the sender's address,
including country, in the upper left corner of the package
or envelope. As a precaution, senders should place a piece

of paper inside the package with the entire address printed on it.

International mail is subject to customs examination when it arrives at its destination. There are exemptions, and individual countries may have specific requirements for mail handling, which are listed at the USPS Web site. There are four basic categories of international mail:

1. *Global Express Guaranteed*™ *(GXG):* This service is the product of an alliance between the USPS and DHL Worldwide Express, Inc. It provides high-speed, reliable delivery service to principal locations in more than 200 countries and territorial possessions. If destination-specific delivery standards are not met, postage will be refunded. Shipments are insured against loss, damage, or rifling, at no additional charge, up to a value of $100, and there is optional insurance for up to a maximum of $2,499. The maximum weight limit for GXG shipments is 70 pounds.

2. *Global Express Mail*™ *(EMS):* EMS is a high-speed, reliable service for mailing time-sensitive items to more than 175 countries and territorial possessions. It provides "on demand" handling and delivery. Insurance is available at no additional charge for values up to $100. Optional insurance is available for values over $100 on merchandise only. EMS does not offer a money-back service guarantee. A return-receipt service for EMS shipments is available to certain countries at no additional charge.

3. *Global Priority Mail*™ *(GPM):* A GPM envelope or sticker furnished by the USPS provides the customer with an accelerated airmail service. It is an economical means of sending correspondence, business documents, printed matter, and lightweight merchandise to areas such as Canada, Mexico, and other specified destination countries. These items receive priority handling in the United States and the destination country. As with domestic priority mail, senders

have the option of flat-rate or variable-weight postage. The maximum weight limit is four pounds.

4. *Letter-post:* "Letter-post" is the accepted term for classes of international mail formerly referred to as LC (Letters and Cards) and AO (Other Articles). It may include letters, packages, postcards, printed matter, and small packets, and can be sent as airmail or economy (surface) mail. The maximum weight is four pounds.

PRIVATE DELIVERY SERVICES

While the USPS is the leading carrier of mail—delivering to over 130 million addresses, including over 20 million post office boxes—several well-established companies (Federal Express, UPS, and Airborne, to name a few) provide delivery services as well. They offer the convenience of pickup and delivery of letters and packages, along with listings of drop-off locations. Supplies of stickers, mailing envelopes, and boxes are offered free of charge by many of these companies, and an account can be opened with them (some charge a monthly fee). They also offer online services and information: drop-off and pick-up times, packaging requirements, rates, and options such as overnight, next-day air, two-day delivery, and so on.

MAIL SAFETY AND SECURITY

After the anthrax incidents that followed the terrorist attacks of September 11, 2001, many people became concerned about the safety of the mail they receive. However, most corporations have had mail safety procedures in place for some time. If your company does not, you may want to take a few precautions when handling the mail:

1. Accept packages for current employees only.
2. Refuse packages without an employee's name, and either discard them or return them to sender.
3. Accept mail only from postal employees, special delivery employees, or courier services known to you. If a courier arrives with a suspicious package, ask to call the courier's dispatcher. If the courier refuses, refuse the package.
4. Learn to be suspicious of certain physical attributes of envelopes and parcels. Certainly, a ticking sound or protruding wires would concern the most careless person, but an alert mail handler will watch for these other signs as well:

> oily stains, leaks, or discoloration
> excessive postage
> handwritten, poorly typed, or cut-and-paste lettering
> an incomplete or generic address, such as "President" or "CEO" but with no name
> misspellings of common words
> no return address
> unusual heaviness
> uneven or lopsided packaging
> excessive wrapping material such as masking tape, string, etc.
> unusual artwork or pictures on the package
> an excessive marking of "Personal" or "Confidential"
> a postmark that does not match the return address

If you do receive a suspicious letter or package, report the package to building security and your supervisor. They should notify local police or other law enforcement officials.

Reducing Mail Theft

A few simple precautions can reduce mail theft:

1. Create a trail for each package that enters the building. Each person who takes possession of a package on and after delivery should sign for it.
2. If a package cannot be delivered immediately to an employee, it should be kept in a secure place with limited access.
3. Do not place new employees in the mail room. New employees should pass their probationary period before handling the mail.
4. Keep outgoing mail in a secure place, and limit access to it.
5. Limit access to the postage meter and account for its use.

Do not shake or open the letter or package. Put the package or letter in a plastic bag, and wash your hands with soap and water. You should make a list of all the people in the room or area when the package was received, and give this list to an official investigator.

If a suspicious package or envelope spills powder or other suspicious substances, do not try to clean it up. Cover the spill immediately with paper or a trash can. Turn off any fans or ventilation systems in the area, if possible. Leave the room and close it off, and wash your hands with soap and water. Notify building security and your supervisor. If powder or another substance has contaminated your clothing, remove the clothing as soon as possible and put it in a plastic bag. Give the bag to law enforcement personnel when they arrive. Shower as soon as possible, but do not use harsh detergents, disinfectant, or bleach on your skin.

E-MAIL

As computer use in the workplace has become increasingly more commonplace, so has the custom of communicating via electronic mail, known more familiarly as "e-mail."

Although hard copy is still kept on file in certain cases, e-mail has largely replaced typewritten, photocopied, and hand-distributed interoffice memos, along with typewritten correspondence sent via the postal service to outside parties. E-mail correspondence saves paper, and a record can be kept of the e-mail by storing it in a customized computer file. Most companies offer the option for, or even encourage, prospective employees to submit their résumés through e-mail.

Among the general guidelines that apply to the drafting and sending of e-mails is the advice not to key the text of a message in all uppercase letters, which is the equivalent of yelling at the recipient. Another advisable practice is to be concise, remembering that many professionals receive a multitude of e-mails throughout the day and often don't have the time to read thoroughly each piece of correspondence. Because the recipient may have to evaluate which incoming messages have the greatest priority, it may be to the sender's advantage to use the subject line as an attention grabber, especially if the objective is to get a response as soon as possible. Also, the subject line can be used to identify the sender, as sometimes the reading of e-mail may be delayed because the recipient does not recognize the sender's name or address. If the sender is unknown, or the subject-line message is particularly obscure or cryptic, there is a chance that the recipient may, as a precautionary measure against viruses, disregard the e-mail altogether and delete the message without opening it.

E-mail messages being sent off-site should end with a closing signature that includes the sender's full name and business affiliation. Most e-mail programs provide an option whereby a closing signature may be created and automatically appended to all outgoing messages.

It is good business practice to use the "reply" option to an existing message rather than opening a "new message" page. The "reply" gives the recipient a link, commonly called a thread, to the original message, and a path to follow if several replies to one message pile up. Or, if the incoming message is lengthy and only certain items require a response, the sender can copy only those relevant parts and paste them into a "new message," then key in the appropriate responses. A standard technique (often performed automatically by e-mail software) for indicating which text was excerpted from the original is to precede that text with a greater-than symbol (>), for example:

> Will you be available for a meeting on Tuesday, March 19?
[from the original incoming message]
Yes, that's fine. [response]

It is important to remember that the e-mail system in the workplace is the property of the employer. It should not be used to send personal messages. It is not private. While passwords safeguard privacy to some extent, they are not a guarantee. (For additional information on business correspondence, see Chapter 8.)

E-Mail Dos and Don'ts

Dos:

1. *Be sure that the people with whom you plan to communicate are comfortable receiving e-mail.* Not everyone is.

2. *Consider your readers.* Ask yourself how they might react to what you've written.

3. *Provide a clear, specific subject line.* Be sure it's meaningful at a glance. If the recipient has an in-box replete with messages (some people receive more than 100 a day), he or she will decide which to read based on the relative importance of senders and subjects. Users often respond to the volume of their e-mail by using filters and rules-based agents. If your message has been filed, the recipient can find it quickly by checking the subject area.

4. *Use excerpts from previous messages to clarify what you're replying to.* To distinguish the earlier text from your current responses, insert the ">" symbol in front of the quoted material and follow it with your response. This example shows how such a text will look on your screen:

>How about 3:00 p.m. on Thursday for the meeting?
That will work for me.
>Can we count on a report from you concerning your group's progress?
Yes. It'll take about five minutes.

This technique is preferable to quoting an entire message and adding "OK," "Me, too," or "I agree."

5. *Remove long lists of recipients' names and addresses.* These require the recipient to scroll down in order to get to your message, and some of your correspondents might not like having their e-mail addresses made available to other people. Use the BCC ("blind carbon copy") feature to suppress the names of other recipients.

6. *Strike a balance between formal and casual language.* Your message creates an image of your company and you. When communicating with upper management or customers, use a business letter format, complete sentences, and a spell-checker. Misspelled or omitted words indicate a lack of attention to detail. If you're just trying to set up a meeting with your colleague in the next cubicle, casual language is appropriate.

(continued)

7. *Read and then reread your message before you send it.* Be sure that your message is clear and grammatical. Attention to detail is as important in e-mail as it is in other forms of written communication. Double-check the spelling of recipients' addresses. A missed keystroke will result in undelivered mail. After sending e-mail, check back in case you've received an "undeliverable" error message. Save a sender's address to your address book, which allows you to avoid retyping the address and introducing errors.

8. *Key in your name at the end of your message.* It identifies you as the sender, and it's common courtesy.

9. *Be careful how you present your message.* Double-check your formatting. Your message may look quite different on your recipient's screen than it does on yours. Avoid fancy fonts and the use of special characters which may result in a garbled message.

10. *Acknowledge receipt of messages promptly.* If you're going to be out of the office, use auto-response messages.

11. *Observe the common practices of your company.* Every company has its own "culture." If you're not familiar with a new system, ask someone who is before sending messages.

Don'ts:
Most of these rules are practices that are inappropriate in any form of business communication because they are either rude or unprofessional. With so many new (and inexperienced) e-mail users going online every day, the rules need to be made explicit.

1. *Never substitute e-mail for necessary face-to-face meetings,* especially when praising work well done, reprimanding someone, or firing someone. Such communications should be handled in person.

2. *Never assume that e-mail is private.* Something can go wrong with any software program, and your e-mail might be misdirected. Also, many companies monitor their employees'

e-mail. Don't send anything via e-mail that you wouldn't post to the company bulletin board. If your message is personal, ask for a face-to-face meeting or send it via regular mail.

3. *Don't assume that everyone reads e-mail immediately.* E-mail travels quickly, but speed of transmission does not guarantee speed of communication. Some people don't check their e-mail in-box every day. Others may set aside a particular time of the day to check their e-mail, but respond only to messages that require immediate attention. Sometimes days or weeks can pass between when a message is sent and when it is read. If you need an immediate response, put "urgent" or "please read immediately" in the subject line, preceding the specific subject of the message.

4. *Never send an angry message via e-mail.* There's no time in business when such correspondence is appropriate.

5. *Never send an e-mail message written in capital letters, LIKE THIS!* Using all capital letters in any context is regarded as the e-mail equivalent of shouting.

6. *Never forward jokes, spam, chain letters, or advertisements.* They will annoy colleagues and potential customers.

7. *Do not reply to everyone who received an e-mail unless it's relevant to them.* If you're simply acknowledging receipt or confirming the time of a meeting, respond only to the sender.

8. *Do not send anyone a large attached file unless the person is expecting it.* If a document is really important, send it by overnight delivery.

9. *Do not send files in HTML unless it's requested.* Some servers cannot handle messages in HTML, and your message will arrive garbled. Such documents can actually cause the recipient's software program to crash.

10. *Do not use e-mail for any illegal or unethical purpose.* This should go without saying.

The Biggest E-Mail Mistakes

E-mail is a great tool but can sometimes be a bit perilous. Sloppiness, and carelessness can not only get you in trouble, they can lead to your company's e-mail system crashing. Anyone who uses e-mail should avoid the following mistakes:

1. *Giving confidential information in an e-mail.* Your credit card number, for instance, can easily be sent throughout in the world.

2. *Opening attachments from strangers.* Never open an e-mail that has an attachment that is vague or says "Check this out!" A virus may spread by invading the contact list on a computer and sending itself to every e-mail address on the list.

3. *Opening unsolicited e-mail without first scanning for viruses.* There are several free anti-virus programs available. Check with your company's IT or MIS department to see what they recommend.

4. *Hitting "reply" to an unsolicited e-mail when asking to be taken off the sender's list.* By hitting "reply" you may be opening up your account to a deluge of spam.

5. *Hitting "reply all" when only the sender needs a response.* If you receive an e-mail from someone in the company who asks for feedback on an issue, remember to hit "reply."

6. *Sending "all@" e-mails.* Being able to send e-mail to everyone in your organization at once is not a right. Very few companies in the world allow employees the right to send e-mails to the entire company without some approval process. So remember, just because you are desperate to sell your 1997 Geo Prism, that doesn't mean the CEO needs an e-mail about it.

7. *Sending an e-mail without a signature.* Your business e-mail should have a preset signature at the bottom. Make

sure you use company colors and logos if provided. Never use a virtual business card attachment (unless it is a company protocol). It may be mistaken for a virus.

8. *Sending an e-mail without spell-checking it.* E-mail is official correspondence. Most e-mail systems spell-check as you type or have a "spell-check before sending" setting.

9. *Sending e-mail without a "subject" line or sending e-mail with a vague subject line.* Be specific. A subject that reads "Lastest Info on Johnson Account" will get more attention than one that reads "FYI" or "new data." A blank subject line may get no attention at all.

—*Evan Schnittman*

CHAPTER 6

Creating Documents

WORD-PROCESSING SKILLS

In this highly technical age, it is becoming more difficult to find an office without a computer. Businesses depend a great deal on office professionals with word-processing skills, whether to create a complicated form, a report, or a simple business letter. Typing speed and accuracy play an important role in document creation, but understanding the word-processing program you are using is just as important. These programs offer many useful features, like choices of typefaces and font size, the cutting and pasting of data, and grammar- and spell-checking. But it still takes a keen eye to proofread the final document before printing. The spell-checking feature will not pick up an error such as "he" in place of "the" because it recognizes both as acceptable words.

These word-processing programs give the business office the capability of creating documents that were once sent out to a local print shop. Keeping such work in-house saves time and money. It offers the convenience of making corrections on-screen without having to redo the document from scratch, another money-saving feature. There is the added benefit of being able to store many documents in a computer file, making searches and retrieval quicker and easier.

Computer Production

Becoming familiar with computer basics, along with the capabilities of your word-processing program, are critical to maintaining cost-efficiency and professionalism in your office. It's up to you to tell the computer what you want it to accomplish for you.

Computer Capabilities

RECEIVING INFORMATION (INPUT).

Input is the information (data) the computer receives, via the keyboard, a mouse, a trackball (for laptop computers), or a scanner. More sophisticated systems may also receive input by voice. Once the computer receives this information, it waits for a command to tell it how to process the information.

PROCESSING INFORMATION.

Once the computer receives information (data), it must process it in some way. In order to process information, computers need software. Depending on the software programs installed in the computer, it can calculate, draw, create graphics for presentations, keep financial records through accounting systems, communicate, and write. The writing feature is the most common use of the computer. Reports, tables, or documents can be keyed and formatted to give an appealing look using various typefaces, point sizes, bold or italic print, justified lines, indents, bulleted or numbered lists, columns, and boxed or lined sections. Multipaged documents can be formatted to include consecutive page numbers. Headers and footers are also a helpful feature. The header, or running head, is placed in the top margin of the page and repeated on each page thereafter. The footer is in the bottom margin and may include the page numbers or even filing information, such as the name of the folder the document is stored in on the hard drive.

RETRIEVING INFORMATION (OUTPUT).

Once the data is processed, it can be retrieved. This is often accomplished by using a printer to produce the information (hard copy), or it can be attached to an e-mail message and sent to a coworker or to a client outside your firm.

STORING INFORMATION.

In most cases, a document is saved on a computer's hard drive in a file you create, much like a manila folder used in a file cabinet. By copying the data onto a floppy disk (diskette), you also create a backup in the event the original file is accidentally deleted or the computer fails.

DESKTOP PUBLISHING

Desktop publishing (DTP) is a step above word processing and enables organizations to produce camera-ready brochures, documents, newsletters, complex reports, calendars, business cards, books, and more, on a computer. The best feature of such a software program is that it shows on-screen exactly what your data will look like in printed form. The initial cost of a DTP program is more than made up in the eventual savings for typesetting, printing, and time. But do some research first to determine if such a program is right for your office. DTP programs require lots of memory and fast processors. A good laser printer is essential in producing high-quality printouts as well.

Those who will be using the program should become familiar with DTP terminology, such as *font, leading, point size, justified type, ragged right, Roman, italic, bold, serif, sans serif*, and so on. Because of the complexity of DTP, it is wise to invest in a training course for such a program. Be sure your office already has the DTP program in place. It is important to have hands-on experience in order to retain what is learned in class.

REPORT PREPARATION

The report plays an important role in the workplace, whether you are preparing one for your supervisor, the executive staff, board of directors, or clients. It may be short and simple, in the form of a memo or e-mail, or it may be more formal and several pages long.

Reports require more preparation time than letters or memoranda, especially if you are creating them from one of the many software programs available for such tasks, and require careful proofreading for accuracy. They often contain tables and graphics, which offer readers facts at a glance, but also break up the monotony of solid text and provide visual appeal. Whatever its length, content, or destination, the end result is the same: a report must be informative, factual, understandable, and neatly presented. This requires research, focus, and patience.

Research

Research for a report may be as simple as questioning key people within the workplace, gathering numbers and information from documents on file, or even pulling data from past minutes of meetings. In some cases, however, contacting other organizations, using the resources of the local library, or browsing the Internet will be necessary. You may even have to enlist the help of others, and, depending on the amount of research needed, assigning specific tasks to each helper.

Before you begin, it is important to have a clear picture of what you need to know. If you are interviewing someone, have a list of questions ready, so as not to waste time. If you are planning to use books, magazines, newspapers, or the Internet for answers, have the topics needing investigation written out, with key questions listed. Sometimes the answer to one question leads to another question not even on your list. It is wise to keep track of your sources, even on the Internet, in case you have to go back to that source for any reason. You'll also need a record of your sources in order to prepare a bibliography for a formal report.

Informal Reports

An informal report may be one or two pages in length and formatted as a letter or memo. It may even be distributed via e-mail. Your company may have a specific format to be followed, so using past reports as a guide will help. Or you may choose a style with headings and subheadings, numbered lists, or an outline style to make reading easier. The title of the report should be introduced as a subject line. Keep in mind who will be receiving your report and use vocabulary and tone appropriate for your audience. Simplicity and accuracy, however, remain key factors.

Formal Reports

The formal report is usually more complex and runs several pages long. Accuracy of facts, spelling, and grammar is a must. Also, if more than one person writes the report, be sure it has continuity (no sudden jumps from one topic to another) and a consistent voice (no jarring contrasts in style). Your company may have its own report format, or you may have to develop one of your own. Whatever the case, some or all of the following sections will probably be required.

COVER PAGE.

Always provide a cover page for a formal report, not only to improve its appearance but to keep it neat as well. Your cover page should usually be of heavier stock paper than the body of the report; it can be any color, or clear or colored plastic. Whatever you choose, the cover page should have a label with the title and author(s) of the report. Your company name should also be provided if the report is going off-site.

FLYLEAF.

A flyleaf is a blank page inserted both after the front cover and before the end cover. The purpose of these pages is to protect the report, but they are also useful for jotting down notes.

TITLE PAGE.

The title page should include the title of the report, the author, the name of the company or organization responsible for it, the name of the company or organization the report was compiled for (if appropriate), and the date. Center all the information, keeping in mind that a wider left margin may be necessary for binding the report. Generally, the title is typed in uppercase, about two inches from the top of the page. All other information is typed in initial caps, centered below the title. The date is usually typed two inches from the bottom of the page.

LETTER OF TRANSMITTAL.

A letter of transmittal acts as an introduction to the report. It may give the reason the report was written, who originally had the idea, and a summary of the report's content. It can be typed on business letterhead or in memorandum style and signed by the person(s) who wrote it.

ACKNOWLEDGMENT PAGE.

If several people, departments, or outside sources contributed to the compilation of your report, you should acknowledge them on this page.

Sample Title Page:

COMPETITORS' PRICING OF SOAP PRODUCTS

Lisa Yu, Jim Martinez, and Wendy Fitzgerald
Four-Way Protection Soap Company
Marketing Division

September 23, 2003

TABLE OF CONTENTS.

The table of contents is the last page to be typed, after the entire report is finished and its pages are numbered. List the chapter or section headings exactly as they appear in the report. If headings are prefaced by Roman numerals, Arabic numbers, capital letters, and so on, be sure to follow that format as well in the table of contents. Each major heading should be listed also, with the corresponding page number. Leaders are also helpful, connecting the entry heading with the page number.

Sample Table of Contents:

LIST OF ILLUSTRATIONS.

Tables, charts, and figures all fall in the category of illustrations. Each illustration should be numbered, listing the caption or title exactly as it appears in the report. If there are several of each, they may each have a separate page, listing them, in the same format as the table of contents. If they can fit nicely on one page, head each section with the proper title, for example, "List of Tables," "List of Figures," and so on.

PREFACE.

The preface allows the author to provide a personal message or explanation that is not otherwise incorporated in the body of the report. It is not a common feature in a report, but it is an option, nonetheless.

SUMMARY.

The summary has the same purpose as, and would supersede, the preface in most cases. It gives the authors the opportunity to discuss their research methods and offer a brief synopsis of the report's conclusions.

BODY.

The body of the report may be single- or double-spaced, depending on the length. The margins should be no less than one inch on each side, and top and bottom, but allow at least an extra half inch where the binding will be.

A heading or subheading usually begins each section. You may choose to use Arabic numbers, Roman numerals, or the alphabetical system to preface each heading. Be consistent throughout.

If you are incorporating illustrations within the body of the report, be sure they are identified in some way, such as with a title or a figure number. The placement should coincide with the corresponding text for easy referral by the reader.

APPENDIX.

If you choose to keep all charts, illustrations, tables, and so forth together, they are placed in an appendix, which follows the body of the report. Supporting material such as maps, notes, or summaries of data may also go here. If you have several items appended, they would be headed as Appendix A, Appendix B, and so on.

FOOTNOTES/ENDNOTES.

The use of reference notes validates the authority of your work and gives proper credit to those whom you quote. A footnote appears at the bottom of the page to which its reference belongs. The numbering of footnotes usually begins with "1" on each new page. Instead of footnotes, you may prefer endnotes, the references to which are numbered consecutively to the end of each chapter or to the end of the entire report. The endnotes thus appear in correspondingly numbered lists at the end of each chapter or at the end of the report. If you choose the latter method, keep in mind that, if you change the number of a note near the beginning of the report, it will affect the numbers thereafter. Note numbers are placed after the appropriate text and are indicated by a superscript, or raised, numeral:

> Human Resources reported a decline in applications that summer.[1]

Footnotes and endnotes that refer to published text should follow a conventional style. A good source of information on acceptable formats is the *Chicago Manual of Style* (14th edition).

Sample Footnotes/Endnotes

1. Irving Blankenship. Index of Soap Manufacturers (Portsmouth, NH: Reference Books, 1986).
2. Irving Blankenship, Mildred Wu, and Darlene Saltzstern. Marketing Soap (New York: Acme Publishing, 2002.
3. Mildred Wu, "The Use of Chemicals in Soap Manufacturing," Journal of Soap and Bath Manufacturers 68 (1966): 9–33.
4. Ken Starbright, "You and Your Soap," Redbook, March 1983, 44–50, 66, 104.
5. Sharon McCoy, "Soap Takes a Bath," Los Angeles Times, 6 July 1991, sec. D, p. 2.

If your report will have numerous reference notes, it may be advantageous to the keyer and the reader to set them as endnotes, after the appendix. While it may sometimes be annoying to the reader to have to flip back and forth from the body of the report to the endnotes, it keeps notes contained in one area and keeps the text flowing without the clutter of footnotes at the bottom of pages.

If you are not familiar with the features of your word-processing software that facilitate the placement and numbering of footnotes and endnotes, consult the help menu or ask an experienced user for assistance. Letting the word processor handle the organization and numeration of notes is both time-saving and accurate.

GLOSSARY.

If your report uses many technical or uncommon terms, a glossary can provide readers with an alphabetical listing with definitions. If you include a glossary of terms, using boldface type to draw your readers' attention to glossary terms in the body of your text will alert them that the term is -included in the glossary.

BIBLIOGRAPHY.

The bibliography lists, in alphabetical order, all published resources used in the compilation of your report. The author's surname is typed first, followed by first name or initials or a period if there is no initial. The year of publication comes immediately after the author's name, also followed by a period. If the source has more than three authors, type the first author, followed by *et al.* If there are several sources by the same author, type the first one according to the usual format. Each source thereafter, use three em-dashes, followed

---

Sample Bibliography

Books
   Single author
      Blankenship, Irving. 1986. *Index of soap manufacturers. Portsmouth*, NH: Reference Books.
   Two or Three Authors:
      ————, Mildred Wu, and Darlene Saltzstern. 2002. Marketing soap. New York: Acme Publishing.

Articles
   In a journal:
      Wu, Mildred. 1966. The use of chemicals in soap manufacturing. *Journal of Soap and Bath Products Manufacturers* 68: 9–33.
   In a magazine:
      Starbright, Ken. 1983. You and your soap. *Redbook*, March, 44–50, 66, 104.
   In a newspaper:
      McCoy, Sharon. 1991. Soap takes a bath. *Los Angeles Times*, 6 July, sec. D, p. 2.

by a period, (or a comma if there is more than one author), to take the place of the author's name. Then proceed with the title of the publication, and so on. In the bibliography, book titles are in italics, and only the first word is capitalized. The rest of the title is lower case, except for proper nouns and the first word following a colon in the title. Article and essay titles are in roman type, and capitalization of words is the same as that for books. A good source of style for the bibliography is the *Chicago Manual of Style* (14th edition).

REFERENCE LIST.

The reference list takes the place of the bibliography and the use of footnotes. Instead of using superscripts within the text, you place the author's name and publication year in parentheses after the quoted material. The detailed reference list is placed at the end of the report in place of a bibliography. The style for the reference list can be the same as that of a bibliography.

INDEX.

Very long reports may require an index. Major headings, sections, or topics are listed in alphabetical order with corresponding page numbers listed. This may be compiled by an outside firm, by available software packages for your computer, or manually.

HEADERS/FOOTERS.

Headers and footers are used to aid the reader in locating specific information or sections. The header is placed at the top of the page, outside the top margin. It may contain the title of the report along with subheadings for that particular section, for example:

LAUNDRY DETERGENTS / Powder

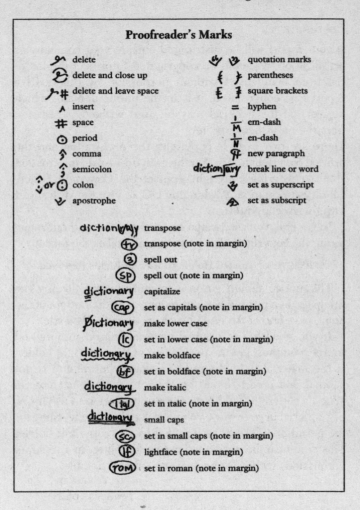

Proofreader's Marks

℘	delete	❣ ❣	quotation marks
℘	delete and close up	( )	parentheses
℘#	delete and leave space	[ ]	square brackets
∧	insert	=	hyphen
#	space	⊢M⊣	em-dash
⊙	period	⊢N⊣	en-dash
⌃	comma	¶	new paragraph
⌃	semicolon	dictionary	break line or word
⁚ or ⊙	colon	∨	set as superscript
⌄	apostrophe	∧	set as subscript

dictionary	transpose
(tr)	transpose (note in margin)
(3)	spell out
(SP)	spell out (note in margin)
dictionary	capitalize
(cap)	set as capitals (note in margin)
Dictionary	make lower case
(lc)	set in lower case (note in margin)
dictionary	make boldface
(bf)	set in boldface (note in margin)
dictionary	make italic
(ital)	set in italic (note in margin)
dictionary	small caps
(sc)	set in small caps (note in margin)
(lf)	lightface (note in margin)
(rom)	set in roman (note in margin)

The footer is placed at the bottom of the page, outside the bottom margin, and may contain the page number, date, or other pertinent information. The header and footer may also be keyed in a slightly smaller point size than the text.

COPYRIGHT.

If your report will be distributed outside your company or organization, it should be copyrighted to protect the material from being used without permission by others. If a report isn't copyrighted, it is in the public domain, which means that the material may be used without permission from the publisher or writer.

There are two parts to copyright: the registration and the printed copyright notice. For the most up-to-date information about registering copyright, contact the Copyright Office, Library of Congress, Washington DC, or visit the Web site at http://www.copyright.gov.

In general, you can print a copyright notice without registering the copyright. This notice usually takes the form:

©2002. Amalgamated Holdings, Inc. All Rights Reserved.

This notice should go on a separate page following the title page in a printed book or report, or at the bottom of the home page and at the end of each section of a Web site.

If you need to use original material from a copyrighted source, you must get the permission of the copyright holder. If the material is in the public domain, permission is not needed, but credit should be given to the original source. When a copyright holder gives you permission to use his or her material in your work, you must use the exact wording for the permissions credit as supplied by the copyright holder. This credit can be positioned in text footnotes, in a separate permissions section, or underneath a figure or table.

CHAPTER 7

Business Writing

INTRODUCTION TO BUSINESS WRITING

Writing is not a gift. It is a skill, learned in the same way as any other activity: by trial and error over a long period of time. Everyone begins as an inexperienced novice who longs for a simple formula: if you follow these six easy steps, you will (presto!) become a fluent writer. While there are formulas for writing specific types of content, for example, the elements that must go into a thank-you letter or a letter of resignation, you will become a skilled writer only by writing, and writing, and writing some more. It is one of the most important skills you will need in the world of business, regardless of the specific culture in which you work.

Writing is not a linear process. It is messy and, frequently, time-consuming. When you confront that blank piece of paper, or, more likely these days, a blank computer screen, you will often find that your mind is just as blank, and that can be frustrating when your boss wants that report on her desk by 5:00 p.m. Gather your wits, the facts and figures you'll need, something to write with and something to write on, and get started. Be prepared to spend a lot of time thinking, not writing—thinking about what you need to say and what you want to say. If you can think well, you can write well. And, take comfort in this: only a few, a very few, writers can truthfully claim that they get "it" right on the first try. Good writing is the product of revising, rereading, revising, . . . you get the idea.

Writing, the process of using written language to communicate, can be intensely personal, as when we write in a diary or write a letter to a loved one, but more often it is a public, social event. That is, although we may sometimes write for our own pleasure we usually write in order to provide a specific group of people with information on a topic we know about. Where do you begin?

There are several identifiable steps in the writing process: define your purpose, audience, and subject; jot down ideas as they come to you; gather information; organize your ideas; prepare a first draft; revise; prepare a second draft; revise. Repeat the drafting and revision steps as many times as you need to. Then type what you hope is a final draft, edit it once more and, if you are satisfied, proofread it. (Yes, neatness counts.) Although not one of these steps can be omitted, they need not be done in a specific order. (Remember, writing is not a linear process.) You will probably find, as you become more and more experienced, that some of the steps do seem to follow logically one from the other.

Identifying Your Purpose

Most of us rarely write without a purpose in mind, and business writing, in particular, always has a goal, something to be accomplished. Clarifying for yourself the reason(s) for your writing will immediately put you on the right track. You can do this by asking yourself three questions:

- Do I want to explain an idea or provide information? (expository writing)
- Do I want to convince others that my point of view is

the best perspective or persuade them to act?
(*argumentative* or *persuasive* writing)
* Do I need to describe a detailed process or an
experiment? (*scientific* or *technical* writing)

Scientific (technical) writing is the most straightforward
because it describes the methodology and steps performed in
an experiment or it lays out, point by point, the course of a
process from beginning to end. Both expository and persuasive writing can be approached in numerous ways, giving
you some latitude in deciding exactly how you want to approach your topic. That decision depends on your assessment of your audience.

Identifying Your Audience

Much of the time, when you write letters or memorandums,
you know exactly who your audience is: a customer who
requested information about a product or informing colleagues about Thursday's meeting. In other situations, however, you will need to think more thoroughly about your
audience, what kinds of people might comprise your audience and what their needs and expectations are. Identifying
your audience early in the writing process will help you
determine what kind of information they need and how
much you need to tell them. One of the crucial aspects of
writing is deciding what information you must provide and
what you can safely omit.

Answering a few questions before you begin to write will
provide you with an initial profile of your audience:

* Who is going to read what I am writing?
* What might a general reader know about my topic,
and what will I need to explain in some detail?
* What might a reader expect to find in terms of
purpose, subject matter, presentation (format),
length, level of formality (tone), and date of delivery?

- How can I interest my reader(s) in what I am saying
  and make reading what I produce an enjoyable,
  rather than frustrating, experience?

Writing for a general audience is quite different from writing for a group of specialists. While general readers might know a few terms in a specific field, you will obviously need to provide them with more detail and explanation than you would a group of colleagues who share your training and expertise. You don't want to lose general readers' interest by assuming they know as much as you do about the topic or overwhelming them with technical jargon. A bit of humor might lighten the reading for a general audience, but it would be out of place in a formal report to the board of directors. Most readers of Standard English, regardless of their interests or expertise, expect informative and persuasive prose to have six characteristics:

1. a clearly stated main point—a central *thesis* that
   governs and unifies the piece of writing;
2. several clearly articulated points that support your
   thesis;
3. several paragraphs, each with its own main idea,
   often explicitly stated;
4. specific details that support or illustrate the main
   idea of each paragraph;
5. concrete language;
6. a more-or-less formal tone that avoids slang or
   colloquial language without sounding stuffy or
   stilted.

Gathering Your Ideas

You've identified the purpose of your writing and the audience for whom you're writing, but what are you going to say and how are you going to organize it? Remember that pen and pad of paper you took out? If you haven't already begun to jot down ideas as they occur to you, start now.

Where do ideas come from? Obviously ideas can come out of your own mind or from reading and talking to others about your topic, but almost anything can ignite that spark of creativity you'll need to generate ideas for your project. Be prepared to have that brilliant realization happen at any time and in any situation. You'll be amazed at the way your sub-conscious mind continues to work on issues and problems associated with your topic long after you've turned off your PC or put your notepad aside, even while you're asleep! (Some professional writers keep a pen [or pencil] and paper on the table beside their bed so that they can record solu-tions and flashes of insight when they come during the night. And those ideas must be recorded at the moment they occur. No, you won't remember them, at least not easily, when you awaken.)

There are also more organized ways of generating ideas. Some people find that keeping a journal in which to record observations, references, and quotations is helpful. Others use a method called "freewriting," writing sessions during which they just start writing whatever comes to mind, allow-ing the words already on the page to generate still more words, without worrying about grammar, organization, or spelling. (Those can be attended to later.) Another way of getting started is to construct an outline, (1) beginning with a broad description of your subject area, and gradually nar-rowing that area to (2) a topic to explore within that subject area, (3) formulating a question about that topic that inter-ests you, and (4) stating your thesis, an opinion or main point that answers the question.

Two other methods you can try are brainstorming (most fruitful when done in a group) and mapping. When you brainstorm, you make a list of ideas as they come to you, whether or not they seem irrelevant or "off the wall" and without worrying about how you might organize them or connect them. The purpose is to generate ideas at this stage, and the more ideas you have, the more likely you are to end up with some that will be useful when you begin to write. Mapping, which can also be done individually or in a group, is a way of using words to construct a conceptual map around your topic. You begin by writing your topic (subject area) in the middle of a page, think of concepts related to your topic and write them down around your topic. As you begin to perceive relationships among those concepts and your topic, you draw lines connecting the supporting details to your main idea.

Finally, there are those reliable standbys—Who? What? When? Where? Why? and How?—used by journalists to make sure that they've answered all of the questions that their readers might ask.

Formulating Your Thesis

Your *thesis* is the main idea you will be writing about, the central point about your topic that you want your audience to remember. Generally, you are prepared to state your thesis after you've chosen a topic, developed a question or opinion to answer or elaborate, and generated ideas from your experience or research.

Your thesis is what all of your preparation has been leading up to, and a good thesis accomplishes several important writing objectives:

- it narrows your topic to one central idea you will write about;
- it states your position clearly;
- it expresses your opinion about or attitude toward the topic;

- it makes a generalization you will support with details, facts, and examples;
- it stimulates the interest of your readers in what you have to say.

Depending on the kind of writing you are doing, for example, expository or persuasive, a good thesis should also do one or more of the following:

- make a firm, controversial statement;
- express a "call to action";
- ask a question that will be answered in the body of your text;
- provide a preview of how your text will be organized.

At some point in the writing process, you will have to decide whether to state your thesis explicitly or leave your readers to infer it from the details, facts, examples, and other information you provide.

EXPOSITORY WRITING

The purpose of expository writing is to provide readers with information. For this reason, it usually contains facts, concrete examples, and specific details about the topic in an objective tone. In this kind of writing, the thesis is usually stated explicitly near the beginning of the essay (or report), and it functions as a touchstone for you as you prepare your first draft—keeping you from straying too far—and prepares your readers for what you will tell them.

PERSUASIVE WRITING

The purpose of persuasive writing (as you would guess) is to convince your readers to agree with you on some point regarding your topic, to adopt your perspective on the topic as the one that best addresses the issues you raise and the questions you ask. In a persuasive piece of writing, the thesis takes a stand on an issue, and, although you should present alternative and competing arguments for your readers' consideration, you will reach a conclusion and clearly state your position on the issue.

Eventually, you will decide where to place your thesis if it's going to be stated explicitly. That placement is up to you. It can be placed at or close to the beginning, especially if it's expository writing, or at the conclusion of your essay if your purpose is to persuade. You state your thesis *after* you've presented all of your evidence and built your case, and it functions as the climax and final outcome of the evidence you've presented.

One other thing to remember: your thesis is not, and should not, be thought of as "engraved in stone." Because writing is a process of discovery, you will probably find that your thesis will change during that process, as it should. It is not unusual for writers to find, at the end of a first draft, that their thesis has changed. If that happens, begin your second draft by focusing on the thesis that emerged at the end of your first draft. Never try to squeeze your evidence into tight boxes to try and make it fit a thesis that doesn't work. It's much easier to change your thesis so that it fits the evidence than to mangle your evidence in an effort to retain an erroneous thesis.

Writing Your Drafts

One of the rewarding outcomes of the writing process is a polished piece of writing of which you can be proud. Unlike speaking, writing gives us the opportunity to refine the way we express our ideas and revise until we are satisfied (within whatever time limit we face). As you learn methods that enable you to produce your best writing and extend the range of your writing ability, you, and your readers as well, will find the results of your hard work highly satisfying. Don't let this go to your head. Note that plural, *drafts*, in the heading. You haven't begun yet, and several drafts (probably) lie between you and that superb piece of writing.

GETTING STARTED

First things first: do not begin at the beginning. The introduction (or first paragraph) is the hardest part of your report or essay, for one simple reason: you have no idea at this point what you're going to say, and your introduction should be the last thing you write, after you know what you've said. You've probably heard the simple formula for writing: (1) Tell your readers what you're going to tell them; (2) tell your readers; (3) tell your readers what you've told them.

Well, yes and no. In actual practice, begin by saying what you want to say. Start by writing those parts of your essay for which you have the most material to write about. After you have something down on paper, you can begin to consider how you want to organize your material.

Next, write that first draft just as quickly as you can. Fill those pages without stopping to worry over spelling, commas, or sentence fragments. This one is for your eyes only, so don't waste your valuable time searching for just the right word or the most eloquent statement of an idea. If you are stymied along the way, make a note to yourself in the margin, leave a space, or insert a blank to remind you that something is missing. If an idea suddenly comes to you that belongs somewhere else, jot it down on that notepad and note approximately where you think it will fit.

Although this first draft will be written quickly, you don't want to write without thinking. Ideally, what appears in this draft should support your thesis. If you find yourself straying from your central idea—what this is all about—stop and ask yourself whether what you're saying is a digression or something that might lead to a more interesting thesis. If you have the time, pursue it and see where it takes you. If not, make a note to yourself and return to your original idea and stick with it.

At this point, don't worry about your language or about being extreme in stating your ideas. What is important now is getting your ideas down on the page. You can tone down your language and adopt a more restrained stance in your next draft, if that's what you decide to do.

Once you're sure you've gotten down everything that you want to say, read through your work, paying particular attention to how you've developed your thesis paragraph by paragraph. Is each sentence in a paragraph related both to what precedes it and what follows it? How does each paragraph relate to the one that immediately precedes it and the one that follows? Is each paragraph coherent, moving smoothly from one sentence to the next, and does each paragraph follow from those before it and provide a link to those that follow? If not, now is the time to pay attention to organizing your ideas in the most logical relationships and ensuring that the entire essay coherently addresses your thesis and presents sufficient examples and specific details to support it.

The Final Work

When you've completed your first draft, you can begin the long process of polishing, rewriting, and rethinking. It is important in business writing to follow the rules of Standard English (which are laid out for you in the next section). Reread your draft several times, preferably several hours to a day after writing it. Check any and all words that you are uncertain about in a dictionary, and ask a trusted friend or colleague to read your work and give you feedback, not only about your grammar and spelling, but also about your word choice and the expression of your thesis and evidence.

Make sure that you've put your final document in the format that was required, and be sure to read it at least once on paper, even if—or perhaps especially if—you have written the entire report on the computer.

Ten Tips for Better Business Writing

1. Use ordinary words. Write *begin* instead of *commence*, and *help* instead of *assist*, for example.
2. Use personal pronouns. It's friendlier and more direct.
3. Use contractions in all but the most formal writing.
4. Use the active voice rather than the passive. Write "We did it," not "It was done."
5. Don't be a slave to certain rules (e.g., "never split an infinitive," "never end a sentence with a preposition") that may make your writing stiff and unfriendly.
6. Put your main point first. (You can reiterate it in your conclusion if necessary.)
7. Use headers and lists to organize your thoughts.
8. Avoid being abstract. Use concrete examples and brief stories to make your points.
9. Avoid fancy fonts.
10. Always proofread your work. (Don't rely on spell-checkers: they can't identify common errors like *your/you're* and *there/their/they're* or omitted words.)

Guide to Composition: Rules of English Grammar

Grammar is the system and structure of a language. It embodies all the principles by which the language works. All good writing begins with an understanding of the fundamentals of grammar:

> parts of speech
> parts of sentences
> sentence structures
> sentence functions

PARTS OF SPEECH

Noun

A **noun** is a word that identifies or names a person, place, thing, action, or quality. There are two types of nouns: proper and common.

PROPER NOUNS

A noun that names a particular person, place, or thing is a **proper noun**. It always begins with a capital letter:

Benito Mussolini
Cairo
Chrysler Building
Jell-O
Mount Everest

COMMON NOUNS

A noun that names a type of person, place, or thing is a **common noun**. There are three kinds of common nouns: concrete, abstract, and collective.

A **concrete noun** names someone or something that you can see or touch:

arm
giraffe
hamburger
lake
stapler

An **abstract noun** names something intangible (that is, something that cannot be seen nor touched):

assistance
bravery

disappointment
flavor
wit

A collective noun names a group of persons or things:

audience
colony
herd
platoon
set

SINGULAR AND PLURAL NOUNS

A noun that names one person, place, or thing is **singular**. A noun that names more than one person, place, or thing is **plural**. The spelling of a singular noun almost always changes when it becomes a plural. Most plurals can be formed by adding –s or –es, but many nouns do not follow this format.

beach/beaches
bean/beans
hairbrush/hairbrushes
leaf/leaves
mouse/mice
party/parties
school/schools
woman/women

If the spelling of a plural noun is in doubt, it is always advisable to consult a dictionary.

APPOSITIVES

An **appositive** is a noun (or a unit of words that acts as a noun) whose meaning is a direct copy or extension of the meaning of the preceding noun in the sentence. In other words, the appositive and the preceding noun refer to the same person, place, or thing. The appositive helps to characterize or elaborate on the preceding noun in a specific way.

The wedding cake, a chocolate <u>masterpiece</u>, was the hit of the reception.

[The noun *cake* and the appositive *masterpiece* are the same thing.]

His primary objective, <u>to write the great American novel</u>, was never realized.

[The noun *objective* and the appositive *to write the great American novel* are the same thing.]

Eleanor's math teacher, <u>Mrs. Kennedy</u>, is retiring next year.

[The noun *teacher* and the appositive *Mrs. Kennedy* are the same person.]

POSSESSIVES

A possessive is a noun whose form has changed in order to show possession. Certain rules can be followed to determine how the form should change for any given noun.

In the case of a singular noun, add an apostrophe and an *s*:

<u>Lincoln's</u> inaugural address
the <u>baby's</u> favorite blanket

Exception: Most singular nouns that end in *s* follow the preceding rule with no difficulty (e.g., Chris's, Dickens's), but some singular nouns that end in *s* may be exempted from the rule because the pronunciation of the plural is less awkward with just an apostrophe and no final *s*:

<u>Ramses'</u> dynasty
<u>Aristophanes'</u> great comedic works

In the case of a plural noun that ends in *s*, add just an apostrophe:

the <u>Lincolns'</u> summer home
our <u>babies'</u> double stroller

In the case of a plural noun that does not end in *s*, add an apostrophe and an *s*:

<u>men's</u> footwear
the <u>fungi's</u> rapid reproduction

In the case of a compound noun (a noun made of more than one word), only the last word takes the possessive form:

my <u>sister-in-law's</u> house
the <u>commander in chief's</u> personal staff

In the case of joint possession (that is, two or more nouns possess the same thing together), only the last of the possessing nouns takes the possessive form:

<u>Ryan and Saul's</u> nickel collection
[There is only one nickel collection, and *both* Ryan and
     Saul own it together.]

<u>Gramma and Grampa's</u> photo albums
[However many photo albums there may be, they all
     belong to *both* Gramma and Grampa *together*.]

In the case of individual possession by two or more nouns (that is, two or more nouns possess the same type of thing, but separately and distinctly), each of the possessing nouns takes the possessive form:

<u>Lenny's and Suzanne's</u> footprints on the beach
[Lenny and Suzanne *each* left *their own distinct*
     footprints on the beach.]

<u>Strauss's and Khachaturian's</u> waltzes
[Strauss and Khachaturian *each* composed *their own
     distinct* waltzes.]

Pronoun

A **pronoun** is a word that represents a person or thing without giving the specific name of the person or thing. There are five classes of pronouns: personal, relative, demonstrative, indefinite, and interrogative.

A **personal pronoun** is used to refer to the person speaking (first person), the person spoken to (second person), or the person or thing spoken about (third person). A pronoun formed from certain personal pronouns by adding the suffix –*self* (singular) or –*selves* (plural) is called "reflexive."

PERSON	SINGULAR	PLURAL	REFLEXIVE SINGULAR	REFLEXIVE PLURAL
first person	*I*	*we*	—	—
	my	*our*	*myself*	*ourselves*
	mine	*ours*	—	—
	me	*us*	—	—
second person	*you*	*you*	—	—
	your	*your*	*yourself*	*yourselves*
	yours	*yours*	—	—
	you	*you*	—	—
third person masculine	*he*	*they*	—	—
	his	*their*	—	—
	his	*theirs*	—	—
	him	*them*	*himself*	*themselves*
third person feminine	*she*	*they*	—	—
	her	*their*	—	—
	hers	*theirs*	—	—
	her	*them*	*herself*	*themselves*
third person neuter	*it*	*they*	—	—
	its	*their*	—	—
	its	*theirs*	—	—
	it	*them*	*itself*	*themselves*

Note that the gender designations of masculine, feminine, and neuter apply only to the third person singular.

Reflexive personal pronouns are so-called because they reflect the action of the verb back to the subject. It is incorrect to use a reflexive pronoun by itself; there must be a subject to which it refers.

> *incorrect:* Denise and <u>myself</u> will fix the car.
> [The reflexive pronoun *myself* has no subject to refer to; the wording should be "Denise and I."]

> *correct:* I will fix the car <u>myself</u>.
> [The reflexive pronoun *myself* refers to the subject *I*.]

A reflexive pronoun that adds force or emphasis to a noun or another pronoun is called "intensive:"

> You <u>yourself</u> must return the ladder.
> Terri and Phil want to wallpaper the kitchen <u>themselves</u>.

A **relative pronoun** introduces a descriptive clause. The relative pronouns are *which*, *that*, *who*, *whoever*, *whose*, *whom*, and *whomever*.

> Wendy was the pianist <u>who</u> won the scholarship.
> Is Mr. Leonard the teacher <u>whose</u> book was just published?
> <u>Whoever</u> wrote the speech is a genius.
> I attended the morning meeting, <u>which</u> lasted for three hours.

A **demonstrative pronoun** is specific. It is used to point out particular persons, places, or things. The demonstrative pronouns are *this*, *that*, *these*, and *those*.

> <u>These</u> are the finest fabrics available.
> I'll look at <u>those</u> first.
> What is <u>this</u>?

An **indefinite pronoun** is nonspecific. It is used to refer to persons, places, or things without particular identification.

There are numerous indefinite pronouns, including the following:

all	everyone	none
any	everything	no one
anybody	few	other
anyone	little	others
anything	many	several
both	most	some
each	much	somebody
either	neither	someone
everybody	nobody	something

George brought two desserts, but I didn't try <u>either</u>.
<u>Many</u> are called, but few are chosen.
Can <u>somebody</u> please answer the phone?

An **interrogative pronoun** is used to ask a question. The interrogative pronouns are *who*, *which*, and *what*.

<u>Who</u> wants to buy a raffle ticket?
<u>Which</u> of the two applicants has more practical
    experience?
<u>What</u> is the purpose of another debate?

PRONOUN CASES

The case of a pronoun is what determines its relation to the other words in the sentence. There are three pronoun cases: nominative, objective, and possessive.

Nominative case

The nominative pronouns are *I*, *we*, *you*, *he*, *she*, *it*, *they*, *who*, and *whoever*.

A pronoun that is the subject (or part of the subject) of a sentence is in the nominative case:

They loved the movie.
Mark and I are going to the Bahamas.

A pronoun that is a predicate is in the nominative case:

It was she who wrote the poem.
The winner will probably be you.

Objective case

The objective pronouns are *me, us, you, him, her, it, them, whom,* and *whomever*.

A pronoun that is the direct object of a verb is in the objective case:

Stephen already invited them.
Should we keep it?

A pronoun that is the indirect object of a verb is in the objective case:

Captain Mackenzie told us many seafaring tales.
I'll give you the recipe tomorrow.

A pronoun that is the object of a preposition is in the objective case:

Does she think this job is beneath her?
To whom was it addressed?

Possessive case

A possessive pronoun shows ownership.

The possessive pronouns used as predicate nominatives are *mine, ours, yours, his, hers, its, theirs,* and *whose*.

The blue station wagon is mine.
None of the cash was theirs.

The possessive pronouns used as adjectives are *my*, *our*, *your*, *his*, *her*, *its*, *their*, and *whose*.

> <u>Whose</u> test scores were the highest?
> I believe this is <u>your</u> package.

TIP

A possessive pronoun never has an apostrophe. Remember, the word *it's* is the contraction of *it is* or *it has*—not the possessive form of *it*.

- possessive:　Life has its ups and downs.
- contraction:　It's good to see you.

SINGULAR AND PLURAL AGREEMENT

It is important to identify a pronoun as singular or plural and to make certain that the associated verb form is in agreement. The pronouns that tend to cause the most problems for writers and speakers are the indefinite pronouns.

Some indefinite pronouns are always singular and therefore always require a singular verb. These include *everybody*, *everyone*, *somebody*, *someone*, *nobody*, *one*, *either*, and *neither*.

> Nobody <u>wants</u> to leave.
> Don't get up unless <u>someone</u> <u>knocks</u> on the door.
> <u>Either</u> of these two colors <u>is</u> fine.

Other indefinite pronouns may be singular or plural, depending on the particular reference. These include *any*, *all*, *some*, *most*, and *none*.

> If <u>any</u> of these marbles <u>are</u> yours, let me know.
> [The noun *marbles* is plural.]

If <u>any</u> of this cake <u>is</u> yours, let me know.
[The noun *cake* is singular.]

<u>Most</u> of the potatoes <u>are</u> already gone.
[The noun *potatoes* is plural.]

<u>Most</u> of the evening <u>is</u> already gone.
[The noun *evening* is singular.]

Verb

A **verb** is a word that expresses an action or a state of being.

An **action verb** expresses a physical or mental action:

break	operate
eat	unveil
intercept	wish

A **state of being verb** expresses a condition or state of being:

be	lack
become	seem
is	smell

TRANSITIVE VERBS

A **transitive verb** expresses an action that is performed on someone or something. The someone or something is the **direct object.** Notice in each of the following examples that the direct object receives the action of the verb.

Ingrid <u>restores</u> antique <u>furniture</u>.
[transitive verb: *restores*; direct object: *furniture*]

Hernandez <u>pitched</u> the <u>ball</u>.
[transitive verb: *pitched*; direct object: *ball*]

Did you <u>feed</u> the <u>animals</u>?
[transitive verb: *feed*; direct object: *animals*]

TIP

Remember: A direct object answers *what?* An indirect object answers *to whom?* (or *to what?*) or *for whom?* (or *for what?*).

direct objects:	*What* does Ingrid restore?	furniture
	What did Hernandez pitch?	ball
	Did you feed *what?*	animals
	What did the captain hand?	orders
	Did you give *what?*	water
	What did I toss?	pen
indirect objects:	*To whom* did the captain hand orders?	us
	Did you give water *to what?*	plants
	To whom did I toss a pen?	Herman

Sometimes a transitive verb has both a direct object and an indirect object. An **indirect object** is the person or thing to whom or for whom the verb's action is being performed. Notice in each of the following examples that the direct object receives the action of the verb, while the indirect object identifies who or what the action affected.

The captain <u>handed us</u> our <u>orders</u>.
[transitive verb: *handed*; direct object: *orders*; indirect object: *us*]

Did you <u>give</u> the <u>plants</u> some <u>water</u>?
[transitive verb: *give*; direct object: *water*; indirect object: *plants*]

I <u>tossed</u> a <u>pen</u> to <u>Herman</u>.
[transitive verb: *tossed*; direct object: *pen*; indirect object: *Herman*]

INTRANSITIVE VERBS

An **intransitive verb** does not have an object. Notice in each of the following examples that the verb expresses an action that occurs without needing to be received.

We <u>marched</u> in the parade.
The tea kettle <u>whistled</u>.
Heidi <u>sleeps</u> on the third floor.

TIP

Remember: Because an intransitive verb does not have an object, the question *what?* will be unanswerable.

What did we march?
What did the kettle whistle?
What does Heidi sleep?

These questions simply cannot be answered; therefore the verbs are intransitive.

LINKING VERBS

A **linking verb** joins a word (or unit of words) that names a person or thing to another word (or unit of words) that renames or describes the person or thing. It is always intransitive and always expresses a state of being. The most common linking verbs are *to be* and all the forms of *to be*, which include *am*, *are*, *is*, *was*, and *were*. Other common linking verbs include the following:

act	feel	remain	sound
appear	grow	seem	taste
become	look	smell	turn

The air <u>seemed</u> humid yesterday.
What <u>smells</u> so good?

The days <u>grow</u> shorter.
I <u>am</u> a registered voter.
Kim <u>remains</u> a devout Catholic.
Butch and Sundance <u>were</u> the title characters.

Predicate adjectives and nominatives
The word (or unit of words) that a linking verb joins to the subject can be either an adjective or a noun, but its function is always the same: to tell something about the subject. An adjective that follows a linking verb is a **predicate adjective**. A noun that follows a linking verb is a **predicate nominative**.

predicate adjective: The air seemed <u>humid</u> yesterday.
                        What smells so <u>good</u>?
                        The days grow <u>shorter</u>.

predicate nominative: I am a registered <u>voter</u>.
                        Kim remains a devout <u>Catholic</u>.
                        Butch and Sundance were the
                            title <u>characters</u>.

Voice

The subject of a transitive verb either performs or receives the action. A verb whose subject performs is said to be in the **active voice**. A verb whose subject receives is said to be in the **passive voice**.

active voice: Brainerd & Sons <u>built</u> the storage shed.
                [The subject *Brainerd & Sons* performed
                    the action of building.]

                Lydia <u>will curry</u> the horses.
                [The subject *Lydia* will perform the action of
                    currying.]

passive voice: The storage shed <u>was built</u> by Brainerd & Sons.
                [The subject *shed* received the action of
                    building.]

> The horses will be curried by Lydia.
> [The subject *horses* will receive the action of
>   currying.]

MOOD

Verbs have a quality that shows the attitude or purpose of the speaker. This quality is called the **mood**. There are three verb moods: indicative, imperative, and subjunctive.

The **indicative mood** shows a statement or question of fact:

> Does Paula <u>know</u> the combination to the safe?
> Dr. Sliva <u>is</u> my dentist.

The **imperative mood** shows a command or request:

> <u>Make</u> the most of your situation.
> <u>Proceed</u> to the third traffic light.

The **subjunctive mood** shows a condition of doubtfulness, possibility, desirability, improbability, or unreality:

> <u>Should</u> you <u>decide</u> to return the blouse, you will need
>   the receipt.
> If I <u>were rich</u>, I'd quit my job.

PERSON AND NUMBER

The **person** (first, second, or third) of a verb depends on to whom or to what the verb refers: the person speaking (first person), the person spoken to (second person), or the person or thing spoken about (third person).

The **number** (singular or plural) of a verb depends on whether the verb refers to a singular subject or a plural subject.

For nearly all verbs, the form of the verb changes only in the third person singular.

PERSON	SINGULAR	PLURAL
first person	I *know*	we *know*
second person	you *know*	you *know*
third person	he *knows* she *knows* it *knows*	they *know*
	Chris *knows* Mrs. Hansen *knows* God *knows* the teacher *knows* the heart *knows*	Chris and Pat *know* the Hansens *know* the gods *know* the teachers *know* our hearts *know*

TENSE

The **tense** of a verb shows the time of the verb's action. There are six verb tenses: present, present perfect, past, past perfect, future, and future perfect.

The **present tense** shows action occurring in the present:

I <u>smell</u> fresh coffee.

The present tense can also show the following:

action that is typical or habitual:	I <u>design</u> greenhouses. Stuart <u>daydreams</u> during math class.
action that will occur:	Lynne <u>retires</u> in six months. Our plane <u>lands</u> at midnight.
facts and beliefs:	March <u>follows</u> February. Greed *destroys* the spirit.

The **present perfect tense** is formed with the word *has* or *have*. It shows action begun in the past and completed by the time of the present:

TIP

Yet another function of the present tense is what is called the **historical present**. This usage allows the writer or speaker to relate past actions in a present tone, which may enhance the descriptive flow of the text.

The United States <u>acquires</u> the Oklahoma Territory from France in 1803 as part of the Louisiana Purchase. Following the War of 1812, the U.S. government <u>begins</u> a relocation program, forcing Indian tribes from the eastern United States to move into certain unsettled western areas, including Oklahoma. Because of their opposition to the U.S. government, most of these native people <u>lend</u> their support to the Confederate South during the American Civil War. In 1865, the war <u>ends</u> in utter defeat for the Confederacy, and all of the Oklahoma Territory soon <u>falls</u> under U.S. military rule.

When using the historical present, writers and speakers must be careful not to lapse into the past tense. For example, it would be an incorrect mix of tenses to say, "In 1865, the war <u>ended</u> in utter defeat for the Confederacy, and all of the Oklahoma Territory soon <u>falls</u> under U.S. military rule."

James <u>has checked</u> the air in the tires at least three
   times.
I <u>have read</u> the book you're talking about.

The **past tense** shows action that occurred in the past:

Greg <u>memorized</u> his speech.
The mouse <u>scurried</u> across the room.

The **past perfect tense** is formed with the word *had*. It shows action that occurred in the past, prior to another past action:

Eugene <u>had finished</u> his story by the time we got to the airport.

The parrot <u>had flown</u> into another room long before we noticed an empty cage.

The **future tense** is formed with the word *will*. It shows action that is expected to occur in the future:

The president <u>will address</u> the nation this evening.

Tempers <u>will flare</u> when the truth comes out.

The **future perfect tense** is formed with the words *will have*. It shows action that is expected to occur in the future, prior to another future or expected action:

Noreen <u>will have finished painting</u> by the time we're ready to lay the carpet.

The candidates <u>will have traveled</u> thousands of miles before this campaign is over.

VERBALS

A verb form that acts as a part of speech other than a verb is a **verbal**. There are three types of verbals: infinitives, participles, and gerunds.

An **infinitive** is a verb form that can act as a noun, an adjective, or an adverb. It is preceded by the preposition *to*:

noun: <u>To steal</u> is a crime.
        [The infinitive *to steal* is the subject.]

        Our original plan, <u>to elope</u>, was never discovered.
        [The infinitive *to elope* is an appositive.]

adjective: Those are words <u>to remember</u>.
        [The infinitive *to remember* modifies the noun *words*.]

adverb: The hill was too icy <u>to climb</u>.
        [The infinitive *to climb* modifies the predicate adjective *icy*.]

He lived <u>to golf</u>.
[The infinitive *to golf* modifies the verb *lived*.]

A **participle** is a verb form that has one of two uses: to make a verb phrase ("they <u>were trying</u>"; "the car <u>has died</u>") or to act as an adjective. A participle is a verbal only when it acts as an adjective.

A **present participle** always ends in *–ing*:

catching
laughing
winding

A **past participle** usually ends in *–ed*, *–en*, or *–t*:

given
lost
toasted

TIP

Remember: Both gerunds and present participles always end in *–ing*, but their functions are quite distinct. Also remember that a present participle is only a verbal when it acts as an adjective, *not* when it acts as a verb phrase.

verbal:	Her <u>singing</u> has improved this year. [Used as a noun, *singing* is a gerund, which is always a verbal.]
	Peterson hired the <u>singing</u> cowboys. [Used as an adjective, *singing* is a present participle that is also a verbal.]
not a verbal:	The birds <u>are singing</u>. [Used as a verb phrase, *singing* is a present participle, but not a verbal]

In the following examples, each participle acts as an adjective and is therefore a verbal:

> Does the zoo have a <u>laughing</u> hyena?
> We live on a <u>winding</u> road.
> It was a <u>lost</u> opportunity.
> Add a cup of <u>toasted</u> coconut.

A **gerund** is a verb form that acts as a noun. It always ends in *–ing*:

> <u>Reading</u> is my favorite pastime.
> The next step, <u>varnishing</u>, should be done in a well-ventilated area.
> The doctor suggested guidelines for sensible <u>dieting</u>.

Adjective

An **adjective** is a word that modifies a noun. There are two basic types of adjectives: descriptive and limiting.

DESCRIPTIVE ADJECTIVES

A **descriptive adjective** describes a noun. That is, it shows a quality or condition of a noun:

> She is an <u>upstanding</u> citizen.
> Josh has invited his <u>zany</u> friends.
> That was a <u>mighty</u> clap of thunder.
> I prefer the <u>white</u> shirt with the long sleeves.

LIMITING ADJECTIVES

A **limiting adjective** shows the limits of a noun. That is, it indicates the number or quantity of a noun, or it points out a certain specificity of a noun. There are three types of limiting adjectives: numerical adjectives, pronominal adjectives, and articles.

A numerical adjective is a number. It may be cardinal ("how many") or ordinal ("in what order"):

cardinal: We have served <u>one million</u> customers.
            There are <u>three</u> prizes.
            After Arizona was admitted, there were <u>forty-eight</u>
                states.

ordinal: You are the <u>one millionth</u> customer.
            We won <u>third</u> prize.
            Arizona was the <u>forty-eighth</u> state to be admitted.

A pronominal adjective is a pronoun that acts as an adjective. A pronominal adjective may be personal (*my, our, your, his, her, their, its*), demonstrative (*this, that, these, those*), indefinite (*all, any, few, other, several, some*), or interrogative (*which, what*).

personal: We loved <u>her</u> goulash.
                 The squirrel returned to <u>its</u> nest.

demonstrative: <u>Those</u> directions are too complicated.
                 <u>This</u> window is broken.

indefinite: Pick <u>any</u> card from the deck.
                 <u>All</u> luggage will be inspected.

interrogative: <u>Which</u> radios are on sale?
                 <u>What</u> color is the upholstery?

There are three **articles** in English: *a, an,* and *the.* Articles are classified as either indefinite (*a, an*) or definite (*the*).

indefinite: At dawn, <u>a</u> helicopter broke the silence.
                 <u>An</u> usher seated us.

definite: <u>The</u> paintings lacked imagination.

Comparison of adjectives
Descriptive adjectives are able to indicate qualities and conditions by three degrees of comparison: positive, compara-

---

TIP

Never "double compare" an adjective. Remember:

* Sometimes a descriptive adjective may use either *–er* or *more*, but it never uses both.

correct: The red grapes are <u>sweeter</u> than the green ones.
           The red grapes are <u>more sweet</u> than the green ones.

incorrect: The red grapes are <u>more sweeter</u> than the green ones.

* Sometimes a descriptive adjective may use either *–est* or *most*, but it never uses both.

correct: Samson is the <u>friendliest</u> dog in the building.
           Samson is the <u>most friendly</u> dog in the building.

incorrect: Samson is the <u>most friendliest</u> dog in the building.

---

tive, and superlative. Adjectives may be compared in downward or upward order.

For **downward comparisons**, all adjectives use the words *less* (comparative) and *least* (superlative).

DOWNWARD COMPARISONS

positive (the quality or condition)	comparative (a degree lower than the positive)	superlative (the lowest degree of the positive)
intelligent	less intelligent	least intelligent
kind	less kind	least kind
salty	less salty	least salty

For **upward comparisons**, there are three different formats:

positive (the quality or condition)	comparative (a degree higher than the positive)	superlative (the highest degree of the positive)

1. Almost all one-syllable adjectives use the endings *-er* (comparative) and *-est* (superlative). Some adjectives with two or more syllables follow this format as well.

kind	kinder	kindest
straight	straighter	straightest
salty	saltier	saltiest

2. Most adjectives with two or more syllables use the words *more* (comparative) and *most* (superlative). Most one-syllable adjectives may use this format as an optional alternative to using *-er* and *-est*.

harmonious	more harmonious	most harmonious
impatient	more impatient	most impatient
talkative	more talkative	most talkative
kind	more kind	most kind

3. Some adjectives have irregular forms.

bad/ill	worse	worst
good/well	better	best
far	farther/further	farthest/furthest
little	less	least
many	more	most

Adverb

An **adverb** is a word that modifies a verb, an adjective, or another adverb.

ADVERB MEANINGS

An adverb usually describes how, where, when, or to what extent something happens.

An **adverb of manner** describes *how*:

They argued <u>loudly</u>.

An **adverb of place** describes *where*:

Please sit <u>near</u> me.

An **adverb of time** describes *when*:

I'll call you <u>later</u>.

An **adverb of degree** describes *to what extent*:

The laundry is <u>somewhat</u> damp.

ADVERB FUNCTIONS

A **relative adverb** introduces a subordinate clause:

I'll be out on the veranda <u>when</u> the clock strikes twelve.

A **conjunctive adverb** (also called a **transitional adverb**) joins two independent clauses:

Dinner is ready; <u>however</u>, you may have to heat it up.

An **interrogative adverb** introduces a question:

<u>Where</u> did Lisa go?

An **independent adverb** functions independently from the rest of the sentence. That is, the meaning and grammatical correctness of the sentence would not change if the independent adverb were removed:

    <u>Besides</u>, I never liked living in the city.

COMPARISON OF ADVERBS

Like adjectives, adverbs of manner may be compared in three degrees: positive, comparative, and superlative.

Most adverbs, especially those that end in *–ly*, take on the upward comparing words *more* and *most*:

positive	comparative	superlative
nicely	more nicely	most nicely
diligently	more diligently	most diligently

Some adverbs take on the upward comparing suffixes *–er* and *–est*:

positive	comparative	superlative
early	earlier	earliest
soon	sooner	soonest
close	closer	closest

Some adverbs have irregular upward comparisons:

positive	comparative	superlative
much	more	most
little	less	least
badly	worse	worst
well	better	best
far	farther	farthest
far	further	furthest

Almost all adverbs take on the downward comparing words *less* and *least*:

positive	comparative	superlative
nicely	less nicely	least nicely
diligently	less diligently	least diligently
early	less early	least early
soon	less soon	least soon
close	less close	least close

TIP

Adverbs ending in *–ly*

A great number of adverbs are created by adding the suffix
–ly to an adjective:

hesitant + *-ly* = hesitantly
strong + *-ly* = strongly

This does not mean, however, that all adverbs end in *–ly*.

adverbs: fast, seldom, now

Nor does it mean that all words ending in *–ly* are
adverbs.

adjectives: friendly, homely, dastardly

The way to determine if a word is an adverb or an
adjective is to see how it is used in the sentence:

- If it modifies a noun, it is an adjective.
- If it modifies a verb, an adjective, or another
  adverb, it is an adverb.

Preposition

A **preposition** is a word or group of words that governs a
noun or pronoun by expressing its relationship to another
word in the clause.

The suspects landed <u>in</u> jail.
[The relationship between the noun *jail* and the verb
  landed is shown by the preposition *in*.]

Please hide the packages <u>under</u> the bed.
[The relationship between the noun *bed* and the noun
  packages is shown by the preposition *under*.]

The guitarist playing <u>with</u> our band is Samantha's
  uncle.

[The relationship between the noun *band* and the
   participle *playing* is shown by the preposition *with*.]

I already knew <u>about</u> it.
[The relationship between the pronoun *it* and the verb
   knew is shown by the preposition *about*.]

Common prepositions:

aboard	beneath	in front of	past
about	beside	in lieu of	per
above	besides	in place of	prior to
according to	between	in regard to	regarding
across	beyond	in spite of	round
after	but	inside	since
against	but for	instead of	thanks to
ahead	by	into	through
along	by means of	like	throughout
along with	by way of	near	till
amid	concerning	next to	to
around	contrary to	of	toward
as	despite	off	under
as far as	down	on	underneath
as for	during	on account of	unlike
as to	except	on behalf of	until
aside from	for	onto	up
at	from	opposite	upon
because of	in	out	up to
before	in addition to	out of	with
behind	in back of	outside	within
below	in case of	over	without

TIP

Many words used as prepositions may be used as other parts
of speech as well.

The closest village is <u>over</u> that hill.	[preposition]
He leaned <u>over</u> and whispered in my ear.	[adverb]

I told no one <u>but</u> Corinne.	[preposition]
We played our best, <u>but</u> the other team won.	[conjunction]
She is <u>but</u> a shadow of her former self.	[adverb]

Conjunction

A **conjunction** is a word (or unit of words) that connects
words, phrases, clauses, or sentences. There are three kinds
of conjunctions: coordinating, subordinating, and correlative.

COORDINATING CONJUNCTIONS

A **coordinating conjunction** connects elements that have
the same grammatical rank—that is, it connects words to
words (nouns to nouns, verbs to verbs, etc.), phrases to
phrases, clauses to clauses, sentences to sentences. A coordinating conjunction is almost always one of these seven
words: *and, but, for, nor, or, so, yet.*

Would you prefer rice <u>or</u> potatoes?
[The coordinating conjunction *or* connects the two
   nouns *rice* and *potatoes*.]

I have seen <u>and</u> heard enough.
[The coordinating conjunction *and* connects the two
   verbs *seen* and *heard*.]

Vinnie's cat lay on the chair purring softly <u>yet</u> twitching its tail.

[The coordinating conjunction *yet* connects the two participial phrases *purring softly* and *twitching its tail*.]

O'Donnell is the reporter whose name is on the story <u>but</u> who denies having written it.

[The coordinating conjunction *but* connects the two subordinate clauses *whose name is on the story* and *who denies having written it*.]

We wanted to see batting practice, <u>so</u> we got to the stadium early.

[The coordinating conjunction *so* connects the two sentences *We wanted to see batting practice* and *We got to the stadium early*, creating one sentence. Notice that a comma precedes the conjunction when two sentences are joined.]

SUBORDINATING CONJUNCTIONS

A **subordinating conjunction** belongs to a subordinate clause. It connects the subordinate clause to a main clause.

I could get there on time <u>if only</u> the ferry were still running.

[The subordinating conjunction *if only* connects the subordinate clause *if only the ferry were still running* to the main clause *I could get there on time*.]

Common subordinating conjunctions:

after	but	since	until
although	even if	so	when
as	even though	so that	whenever
as if	how	than	where
as long as	if	that	whereas
as though	if only	though	wherever
because	in order that	till	while
before	rather than	unless	why

TIP

A noun clause or an adjective clause may or may not be introduced by a subordinating conjunction, but an adverb clause always is introduced by a subordinating conjunction.

- noun clause introduced by subordinating conjunction:
  Jack asked the question <u>even though he knew the answer</u>.

- noun clause with no subordinating conjunction:
  We gave <u>every single detail</u> our fullest attention.

- adjective clause introduced by subordinating conjunction:
  This is the farm <u>where we boarded our horses</u>.

- adjective clause with no subordinating conjunction:
  The people <u>we met last night</u> are Hungarian.

- adverb clause with subordinating conjunction (as always):
  I will speak <u>as soon as the crowd quiets down</u>.

CORRELATIVE CONJUNCTIONS

Two coordinating conjunctions that function together are called a pair of correlative conjunctions. These are the most common pairs of **correlative conjunctions**:

both . . . and	not only . . . but
either . . . or	not only . . . but also
neither . . . nor	whether . . . or

TIP

It would be incorrect to say:

Their dog is <u>neither</u> quiet <u>nor</u> obeys simple commands.

Why? Because the pair of correlative conjunctions *neither . . . nor* is being used to connect the adjective *quiet* to the verb phrase *obeys simple commands*. This is not a grammatically valid connection.

Remember: A pair of correlative conjunctions is comprised of two coordinating conjunctions, and a coordinating conjunction must connect elements that have the same grammatical rank—that is, it must connect words to words (nouns to nouns, verbs to verbs, etc.), phrases to phrases, clauses to clauses, sentences to sentences.

Therefore, the sentence must be reworded to make the grammatical ranks match. Here are two such corrected versions:

Their dog is <u>neither</u> quiet <u>nor</u> obedient.
[The adjective *quiet* is connected to the adjective *obedient*.]

Their dog <u>neither</u> stays quiet <u>nor</u> obeys simple commands.
[The verb phrase *stays quiet* is connected to the verb phrase *obeys simple commands*.]

The site in Denver offers the potential for <u>both</u> security and expansion.
[The pair of correlative conjunctions *both . . . and* connects the two nouns *security* and *expansion*.]

I'm running in tomorrow's race <u>whether</u> it is sunny <u>or</u> rainy.
[The pair of correlative conjunctions *whether . . . or* connects the two adjectives *sunny* and *rainy*.]

Interjection

An interjection is a word or phrase that expresses emotion, typically in an abrupt or emphatic way. It is not connected grammatically to the rest of the sentence. When the emotion expressed is very strong, the interjection is followed by an exclamation point. Otherwise it is followed by a comma:

<u>Stop</u>! I can't let you in here.
<u>Yeah</u>! Dempsey has won another fight.

<u>Ah</u>, that was a wonderful meal.
<u>Oh no</u>, I left my sweater on the train.

TIP

Interjections occur more often in speech than in writing. It is not wrong to use interjections in writing, but writers should do so sparingly. Remember, an interjection is essentially an interruption, and too many may disrupt the flow of the text.

PHRASES, CLAUSES, SENTENCES, AND PARAGRAPHS

Phrases

A **phrase** is a unit of words that acts as a single part of speech.

NOUN PHRASES

A phrase made up of a noun and its modifiers is a **noun phrase**:

> The biggest pumpkin won a blue ribbon.
> A magnificent whooping crane flew overhead.

Most noun phrases can be replaced with a pronoun:

> Give the tickets to the tall, dark-haired gentleman.
> Give the tickets to him.

VERB PHRASES

A phrase made up of a main verb and its auxiliaries is a **verb phrase** (also called a **complete verb**):

> We have been waiting for three hours.
> What type of music do you prefer?

ADJECTIVE PHRASES

A phrase made up of a participle and its related words is an **adjective phrase** (also called an **adjectival phrase** or a **participial phrase**). Acting as a single adjective, it modifies a noun or pronoun:

> Awakened by the siren, we escaped to safety.
> [The adjective phrase *Awakened by the siren* modifies
>   the pronoun *we*.]

> Following his grandmother's directions, Harry baked a
>   beautiful apple pie.

[The adjective phrase *Following his grandmother's directions* modifies the noun *Harry*.]

PREPOSITIONAL PHRASES

A phrase that begins with a preposition is a **prepositional phrase**. It can act as an adjective or an adverb:

adjective: The car <u>with the sunroof</u> is mine.
              [The noun *car* is modified by the prepositional phrase *with the sunroof*.]

adverb: <u>After the storm</u>, we gathered the fallen branches.
              [The verb *gathered* is modified by the prepositional phrase *After the storm*.]

Clauses

A clause is a unit of words that contains a subject and a predicate.

INDEPENDENT CLAUSES

A clause that can stand by itself as a complete thought is an **independent clause**. Any independent clause can stand alone as a complete sentence:

<u>The Milwaukee Brewers joined the National League in November 1997.</u>
<u>It is snowing.</u>
<u>Vitus is the patron saint of actors.</u>
<u>Bob called.</u>
<u>The Celts were highly ritualistic.</u>
<u>Read what child development experts have to say.</u>

SUBORDINATE CLAUSES

A clause that cannot stand by itself as a complete thought is a **subordinate clause** (also called a **dependent clause**). It cannot be a part of a sentence unless it is related by meaning to the independent clause. Essentially, it exists to build upon the information conveyed by the independent clause. A subordinate clause can relate to the independent clause as an adjective, an adverb, or a noun:

adjective: The Milwaukee Brewers, <u>who play at Miller Park</u>, joined the National League in November 1997.

adverb: Bob called <u>when you were at the store</u>.

noun: Read what child development experts have to say <u>about the virtues and drawbacks of homeschooling</u>.

ELLIPTICAL CLAUSES

An **elliptical clause** deviates from the rule that states "a clause contains a subject and a predicate." What an elliptical clause does is *imply* both a subject and a predicate, even though both elements do not in fact appear in the clause:

<u>While vacationing in Spain</u>, Jo received word of her promotion.
[The elliptical clause implies the subject "she" and the predicate "was vacationing"—that is, it implies "While she was vacationing in Spain."]

Myers arrived on Saturday the 12th; <u>Anderson, the following Monday</u>.
[The elliptical clause implies the predicate "arrived the following Monday"—that is it implies "Anderson arrived the following Monday."]

Elliptical clauses are valuable devices, as they allow the writer to avoid excessive wordiness, preserve a sense of variety, and enhance the rhythm of the text.

RESTRICTIVE CLAUSES

A clause that is essential to the meaning of the sentence—
that is, it *restricts* the meaning of the sentence—is a **restrictive clause**. The content of a restrictive clause identifies a
particular person, place, or thing. If the restrictive clause
were to be removed, the meaning of the sentence would
change. A restrictive clause begins with the relative pronoun *that*, *who*, or *whom*. It should never be set off with
commas.

> I'm returning the coat <u>that I bought last week</u>.
> [The identification of the coat is important. It's not just
> any coat. It's specifically the one and only coat "that I
> bought last week." Without the restrictive clause, the
> identification would be lost.]

> The president <u>who authorized the Louisiana Purchase</u>
> was Thomas Jefferson.
> [The point of this sentence is to identify specifically the
> one and only president responsible for the Louisiana
> Purchase. Without the restrictive clause, the point of
> the sentence would be lost.]

NONRESTRICTIVE CLAUSES

A clause that is not essential to the meaning of the sentence—that is, it does *not restrict* the meaning of the sentence—is a **nonrestrictive clause**. The content of a
nonrestrictive clause adds information to what has already
been identified. If the nonrestrictive clause were to be removed, the meaning of the sentence would not change. A
nonrestrictive clause begins with the relative pronoun
which, *who*, or *whom*. It should always be set off with commas.

I'm returning my new coat, <u>which doesn't fit</u>.

President Jefferson, <u>who authorized the Louisiana Purchase</u>, was the third U.S. president.

[The clauses *which doesn't fit* and *who authorized the Louisiana Purchase* are informative but not necessary. Without them, the meaning of each sentence is still clear.]

Sentences

Properly constructed sentences are integral to good communication. By definition, a sentence is "a set of words that is complete in itself, typically containing a subject and predicate, conveying a statement, question, exclamation, or command, and consisting of a main clause and sometimes one or more subordinate clauses." Simply put, a sentence is a group of words that expresses a complete thought.

SUBJECT AND PREDICATE

The primary building blocks of a sentence are the subject and the predicate.

The **subject** (usually a noun or pronoun) is the part that the sentence is telling about. A **simple subject** is simply the person, place, or thing being discussed. A **complete subject** is the simple subject along with all the words directly associated with it:

<u>The large tropical plant in my office</u> has bloomed every summer.
[Here, the simple subject is *plant*. The complete subject is *The large tropical plant in my office*.]

Two or more subjects that belong to the same verb comprise what is called a **compound subject**:

> <u>Stan Garrison</u> and the <u>rest of the department</u> are relocating next week.
> [Here, the compound subject consists of *Stan Garrison* and *the rest of the department*. They share the verb phrase *are relocating*.]

The **predicate** (a verb) is the "action" or "being" part of the sentence—the part that tells something about the subject. A **simple predicate** is simply the main verb and its auxiliaries. A **complete predicate** is the simple predicate along with all the words directly associated with it:

> The setting sun <u>has cast a scarlet glow across the skyline</u>.
> [Here, the simple predicate is has cast. The complete predicate is *has cast a scarlet glow across the skyline*.]

Two or more predicates that have the same subject comprise what is called a **compound predicate**.

> I <u>wanted to buy some art</u> but <u>left empty-handed</u>.
> [Here, the compound predicate consists of *wanted to buy some art* and *left empty-handed*. They share the subject *I*.]

FOUR SENTENCE STRUCTURES

A **simple sentence** contains one independent clause. Its subject and/or predicate may or may not be compound, but its one and only clause is always independent:

> Paula rode her bicycle. [subject + predicate]
> Honus Wagner and Nap Lajoie are enshrined in the Baseball Hall of Fame. [compound subject + predicate]
> The correspondents traveled across the desert and slept in makeshift shelters. [subject + compound predicate]

Lunch and dinner are discounted on Sunday but are full price on Monday. [compound subject + compound predicate]

A **compound sentence** contains two or more independent clauses. The following examples show the various ways that coordinating conjunctions (e.g., *and*, *but*, *yet*), conjunctive adverbs (e.g., *however*, *therefore*), and punctuation may be used to join the clauses in a compound sentence:

Ken made the phone calls and Maria addressed the envelopes.

The war lasted for two years, but the effects of its devastation will last for decades.

Judges and other officials should sign in by noon; exhibitors will start arriving at 2:00.

I have decided to remain on the East Coast; however, I am willing to attend the monthly meetings in Dallas.

FDR initiated the New Deal, JFK embraced the New Frontier, and LBJ envisioned the Great Society.

A **complex sentence** contains one independent clause and one or more subordinate clauses:

Even though I majored in English, I was hired to teach applied physics.

We can have the party indoors if it gets too windy.

Before I agree, I have to read the final report that you drafted.

[The independent clauses are *I was hired to teach applied physics; We can have the party indoors; I have to read the final report.* The subordinate clauses are *Even though I majored in English; if it gets too windy; Before I agree; that you drafted.*]

A **compound-complex sentence** contains two or more independent clauses and one or more subordinate clauses:

> Because the candidates have been so argumentative, some voters are confused and many have become disinterested.
>
> We will begin painting tomorrow if the weather's nice; if it rains, we will start on Thursday.
>
> [The independent clauses are *some voters are confused; many have become disinterested; We will begin painting tomorrow; we will start on Thursday.* The subordinate clauses are *Because the candidates have been so argumentative; if the weather's nice; if it rains.*]

FOUR SENTENCE FUNCTIONS

A **declarative sentence** states a fact, an assertion, an impression, or a feeling. It ends with a period:

> Florence is a beautiful city.
> Lewis Carroll died in 1898.
> I'm sorry I missed the end of your speech.

An **interrogative sentence** asks a question. It ends with a question mark:

> Did you read the article about migrating geese patterns?
> How do spell your last name?
> Mr. Young owns a kennel?

An **imperative sentence** makes a request or gives an order. It typically ends with a period but occasionally may end with an exclamation point:

> Please lock the doors.
> Do not throw trash in the recycling bins.
> Think before you speak!

An **exclamatory sentence** expresses surprise, shock, or strong feeling. It ends with an exclamation point:

Look at this mess!
I can't believe how great this is!
I lost my purse!

Paragraphs

A paragraph is a series of sentences that conveys a single theme. Paragraphs help writers organize thoughts, actions, and descriptions into readable units of information. The paragraph, as a unit of text, may have one of several functions. It may be descriptive, giving certain details or impressions about a person, thing, or event. It may be instructive, explaining a method or procedure. It may be conceptual, stating thoughts, feelings, or opinions.

Every paragraph should contain a sentence that states the main idea of the paragraph. This is called the **topic sentence**. The other sentences in the paragraph are the **supporting sentences**, and their function is just that—to support or elaborate on the idea set forth in the topic sentence. Most paragraphs begin with the topic sentence, as in the following example:

Each Thanksgiving we make place cards decorated with pressed autumn leaves. After gathering the smallest and most colorful leaves from the maples and oaks in our backyard, we place the leaves between sheets of blotter paper, which we then cover with a large, heavy book. In just a day or two, the leaves are ready to be mounted on cards. We use plain index cards, folded in half. Using clear adhesive paper, we put one leaf on each card, leaving room for the guest's name.

Try reading the preceding paragraph without the topic sentence (the first sentence). The supporting information becomes less unified because it has no main idea to support.

Now imagine adding to the paragraph the following sentence:

Last year, three of our guests were snowed in at the
airport.

This would be a misplaced addition to the paragraph, as it is
unrelated to the topic sentence (that is, it has nothing to do
with making Thanksgiving place cards). Because it introduces a new and distinct idea, it should become the topic
sentence for a new and distinct paragraph.

SENTENCE DEVELOPMENT:
AVOIDING PROBLEMS

Sentence style

Getting one's ideas across in words is the core of communication. Sentences provide the means to arrange ideas in a
coherent way. Certainly, the rules of grammar should be
observed when constructing a sentence, but the general
rhythm of the sentence is also important. Sentences may be
categorized into three general types: loose, periodic, and balanced. Good writers typically use a combination of these
styles in order to create a flow of ideas that will hold the
reader's interest.

A **loose sentence** gets to the main point quickly. It begins
with a basic and complete statement, which is followed by
additional information:

The power went out, plunging us into darkness,
silencing the drone of the television, leaving our
dinner half-cooked.
[The basic statement is *The power went out*.
Everything that follows is additional information.]

A **periodic sentence** ends with the main point. It begins with additional information, thus imposing a delay before the basic statement is given:

> With no warning, like a herd of stampeding bison, a
>   mob of fans crashed through the gate.
> [The basic statement is *a mob of fans crashed through
>   the gate*. Everything that precedes is additional
>   information.]

A **balanced sentence** is comprised of grammatically equal or similar structures. The ideas in the sentence are linked by comparison or contrast:

> To visit their island villa is to sample nirvana.

As writers become more comfortable with the basic rules of grammar and the general patterns of sentence structure, they are able to remain compliant with the rules while getting more creative with the patterns. Many well-constructed sentences will not agree precisely with any of the three preceding examples, but they should always evoke an answer of "yes" to two fundamental questions:

> Is the sentence grammatically correct?
> Will the meaning of the sentence be clear to the
>   reader?

Flawed sentences

Three types of "flawed sentences" are sentence fragments, run-on sentences, and sentences with improperly positioned modifiers.

SENTENCE FRAGMENTS

A **sentence fragment** is simply an incomplete sentence. Fundamental to every sentence is a complete thought that is able to stand on its own. Because a phrase or subordinate clause is not an independent thought, it cannot stand on its own as a sentence. To be a part of a sentence, it must either be connected to an independent clause or be reworded to become an independent clause. Consider this sentence fragment:

My English guest who stayed on for Christmas.

Here are three possible ways to create a proper sentence from that fragment:

Everyone left on Tuesday except Dan, my English
    guest who stayed on for Christmas.
[The fragment is added to the independent clause
    Everyone left on Tuesday except Dan.]

My English guest stayed on for Christmas.
[The fragment becomes an independent clause by
    removing the word *who*.]

Dan was my English guest who stayed on for
    Christmas.
[The fragment becomes an independent clause by
    adding the words *Dan was*.]

RUN-ON SENTENCES

A **run-on sentence** results when two or more sentences are improperly united into one sentence. Characteristic of a run-on sentence is the absence of punctuation between the independent clauses or the use of incorrect punctuation (typically a comma) between the independent clauses:

Our flight was canceled we had to spend the night in
    Boston.
Our flight was canceled, we had to spend the night in
    Boston.

Here are three possible ways to correct the preceding run-on sentences:

> Our flight was canceled; we had to spend the night in Boston.
>
> [A semicolon provides a properly punctuated separation of the two independent clauses.]
>
> Our flight was canceled, so we had to spend the night in Boston.
>
> [A comma followed by a conjunction (*so*) provides a properly worded and punctuated separation of the two independent clauses.]
>
> Our flight was canceled. We had to spend the night in Boston.
>
> [The creation of two distinct sentences provides an absolute separation of the two independent clauses.]

MODIFIER PROBLEMS

The improper placement of modifying words, phrases, and clauses is a common mistake. The result is a sentence in which the modifier unintentionally refers to the wrong person or thing. The three principal culprits are dangling modifiers, misplaced modifiers, and squinting modifiers. Writers must be careful to avoid these troublesome errors in sentence construction. Review the following examples to see how an improperly placed modifier can be confusing to the reader. It is important to recognize the subtle differences between the incorrect sentences and their corrected versions.

A **dangling modifier** is an adjectival phrase or clause that lacks a proper connection because the word it is supposed to modify is missing.

dangling: While waiting for my son, a cat jumped onto the hood
               of my car.
               [This wrongly implies that "a cat was waiting for my
               son."]

correct: While I was waiting for my son, a cat jumped onto the
               hood of my car.
               While waiting for my son, I saw a cat jump onto the
               hood of my car.
               A cat jumped onto the hood of my car while I was
               waiting for my son.
               [The word that was missing is "I."]

dangling: At age seven, her grandfather died of diphtheria.
               [This wrongly implies that "her grandfather died when
               he was seven."]

correct: When she was seven, her grandfather died of
               diphtheria.
               Her grandfather died of diphtheria when she was
               seven.
               At age seven, she lost her grandfather when he died of
               diphtheria.
               [The word that was missing is "she."]

A misplaced modifier is a phrase or clause that is not positioned close enough to the word it is supposed to modify. It will seem to the reader that a different word is being modified.

misplaced: There was an outbreak in our school of chicken pox.
               [This wrongly implies that there is "a school of chicken
               pox."]

correct: There was an outbreak of chicken pox in our school.
               In our school there was an outbreak of chicken pox.
               Our school experienced an outbreak of chicken pox.

misplaced: I was stopped by a policeman without a driver's
             license.
             [This wrongly implies that there was "a policeman
                without a driver's license."]

correct: Driving without a license, I was stopped by a
                policeman.
             I was stopped by a policeman, and I did not have a
                driver's license.

A **squinting modifier** is an adverb placed between two
verbs. For the reader, it is often difficult to determine which
verb the adverb is supposed to modify.

squinting: The stack of chairs she had arranged carefully
                collapsed in the wind.
             [Was the stack of chairs "arranged carefully" or did it
                "carefully collapse"?]

correct: The stack of chairs she had carefully arranged
                collapsed in the wind.
             [Of the two possible meanings, this is only one that
                makes sense.]

squinting: The stack of chairs she had arranged quickly collapsed
                in the wind.
             [Was the stack of chairs "arranged quickly" or did it
                "quickly collapse"?]

correct: The stack of chairs she had quickly arranged collapsed
                in the wind.
             The stack of chairs she had arranged collapsed quickly
                in the wind.
             [Either meaning could make sense, so only the writer
                would know which version is correct.]

Guide to Spelling

Any reader or writer knows that spelling is an important component of writing. Some individuals seem to have little or no trouble spelling words correctly, while others seem to struggle with spelling, often misspelling the same words over and over.

For those who have experienced the struggle, it is important to remember that spelling is a skill that improves with practice. Regular reading and writing, accompanied by a dictionary for consultation, are the best methods for improving one's spelling. Anyone who has encountered trouble with spelling knows that the English language contains numerous irregularities. Even so, there are basic spelling rules that can be followed in most cases.

[For spelling guidelines for plural nouns and possessive nouns, refer to the "Noun" section under "Parts of Speech."]

TIP

Keep a list of words that you find difficult to spell. Use a dictionary to confirm the correct spellings. Add to your list whenever you encounter a troublesome word. Refer to your list often, and quiz yourself. Make up sentences that include words from the list, writing them without going back and forth to double-check the spelling. Compare the words in your sentences to the words on your list. Make a note of the words that continue to give you trouble, and write these words in sentences every day until you have learned to spell them.

COMPOUND ADJECTIVES AND NOUNS

A compound adjective or noun is a single term formed from two or more distinct words. There are three spelling formats for compounds: open, hyphenated, and closed.

In an **open compound**, the component words are
separate, with no hyphen (*well fed; wagon train*).
In a **hyphenated compound**, the component words are
joined by a hyphen (*half-baked; city-state*).
In a **closed compound**, the component words are
joined into a single word (*hardheaded; campfire*).

Compound Adjectives

For most cases of open compound adjectives, there is a general rule of thumb: the compound is left open when it is not followed by the modified noun; the compound is hyphenated when it is followed by the modified noun:

She was well known in the South for her poetry.
[The compound *well known* is open because it is not
followed by the modified noun *She*.]

In the South, she was a well-known poet.
[The compound *well-known* is hyphenated because it is
followed by the modified noun *poet*.]

A notable exception occurs when the first part of the compound adjective is an adverb that ends in *–ly*. In this case, the compound remains open, even when it is followed by the noun:

The woman who met us in the lobby was beautifully
dressed.
A beautifully dressed woman met us in the lobby.

Compound Nouns

For spellers, the least troublesome compound nouns are familiar closed compounds:

briefcase   downstairs
cupcake   fireplace

Other compound nouns can be troublesome. Although certain ones, such as *mother-in-law*, are always hyphenated, many compound nouns commonly occur in more than one acceptable format, such as *ice cap* or *icecap* and *vice president* or *vice-president*. For most spelling questions, the best resource is a dictionary; for questions pertaining specifically to compounds, an unabridged edition is recommended.

TIP

Different dictionaries often disagree on the preferred spelling formats for a number of compounds, so writers are well advised to consult just one dictionary when establishing a spelling style.

PREFIXES

A prefix is group of letters added to the beginning of a word to adjust its meaning.

In most cases, prefixes are affixed to the root word without hyphenation:

antibacterial
postwar
semicircle

Often, however, a hyphen is customary, necessary, or preferable.

Certain prefixes almost always take a hyphen: *all-*, *ex-*, *full-*, *quasi-*, *self-*:

all-encompassing   quasi-liberal
ex-partner   self-confidence
full-bodied

When the root word begins with a capital letter, the prefix takes a hyphen:

anti-American
pre-Conquest

Sometimes, without a hyphen, a word could be easily confused with another:

We <u>recovered</u> our furniture.

Does this mean we *found* our *missing* furniture? Or did we *put new coverings on* our furniture? If the latter is meant, a hyphen would have avoided confusion:

We <u>re-covered</u> our furniture.

Sometimes, a hyphen is not necessary but preferable. Without it, the word may look awkward. One such circumstance is when the last letter of the prefix and the first letter of the root word are both vowels, or when an awkward double consonant is created. For each of the following pairs of words, either spelling is acceptable:

TIP

Regarding the use of optional hyphens, the writer should establish a preferred style. Keeping a running list of hyphenated terms can help writers keep track of which spellings they have already used in their text, thus making the style consistent.

antiknock / anti-knock
preadapt / pre-adapt
semiindependent / semi-independent
nonnegative/non-negative

SUFFIXES

A suffix is group of letters added to the end of a word to create a derivative of the word. There are exceptions to the following guidelines on how to spell with suffixes, but in most cases these rules apply:

A root word that ends in *e* drops the *e* when the suffix begins with a vowel:

rehearse / rehearsing

However, most words that end in *ce* or *ge* keep the *e* when the suffix begins with *a* or *o*:

service / serviceable
advantage / advantageous

A root word that ends in *e* keeps the *e* when the suffix begins with a consonant:

wise / wisely

A root word that ends in a *y* preceded by a consonant changes the *y* to *i* when the suffix begins with any letter other than *i*:

satisfy / satisfies / satisfying

A root word that ends in *ie* changes the *ie* to *y* when the suffix is *–ing*:

lie / lying

A root word that ends in *oe* keeps the *e* when the suffix begins with a vowel, unless the vowel is *e*:

toe / toeing / toed

A one-syllable root word that ends in a single consonant preceded by a single vowel doubles the consonant when the suffix is *–ed*, *–er*, or *–ing*. This rule also applies to root words with two or more syllables if the accent is on the last syllable.

stir / stirred
refer / referring

WORD DIVISION

Sometimes it is necessary to "break" a word when the line on the page has run out of space. Dividing a word at the end of a line is perfectly acceptable, as long as two conditions are met: the word must be divisible, and the division must be made in the right place.

When a word is properly divided, a hyphen is attached to its first part, so that the hyphen is at the end of the line:

At the conclusion of the interview,
I had two minutes to sum-
marize my management experiences.

What words are never divisible?	for example:
• one-syllable words	catch; flutes; strange; through
• contractions	didn't; doesn't; wouldn't; you're
• abbreviations	Calif.; NASCAR; RSVP; YMCA
• numbers written as numerals	1776; $2,800; 9:45; 0.137

Where is a correct place to divide a word?	good break:	bad break:
• after a prefix	inter-national	interna-tional
• before a suffix that has more than two letters	govern-ment	gov-ernment
• between the main parts of a closed compound	nut-cracker	nutcrack-er
• at the hyphen of a hyphenated compound	gender-neutral	gen-der-neutral
• after double consonants if the root word ends in the double consonants	address-ing	addres-sing
• otherwise, between double consonants	rib-bon	ribb-on
• in general (for words that don't fall into the previous categories), between syllables	whis-per	whi-sper

Where is an incorrect place to divide a word?	good break:	bad break:
• before a two-letter suffix	——	odd-ly
• after the first syllable if it has only one letter	Ameri-can	A-merican
• before the last syllable if it has only one letter	nu-tria	nutri-a
• before the ending –ed if the –ed is not pronounced	——	abash-ed

---

TIP

When dividing a word at the end of a line, it is always a good idea to use a dictionary to verify the word's proper syllabification.

NUMBERS

Numbers are an important part of everyday communication, yet they often cause a writer to stumble, particularly over questions of spelling and style. The guidelines on *how* to spell out a number are fairly straightforward. The guidelines on *when* to spell out a number are not so precise.

How to spell out numbers

CARDINAL NUMBERS

The most common problem associated with the spelling of whole cardinal numbers is punctuation. The rules are actually quite simple: Numeric amounts that fall between twenty and one hundred are always hyphenated. No other punctuation should appear in a spelled-out whole number, regardless of its size.

26	twenty-six
411	four hundred eleven
758	seven hundred fifty-eight
6,500	six thousand five hundred
33,003	thirty-three thousand three
972,923	nine hundred seventy-two thousand nine hundred twenty-three

Note: The word *and* does not belong in the spelling of a number. For example, "758" should not be spelled "seven hundred and fifty-eight."

ORDINAL NUMBERS

The punctuation of spelled-out ordinal numbers typically follows the rules for cardinal numbers.

What should we do for their <u>fifty-fifth</u> anniversary?
He graduated <u>two hundred twenty-ninth</u> out of a class of two hundred thirty.

When ordinal numbers appear as numerals, they are affixed with –th, with the exception of those ending with the ordinal *first*, *second*, or *third*.

1st
2nd
3rd
4th

Note: Sometimes *2nd* is written as *2d*, and *3rd* as *3d*.

FRACTIONS

A fraction can appear in a number of formats, as shown here:

$\frac{3}{8}$	case fraction (or split fraction)
3/8	fraction with solidus
0.375	decimal fraction
three-eighths	spelled-out fraction

When acting as an adjective, a spelled-out fraction should always be hyphenated.

The Serbian democrats have won a <u>two-thirds</u> majority.

When acting as a noun, a spelled-out fraction may or may not be hyphenated, according to the writer's or publisher's preferred style.

At least <u>four-fifths</u> of the supply has been depleted.
  or
At least <u>four fifths</u> of the supply has been depleted.

When to Spell Out Numbers

When to spell out a number, whole or fractional, is as much a matter of sense as of style. Text that is heavy with numbers, such as scientific or statistical material, could become virtually unreadable if the numbers were all spelled out. Conversely, conventional prose that occasionally makes mention of a quantity may look unbalanced with an occasional numeral here and there.

Often, the decision to spell or not to spell comes down to simple clarity:

> Our standard paper size is 8½ by 11.
> Our standard paper size is 8 1/2 by 11.
> Our standard paper size is eight and a half by eleven.
> Our standard paper size is eight and one-half by eleven.

The preceding four sentences say exactly the same thing, but the best choice for readability is the first.

Even the most comprehensive books of style and usage do not dictate absolute rules regarding the style of numbers in text. When writing, it is most important to be as consistent as possible with a style once one has been established. For example, some writers or publishers may adopt a policy of spelling out the numbers zero through ten. Others may prefer to spell out the numbers zero through ninety-nine. Either style is perfectly acceptable, as long as the style is followed throughout the written work.

Sometimes, even after adopting a basic number style, the writer may wish to incorporate certain style allowances and exceptions. Perhaps the decision has been made to spell out only the numbers zero though ninety-nine. But in one paragraph, a sentence reads, "There must have been more than 1,000,000 people there." In this case, it may be better to write, "There must have been more than a million people there."

SYMBOLS

In most contexts of formal writing, the use of symbols should be strictly limited, but there are occasions when a symbol may be a better choice than a word. Text that deals largely with commerce, for instance, may rely on the use of various monetary symbols to keep the text organized and readable. In any text, mathematical equations and scientific formulas are much easier to read if written with symbols rather than words. Also, it is usually appropriate to use symbols within tables and charts; as symbols conserve space, they prevent a "cluttered look."

Here are some of the most common symbols found in print:

@	at	≈	is approximately equal to
c/o	care of	≠	is not equal to
$	dollar	<	is less than
¢	cent	>	is greater than
Can$	Canadian dollar	≤	is less than or equal to
£	pound sterling	≥	is greater than or equal to
¥	yen	√	square root
#	number or pound	∞	infinity
/	per *or* solidus	©	copyright
%	percent	®	registered
°	degree	™	trademark
+	plus	¶	paragraph
−	minus	§	section
÷	divided by	*	asterisk
×	times	†	dagger
±	plus or minus	‡	double dagger
=	equals	‖	parallels or pipes

Symbols are sometimes used to point out note references to the reader. In a table or chart, for instance, the writer may wish to indicate that an item is further explained or identified elsewhere on the page. A symbol placed with the item signals the reader to look for an identical symbol, which precedes the additional information. Sometimes, numerals are the symbols of choice, but if the material within the table or chart consists of numerals, it is probably better to use non-

---

TIP

Numerals and other symbols should never begin a sentence. If the symbol should not or cannot be spelled out, the sentence needs to be reworded.

19 students have become mentors.
should be:
Nineteen students have become mentors.

2004 is the year we plan to get married.
should be:
We plan to get married in 2004.

$10 was found on the stairs.
should be:
Ten dollars was found on the stairs.

6:00 is the earliest I can leave.
should be:
Six o'clock is the earliest I can leave.
or:
The earliest I can leave is 6:00.

$y = 2x + 1$ is a line with a slope of 2.
should be:
The line $y = 2x + 1$ has a slope of 2.

---

numeric symbols for the note references. The conventional set of symbols used for this purpose, in the conventional sequence in which to use them, is *, †, ‡, §, ||, #.

FOREIGN TERMS

Foreign words and phrases that are likely to be unfamiliar to the reader should be set in italics. When such terms are to be included in writing or speech, a dictionary should be consulted by the writer to insure proper placement of accents and other diacritical marks and by the speaker to insure correct pronunciations. Each of the following sample terms gives the literal translation, the English-usage definition, and an example sentence.

annus mirabilis: [Latin, 'wonderful year'] a remarkable or auspicious year.
This has been our team's *annus mirabilis*.

cause célèbre: [French, 'famous case'] a controversial issue that attracts a great deal of public attention.
The trial of Lizzie Borden became a *cause célèbre* throughout New England.

Weltschmerz: [German, 'world pain'] a feeling of melancholy and world-weariness.
A sense of *Weltschmerz* permeated his later works of art.
[Note that it is correct to capitalize a German noun.]

Familiar Foreign Terms

Many foreign terms have become so familiar and well-established in standard English usage that it is not necessary to put them in italic type. For most of these words, it is also not necessary to use accents and other diacritical marks, but in certain cases the inclusion of diacritics remains customary. There are, however, no absolute rules regarding when to italicize and when not to italicize, when to use diacritics and when not to use diacritics. Some foreign words may be more familiar to one group of readers than to another; therefore, targeted readership should be considered. Often, the style adopted is a matter of preference. As always, it is important for the writer to be consistent once this preference has been introduced.

Some familiar foreign terms:

ad absurdum
ad hoc
ad infinitum
ad interim
ad lib
ad nauseam
aficionado
à la carte (*or* a la
    carte)
à la king (*or* a la
    king)
à la mode (*or* a la
    mode)
al fresco
alter ego
annus mirabilis
Anno Domini
apartheid
aperitif
a priori
apropros
au contraire
au courant
au fait
au fond
au gratin
au jus
au naturel
au pair
avant-garde
ballet
basmati
bas-relief

baton
beau
beau monde
belle
bête noire
billet doux
bona fide
bonbon
bon mot
bon vivant
bouclé
boudoir
bouffant
bouillabaisse
bouillon
bouquet
bouquet garni
bourgeois
bric-a-brac
burka (*or* burkha)
burrito
cabaret
café (*or* cafe)
camisole
canapé
capo
carafe
carpe diem
carte blanche
cause célèbre
chaise longue
chalet
chamois

chapeau
chateau (*or*
    château)
chauffeur
chic
ciao
cognac
coiffeur
connoisseur
consommé
contretemps
corps
crepe (*or* crêpe)
croquette
cul-de-sac
de facto
déjà vu
de jure
de rigueur
dolce vita
Doppelgänger
élan
elite
enchilada
enfant terrible
en masse
en route
entourage
entrée (*or* entree)
entre nous
eureka
ex cathedra
ex post facto

fait accompli
fajita
faux
faux pas
fiancé (or fiance)
fiancée (or fiancee)
fiesta
flagrante delicto
glasnost
gourmand
gourmet
hacienda
haute cuisine
hoi polloi
hors d'oeuvre
incognito
ingénue
in loco parentis
in re
in situ
in toto
in vitro
in vivo
jabot
judo
julienne
karma
karate
kasha
kibitz
kitsch
laissez-faire
lanai
lèse-majesté

loco
lorgnette
madame
mademoiselle
maître d' (or
    maitre d')
mañana
masseur
masseuse
materiel (or
    matériel)
mea culpa
modus operandi
monsieur
mot juste
née
ne plus ultra
nom de guerre
nom de plume
non sequitur
nota bene
nouveau riche
objet d'art
objet trouvé
pace
par excellence
pasha
pâté de foie gras
patio
per capita
persona non grata
pièce de résistance
pied-à-terre
piccolo

poncho
portière (or
    portiere)
post mortem
prima donna
prima facie
pro bono
pro forma
pronto
protégé (or
    protege)
purée (or puree)
quid pro quo
qui vive
raisond'être
re
rendezvous
repertoire
résumé (or
    resume)
revue
roué
roulette
sachet
salsa
samovar
samurai
sang froid
sans souci
savoir faire
seance
serape
siesta
sine die

sine qua non	tango	viva voce
sombrero	terra incognita	viz.
soufflé	tête-à-tête	vox populi
status quo	tour de force	Wanderjahr
sub judice	tout le monde	Weltanschauung
suede	trompe l'oeil	Weltschmerz
tableau	trousseau	yin/yang
table d'hôte	verboten	yoga
tabula rasa	vice versa	Zeitgeist
taco	villa	

Commonly Misspelled Words

abbreviated	advertisement	answer
absence	advisable	anticipate
absolutely	affectionate	anxiety
acceptance	affidavit	apartheid
accessible	aficionado	aperitif
accidentally	afraid	apology
accommodate	again	apparatus
accompany	aggravate	apparent
accuracy	aghast	appearance
ache	aisle	appetite
achieve	allege	appreciate
achievement	allotment	approach
acquaintance	ally	appropriate
acquire	amateur	approximately
acre	analysis	argue
across	analyze	argument
actually	anesthetic	arithmetic
administration	angel	arrangement
admittance	angle	ascend
adolescent	annihilation	ascertain
advantageous	annually	assistant

Commonly Misspelled Words (cont.)

athletic	changeable	controlled
attendance	character	controversial
authority	characteristic	conversant
auxiliary	chauffeur	convertible
available	chic	cooperate
awkward	chief	copyright
bachelor	chocolate	corps
because	choice	correspondence
beggar	choose	counterfeit
beginning	chose	courageous
behavior	Christian	courteous
believe	clothes	criticism
benefit	collateral	criticize
benefited	colonel	cruelly
bicycle	color	curiosity
bouillon	column	curious
boundary	commercial	cylinder
bulletin	commission	dealt
bureau	committee	debtor
buried	community	deceive
business	compel	decision
cafeteria	competitor	definite
calendar	completely	dependent
campaign	conceivable	describe
cancellation	concentrate	despair
captain	condemn	desperate
carburetor	confidence	despise
career	confidential	develop
ceiling	confusion	difference
cemetery	connoisseur	dilemma
census	conscience	diphthong
certificate	conscious	disappearance
chamois	continuous	disappoint

disastrous
discipline
discrepancy
disease
diuretic
doctor
duplicate
easily
ecclesiastical
ecstasy
effect
efficient
eighth
elementary
eligible
embarrass
eminent
emphasize
encouragement
encumbrances
enforceable
entirely
entourage
envelope
environment
equipped
escape
especially
essential
et cetera
  (abbreviated
  etc.)
exaggerate
excellent
exciting

exercise
exhilarating
exhort
existence
expense
experience
experiment
extraordinary
extremely
facsimile
familiar
fantasy
fascinate
fashionable
fasten
fatal
favorite
February
field
fiery
finally
financial
fluorescent
forehead
foreign
forfeit
fortunately
forty
forward
fourth
freight
friend
fulfill
further
gauge

genius
gourmet
government
governor
gracious
grammar
guarantee
guerrilla
guess
guidance
gymnasium
gypsy
handsome
hangar
hanger
happened
happiness
harass
Hawaii
heavily
height
heinous
heroine
hors d'oeuvre
hospital
humor
humorous
hungrily
hygiene
hypocrisy
hypocrite
hysterical
ignorance
illiterate
imagine

Commonly Misspelled Words (cont.)

immediately	lieutenant	Massachusetts
impossible	lightning	misspell
incidentally	likely	mortgage
increase	liquefy	muscle
indefinite	liquidate	mysterious
independent	listener	narrative
indictment	literature	naturally
indispensable	livelihood	necessary
individually	lively	nickel
inevitable	loneliness	niece
influence	luxury	ninety
ingredient	magazine	noisily
innocence	magnificent	non sequitur
inoculate	maintenance	noticeable
insurance	maneuver	obstacle
intelligence	manufacturer	occasionally
intelligent	marriage	occurrence
interference	marvelous	offensive
interrupt	mathematics	official
iridescent	meant	often
irrelevant	mechanic	omission
itinerary	medical	omit
jealous	medicine	omitted
jewelry	melancholy	once
knowledge	merchandise	operate
laboratory	millionaire	opponent
laborer	miniature	opportunity
laid	minimum	optimistic
legitimate	minuscule	orchestra
leisure	minute	ordinarily
liaison	miscellaneous	organization
library	mischief	originally
license	mischievous	outrageous

pageant	pressure	religious
paid	pretension	removal
parallel	privilege	rendezvous
paralleled	probably	repertoire
paralyze	procedure	repetition
parliament	proceed	rescind
particular	procure	reservoir
pastime	professor	resistance
peaceful	proffered	resource
peculiar	promissory	responsibility
performance	pronunciation	restaurant
permanent	propaganda	rheumatism
perseverance	psychic	rhythm
personality	psychology	ridiculous
personnel	pumpkin	roommate
perspiration	punctual	sachet
persuade	punctuation	sacrifice
pessimistic	pursuit	sacrilegious
phenomenal	questionnaire	safety
Philippines	quiet	satisfied
philosophy	quite	scarcely
physical	quotient	scarcity
picnicking	raspberry	scene
pleasant	realize	schedule
politician	really	scholar
Portuguese	realtor	scissors
possession	realty	scurrilous
possibility	receipt	seance
practically	recipe	secretary
practice	recognize	seize
prairie	recommend	semester
preferred	referred	separate
prejudice	reign	sergeant
preparation	relevant	shepherd
presence	relieve	siege

Commonly Misspelled Words (cont.)

similar	summary	unanimous
sincerely	superintendent	unnecessary
skein	supersede	useful
skiing	surgeon	useless
skillful	surprise	usually
sophomore	susceptible	vacillate
soufflé	suspense	vacuum
source	swimming	vague
souvenir	sympathetic	valuable
specialty	synonym	variety
specifically	temperamental	various
specimen	temperature	vegetable
sponsor	tendency	vengeance
statistics	therefore	vilify
straight	thorough	villain
strength	though	warrant
stretch	thoughtful	weather
strictly	tomorrow	Wednesday
stubborn	tragedy	weird
substitute	transferred	whether
subtle	traveled	whole
succeed	tremendous	yacht
successful	truly	yield
suede	twelfth	
sufficient	typical	

Guide to Capitalization and Punctuation

CAPITALIZATION

Beginnings

The first word in a sentence is capitalized:

Dozens of spectators lined the street.

The first word in a direct quotation is capitalized:

Andy stood by the window and remarked, "The view from here is spectacular."

If a colon introduces more than one sentence, the first word after the colon is capitalized:

We went over our findings, one piece of evidence at a time: The custodian had discovered the body just before midnight. The keys to the victim's office were found in the stairwell. In the adjoining office, three file cabinets had been overturned.

If a colon introduces a formal and distinct statement, the first word after the colon is capitalized:

All my years on the basketball court have taught me one thing: Winning is more of a process than an outcome.

If a colon introduces a complete statement that is merely an extension of the statement preceding the colon, the first word after the colon is usually lowercased:

Everything in the house was a shade of pink: the sofa was carnation blush, the tiles were misty mauve, and the carpet was dusty rose.

If a colon introduces an incomplete statement, the first word after the colon is lowercased:

> The caterer provided three choices: <u>chicken</u>, beef, and shrimp.

Proper names

Proper names are capitalized. This is true of all proper names, including those of persons, places, structures, organizations, vessels, vehicles, brands, etc. Notice from the following examples that when a properly named entity is referred to in a "non-named" general sense, the general sense is almost always lowercased:

Eleanor Roosevelt
J. D. Salinger
Carson City / a city in Nevada
Ural Mountains / a view of the mountains
New York Public Library / borrowing books from the
    public library
Washington Monument / our photos of the monument
Calvin Leete Elementary School / the rear entrance of
    the school
Amherst Historical Society / when the society last met
Boeing 747
USS *Missouri* [note that the names of specific ships,
    aircraft, spacecraft, etc., are italicized]
Chevy Malibu
Slinky

Titles

The titles of works are capitalized. Titled works include:

> written material (books, periodicals, screenplays, etc.)
> components of written material (chapters, sections,
> etc.)

- filmed and/or broadcast works (movies, television shows, radio programs, etc.)
- works of art (paintings, sculptures, etc.)
- musical compositions (songs, operas, oratorios, etc.)

There are certain rules of convention regarding which words in the titles are capitalized.

Capitalize:

- first word in the title
- last word in the title
- nouns and pronouns
- adjectives
- verbs
- adverbs
- subordinating conjunctions (*although, as, because, if, since, that, whenever*, etc.)

Do not capitalize (unless they are first or last words in the title):

- articles (a, an, the)
- coordinating conjunctions (*and, but, for, nor, or, so, yet*)
- prepositions (although some guides suggest capitalizing prepositions of more than four letters)
- the word *to* in infinitives

The King, the Sword, and the Golden Lantern
A Room within a Room
Seventy Ways to Make Easy Money from Your Home
The Stars Will Shine Because You Are Mine

If a subtitle is included, it typically follows a colon. It follows the capitalization rules of the main title, thus its first word is always capitalized:

Aftermath Explored: The Confessions of a Nuclear Physicist

The first element in a hyphenated compound is always capitalized. The subsequent elements are capitalized unless they are articles, prepositions, or coordinating conjunctions. But if the compound is the last word in the title, its final element is always capitalized, regardless of its part of speech:

Nineteenth-Century Poets
Over-the-Top Desserts
The Love-in of a Lifetime
The Year of the Love-In

TIP

Which titles should be set in italics, and which should be set off by quotation marks? In printed material, the distinction can be significant. Here's a handy list of the most common categories of titles and their standard treatments in type:

italics:

- books
  Crossroads of Freedom: Antietam, by James M. McPherson
- pamphlets
  Thomas Paine's *Common Sense*
- magazines
  Popular Mechanics
- newspapers
  USA Today
- movies
  One Flew Over the Cuckoo's Nest
- television or radio series
  This Week in Baseball
- plays
  Neil Simon's *Lost in Yonkers*
- long poems
  Beowulf

An element that follows a hyphenated prefix is capitalized only if it is a proper noun or adjective:

Pre-Columbian Artifacts
Memoirs of a Semi-independent Child

Education

An academic title is capitalized (whether it is spelled out or abbreviated) when it directly accompanies a personal name. Otherwise, it is lowercased:

- collections of poems and other anthologies
  The Collected Poems of Emily Dickinson
- operas, oratorios, and other long musical compositions
  Madame Butterfly
- painting, sculptures, and other works of art
  Thomas Cole's *Mount Etna from Taormina*

quotation marks:

- articles
  "How to Remove Wallpaper"
- chapters
  "Betsy Saves the Day"
- short stories
  "The Pit and the Pendulum," by Edgar Allan Poe
- short poems
  "Tree at My Window," by Robert Frost
- essays
  Emerson's "Spiritual Laws"
- television or radio episodes
  "Lucy Does a TV Commercial"
- songs and other short musical compositions
  "Are You Lonesome Tonight?"

Professor Sarah McDonald
Assoc. Prof. Brown
my chemistry professor

An academic degree or honor is capitalized (whether it is spelled out or abbreviated) when it directly accompanies a personal name. Otherwise, it is lowercased:

Harold L. Fox, Ph.D.
Charles Gustafson, Fellow of the Geological Society
working toward her master's degree

Academic years are lowercased:

the senior prom
he's a sophomore
the fourth grade

The course name of a particular school subject is capitalized. A general field of study is lowercased (unless the word is normally capitalized, such as "English"):

Astronomy 101
Algebra II
taking classes in psychology, French literature, and
chemistry

Calendar terms and time

The names of the days of the week and months of the year are capitalized:

Sunday	September
Monday	October
Tuesday	November

The names of the four seasons are lowercased:

winter	fall
spring	autumn
summer	

The names of holidays (religious and secular) and periods of religious observance are capitalized:

Arbor Day
Easter
Halloween
Lent
Memorial Day
Ramadan

The names of time zones and the time systems they designate are lowercased (except for any words that are proper names). Their abbreviations are capitalized:

eastern daylight time (EDT)
Greenwich mean time (GMT)
Pacific standard time (PST)

Legislation, treaties, etc.

The formal name of a policy, treaty, piece of legislation, or similar agreement is capitalized. A general reference to such is lowercased:

Volstead Act
the act sponsored by Congressman Volstead
Treaty of Versailles
the treaty at Versailles
Bottle Bill
Articles of Confederation
Connecticut Constitution
Connecticut's constitution
North American Free Trade Agreement

Military service

A military title or rank is capitalized (whether it is spelled out or abbreviated) when it directly accompanies a personal name. Otherwise, it is lowercased:

Gen. George Patton
Ensign Irene Mahoney
promoted to admiral
James Kirk, captain of the USS *Enterprise*

There are two significant exceptions to the preceding rule: the U.S. military titles "Fleet Admiral" and "General of the Army" should always be capitalized, even when not directly accompanying a personal name:

became General of the Army in 1950
a visit from the Fleet Admiral

The full official name of a military group or force is capitalized. A general reference to a military group or force is lowercased:

the Royal Air Force
the British air force
the Army Corps of Engineers
the Third Battalion
our battalion
the U.S. Navy
joined the navy

The full name of a battle or war is capitalized. A general reference to a battle or war is lowercased:

the Russian Revolution
fought in the revolution
the Spanish-American War
the war in Vietnam
the Battle of the Bulge
the first battle of the campaign
the Norman Conquest

The official name of a military award or medal is capitalized:

the Purple Heart
the Silver Star
the Victoria Cross
the Congressional Medal of Honor

Science

The capitalization rules governing scientific terminology cover a wide range of categories and applications. Some of the basic rules are discussed here.

Taxonomic nomenclature—that is, the scientific classification of plants and animals—follows specific rules for both capitalization and italics.

The names of the phylum, class, order, and family of a plant or animal are capitalized and set in roman type. This format also applies to the intermediate groupings (suborder, subfamily, etc.) within these divisions:

The North American river otter belongs to the phylum
Chordata, the subphylum Vertebrata, the class
Mammalia, the order Carnivora, and the family
Mustelidae.

The divisions lower than family— that is, genus, species, and subspecies—are set in italic type. Of these, only the genus is capitalized. When a plant or animal is identified by its "scientific name" or "Latin name," the name given is the genus and species (and, when applicable, the subspecies):

The scientific name of the river otter is *Lutra canadensis*.
The Manitoban elk (*Cervus elaphus manitobensis*) is a subspecies of the North American elk.

The common names of plants and animals, as well as their
hybrids, varieties, and breeds, are lowercased and set in
roman type. A part of the name may be capitalized if that
part is a term normally capitalized (that is, a proper name). If
there is doubt, a dictionary should be consulted.

Alaskan malamute
Christmas cactus
Johnny-jump-up
maidenhair fern
rainbow trout
rose-breasted grosbeak
Swainson's hawk
Vietnamese potbellied pig

The names of astronomical entities, such as planets, stars,
constellations, and galaxies, are capitalized:

Alpha Centauri
Canis Major
Crab Nebula
Ganymede
Mercury
Milky Way
Orion
Sirius

The names of geological eras, periods, epochs, etc., are capitalized. When included with the name, the words *eras, periods, epochs,* etc., are lowercased:

Mesozoic era
Quaternary period
Oligocene epoch
Upper Jurassic

TIP

The names *sun*, *moon*, and *earth* are frequently lowercased. It is customary to capitalize them only when they are being referred to as components of the solar system. Also noteworthy is the fact that, in any context, the words *sun* and *moon* typically are preceded by the definite article, *the*. In non-astronomical contexts, the word *earth* often is preceded by *the*, but it is never preceded by *the* when used specifically as the name of a planet. Hence, *the Earth* would not be an appropriate use of capitalization.

We enjoyed the warmth of <u>the sun</u>.
The glow of <u>the moon</u> has inspired poets for
    centuries.
Countless species inhabit <u>the earth</u>.
What on <u>earth</u> are you doing?
In size, Venus is comparable to <u>Earth</u>.
The eclipse of <u>the Moon</u> will be visible from the
    night side of <u>Earth</u>.
They made observations of Neptune's orbit around
    <u>the Sun</u>.

Abbreviations

Although the use of abbreviations in formal writing should be limited, abbreviations are legitimate components of the language and deserve the same attention to spelling as do other words. Certain capitalization guidelines for a few types of abbreviations are given below. Because the possible variations are numerous, a standard dictionary should be consulted for more thorough guidance on the spelling, capitalization, and punctuation of a specific abbreviation.

When a capitalized term is abbreviated, the abbreviation is capitalized. If the abbreviation is comprised of initials, all the initials are capitalized:

Professor J. Leggett / Prof. J. Leggett
Sergeant David Potter / Sgt. David Potter
Master of Business Administration / MBA
United States Marine Corps / USMC

When a lowercased term is abbreviated as a simple shortening, the abbreviation is usually lowercased. But if the abbreviation is comprised of initials, all the initials are usually capitalized. When there is a compound word in the term, the initials may include the first letter of the root word:

especially / esp.
teaspoon / tsp.
deoxyribonucleic acid / DNA
monosodium glutamate / MSG
most favored nation / MFN

Usually, an abbreviation that ends in a capital letter is not followed by a period. An abbreviation that ends in a lowercase letter usually is followed by a period, although the period may be optional, depending on the prevailing style of the particular piece of writing.

One group of abbreviations that never ends with a period is the set of chemical symbols. Also, these abbreviations are always initially capitalized even though the terms they represent are lowercased:

Ar	argon	Na	sodium
Dy	dysprosium	Sb	antimony
H	hydrogen	Sn	tin
Kr	krypton	U	uranium
Lr	lawrencium	Xe	xenon

TIP

If the name of an entity such as an organization, institution, or movement is to be abbreviated, its full name should be identified. Upon first mention, both abbreviation and full name should appear together, with either one being set within parentheses. (Usually the lesser known format goes in the parentheses.) Thereafter in the text, only the abbreviation need appear:

> In February 1909, a group of activists founded what would become the NAACP (National Association for the Advancement of Colored People). For more than ninety years, the NAACP has persevered to honor its founders' vision of racial equality and social justice.

> Plans to rebuild at the site of the World Trade Center (WTC) are being discussed today. Various designs for new office space are expected to be considered. Thousands of suggestions for a WTC memorial have already been submitted.

Note that some chemical symbols appear to be straightforward abbreviations (*Ca* for *calcium*) while others seem unrelated to their corresponding terms (*Au* for *gold*). In fact, these symbols are abbreviations of the official scientific, or Latin, names (*Au* for *aurum*, which is Latin for *gold*).

PUNCTUATION

Punctuation is an essential element of good writing because it makes the author's meaning clear to the reader. Although precise punctuation styles may vary somewhat among published sources, there are a number of fundamental principles worthy of consideration. Discussed below are these punctuation marks used in English:

comma
semicolon
colon
period
question mark
exclamation point
apostrophe
quotation marks
parentheses
dash
hyphen

Comma

The comma is the most used mark of punctuation in the English language. It signals to the reader a pause, which generally clarifies the author's meaning and establishes a sensible order to the elements of written language. Among the most typical functions of the comma are the following:

1. It can separate the clauses of a compound sentence when there are two independent clauses joined by a conjunction, especially when the clauses are not very short:

   It never occurred to me to look in the attic, and I'm sure it didn't occur to Rachel either.

   The Nelsons wanted to see the Grand Canyon at sunrise, but they overslept that morning.

2. It can separate the clauses of a compound sentence when there is a series of independent clauses, the last two of which are joined by a conjunction:

The bus ride to the campsite was very uncomfortable, the cabins were not ready for us when we got there, the cook had forgotten to start dinner, and the rain was torrential.

3. It is used to precede or set off, and therefore indicate, a nonrestrictive dependent clause (a clause that could be omitted without changing the meaning of the main clause):

I read her autobiography, which was published last July.

They showed up at midnight, after most of the guests had gone home.

The coffee, which is freshly brewed, is in the kitchen.

4. It can follow an introductory phrase:

Having enjoyed the movie so much, he agreed to see it again.

Born and raised in Paris, she had never lost her French accent.

In the beginning, they had very little money to invest.

5. It can set off words used in direct address:

Listen, people, you have no choice in the matter.

Yes, Mrs. Greene, I will be happy to feed your cat.

6. It can separate two or more coordinate adjectives (adjectives that could otherwise be joined with *and*) that modify one noun:

The cruise turned out to be the most entertaining, fun, and relaxing vacation I've ever had.

The horse was tall, lean, and sleek.

Note that cumulative adjectives (those not able to be joined with *and*) are not separated by a comma:

She wore bright yellow rubber boots.

7. It is used to separate three or more items in a series or list:

Charlie, Melissa, Stan, and Mark will be this year's soloists in the spring concert.

We need furniture, toys, clothes, books, tools, housewares, and other useful merchandise for the benefit auction.

Note that the comma between the last two items in a series is sometimes omitted in less precise style:

The most popular foods served in the cafeteria are pizza, hamburgers and nachos.

8. It is used to separate and set off the elements in an address or other geographical designation:

My new house is at 1657 Nighthawk Circle, South Kingsbury, Michigan.

We arrived in Pamplona, Spain, on Thursday.

9. It is used to set off direct quotations (note the placement or absence of commas with other punctuation):

"Kim forgot her gloves," he said, "but we have a pair she can borrow."

There was a long silence before Jack blurted out, "This must be the world's ugliest painting."

"What are you talking about?" she asked in a puzzled manner.

"Happy New Year!" everyone shouted.

10. It is used to set off titles after a person's name:

Katherine Bentley, M.D.

Martin Luther King, Jr., delivered the sermon.

Semicolon

The semicolon has two basic functions:

1. It can separate two main clauses, particularly when these clauses are of equal importance:

   The crowds gathered outside the museum hours before the doors were opened; this was one exhibit no one wanted to miss.

   She always complained when her relatives stayed for the weekend; even so, she usually was a little sad when they left.

2. It can be used as a comma is used to separate such elements as clauses or items in a series or list, particularly when one or more of the elements already includes a comma:

   The path took us through the deep, dark woods; across a small meadow into a cold, wet cave; and up a hillside overlooking the lake.

   Listed for sale in the ad were two bicycles; a battery-powered, leaf-mulching lawn mower; and a maple bookcase.

Colon

The colon has five basic functions:

1. It can introduce something, especially a list of items:

   In the basket were three pieces of mail: a postcard, a catalog, and a wedding invitation.

   Students should have the following items: backpack, loose-leaf notebook, pens and pencils, pencil sharpener, and ruler.

2. It can separate two clauses in a sentence when the second clause is being used to explain or illustrate the first clause:

We finally understood why she would never go sailing with us: she had a deep fear of the water.

Most of the dogs in our neighborhood are quite large: two of them are St. Bernards.

3. It can introduce a statement or a quotation:

His parents say the most important rule is this: Always tell the truth.

We repeated the final words of his poem: "And such is the plight of fools like me."

4. It can be used to follow the greeting in a formal or business letter:

Dear Ms. Daniels:

Dear Sir or Madam:

5. It is used (in the U.S.) to separate minutes from hours, and seconds from minutes, in showing time of day and measured length of time:

Please be at the restaurant before 6:45.

Her best running time so far has been 00:12:35.

Period

The period has two basic functions:

1. It is used to mark the end of a sentence:

It was reported that there is a shortage of nurses at the hospital. Several of the patients have expressed concern about this problem.

2. It is often used at the end of an abbreviation:

On Fri., Sept. 12, Dr. Brophy noted that the patient's weight was 168 lb. and that his height was 6 ft. 2 in.

Note that another period is not added to the end of the sentence when the last word is an abbreviation.

Question Mark and Exclamation Point

The only sentences that do not end in a period are those that end in either a question mark or an exclamation point.

Question marks are used to mark the end of a sentence that asks a direct question (generally, a question that expects an answer):

Is there any reason for us to bring more than a few dollars?

Who is your science teacher?

Exclamation points are used to mark the end of a sentence that expresses a strong feeling, typically surprise, joy, or anger:

I want you to leave and never come back!

What a beautiful view this is!

Apostrophe

The apostrophe has two basic functions:

1. It is used to show where a letter or letters are missing in a contraction.

The directions are cont'd [continued] *on the next page. We've* [we have] *decided that if she can't* [cannot] *go, then we aren't* [are not] *going either.*

2. It can be used to show possession:

The possessive of a singular noun or an irregular plural noun is created by adding an apostrophe and an s:

the pilot's uniform
Mrs. Mendoza's house
a tomato's bright red color
the oxen's yoke

The possessive of a plural noun is created by adding just an apostrophe:

the pilots' uniforms [referring to more than one pilot]
the Mendozas' house [referring to the Mendoza family]
the tomatoes' bright red color [referring to more than one tomato]

Quotation Marks

Quotation marks have two basic functions:

1. They are used to set off direct quotations (an exact rendering of someone's spoken or written words):

   "I think the new library is wonderful," she remarked to David.

   We were somewhat lost, so we asked, "Are we anywhere near the gallery?"

   In his letter he had written, "The nights here are quiet and starry. It seems like a hundred years since I've been wakened by the noise of city traffic and squabbling neighbors."

   Note that indirect quotes (which often are preceded by *that, if,* or *whether*) are not set off by quotation marks:

   He told me that he went to school in Boston.

   We asked if we could still get tickets to the game.

2. They can be used to set off words or phrases that have specific technical usage, or to set off meanings

of words, or to indicate words that are being used in a special way in a sentence:

The part of the flower that bears the pollen is the "stamen."

When I said "plain," I meant "flat land," not "ordinary."

Oddly enough, in the theater, the statement "break a leg" is meant as an expression of good luck.

What you call "hoagies," we call "grinders" or "submarine sandwiches."

He will never be a responsible adult until he outgrows his "Peter Pan" behavior.

Note that sometimes single quotation marks, rather than double quotation marks may be used to set off words or phrases:

The part of the flower that bears the pollen is the 'stamen.'

What is most important is to be consistent in such usage. Single quotation marks are also used to set off words or phrases within material already in double quotation marks, as:

"I want the sign to say 'Ellen's Bed and Breakfast' in large gold letters," she explained.

Parentheses

Parentheses are used, in pairs, to enclose information that gives extra detail or explanation to the regular text. Parentheses are used in two basic ways:

1. They can separate a word or words in a sentence from the rest of the sentence:

   On our way to school, we walk past the Turner Farm (the oldest dairy farm in town) and watch the cows being fed.

The stores were filled with holiday shoppers (even more so than last year).

Note that the period goes outside the parentheses' because the words in the parentheses are only part of the sentence.

2. They can form a separate complete sentence:

Please bring a dessert to the dinner party. (It can be something very simple.) I look forward to seeing you there.

Note that the period goes inside the parentheses, because the words in the parentheses are a complete and independent sentence.

Dash

A dash is used most commonly to replace the usage of parentheses within sentences. If the information being set off is in the middle of the sentence, a pair of long (or "em") dashes is used; if it is at the end of the sentence, just one long dash is used:

On our way to school, we walk past the Turner Farm—the oldest dairy farm in town—and watch the cows being fed

The stores were filled with holiday shoppers—even more so than last year.

Hyphen

A hyphen has three basic functions:

1. It can join two or more words to make a compound, especially when so doing makes the meaning more clear to the reader:

We met to discuss long-range planning.

There were six four-month-old piglets at the fair.

That old stove was quite a coal-burner.

2. It can replace the word "to" when a span or range of data is given. This kind of hyphen is sometimes keyed as a short (or "en") dash:

John Adams was president of the United States 1797–1801.

Today we will look for proper nouns in the L–N section of the dictionary.

The ideal weight for that breed of dog would be 75–85 pounds.

3. It can indicate a word break at the end of a line. The break must always be between syllables:

It is important for any writer to know that there are numerous punctuation principles that are considered standard and proper, but there is also flexibility regarding acceptable punctuation. Having learned the basic "rules" of good punctuation, the writer will be able to adopt a specific and consistent style of punctuation that best suits the material he or she is writing.

WORDS: MAKING THE RIGHT CHOICES

The building blocks of written or spoken communication are, of course, words. When we speak informally to one another throughout the day, we use our familiar vocabulary and patterns of expression without giving the individual words much thought. When our communication is more formal—as in a letter, an article, or a speech—our choice of words becomes more important.

Synonyms

Knowing which words to choose depends largely on knowing how to use synonyms. A **synonym** is a term that means exactly or nearly the same as another term in the same language. For example, *glad* is a synonym of *pleased*. By exploring synonym choices, writers are likely to keep their writing fresh and interesting.

Thoughtfully selected words not only convey the writer's message, they can enhance readability and demonstrate the writer's competency. It is usually well worth the writer's time to be guided by such resources as thesauruses and synonym studies.

USING THESAURUSES

A thesaurus, essentially a book of synonyms, can be an indispensable tool for the writer. There are two conventional types of thesauruses: one arranges the material by theme; the other arranges the headwords in an A-to-Z format, much like a dictionary. Most modern thesauruses are compiled in the latter format.

There are several reasons that one might consult a thesaurus. Perhaps "the right word" is somewhere in the writer's mind, but it just isn't coming to the writer at that moment. The writer thinks, "The word means something like *to pause*." When the writer looks up *pause* in the thesaurus, there in a list of synonyms is the very word! The writer is relieved and thinks, "Yes, that's what I was thinking of—the word *hesitate*."

Another valuable function of a thesaurus is to help the writer avoid repetition. Using the same word over and over again can be monotonous to the reader and may suggest weak vocabulary skills on the part of the writer. Consider the following paragraph:

> The movie we saw last night was very exciting. It started with an exciting car chase, and it just got more and more exciting as the plot developed. There were many moments that had me on the edge of my seat, but the scene in the train station was definitely the most exciting part of the story.

The writer risks losing the reader's attention because the reader may be thinking, "Doesn't this person know any word other than *exciting*?" If the writer were to consult a thesaurus, the paragraph could be greatly improved. One such revision might read as follows:

> The movie we saw last night was very <u>exciting</u>. It started with a <u>sensational</u> car chase, and it just got more and more <u>thrilling</u> as the plot developed. There were many moments that had me on the edge of my seat, but the scene in the train station was definitely the most <u>electrifying</u> part of the story.

A thesaurus can expand a writer's use of vocabulary and perk up a piece of writing, but it is the writer's responsibility to make certain that the words chosen are appropriate for the intended context. If a writer is not certain of the precise meaning or correct usage of a term listed in a thesaurus, a dictionary should be consulted as well.

USING SYNONYM STUDIES

Many dictionaries feature synonym studies, which expound on the usage of synonyms for selected terms. They offer an analytical treatment of the nuances of meaning that distinguish a set of closely related synonyms. If a synonym study were to appear at the dictionary entry for *despise*, for example, it might look like this:

> **SYNONYM STUDY: distinguish**
> DESCRY, DIFFERENTIATE, DISCERN, DISCRIMINATE. What we **discern** we see apart from all other objects (*to discern the lighthouse beaming on the far shore*). **Descry** puts even more emphasis on the distant or unclear nature of what we're seeing (*the lookout was barely able to descry a man approaching*). To **discriminate** is to perceive the differences between or among things that are very similar; it may suggest that some aesthetic evaluation is involved (*to discriminate between two singers' styles*). **Distinguish** requires making even finer distinctions among things that resemble each other even more

closely (*unable to distinguish the shadowy figures moving through the forest*). *Distinguish* can also mean recognizing by some special mark or outward sign (*the sheriff could be distinguished by his badge*). **Differentiate**, on the other hand, suggests the ability to perceive differences between things that are easily confused. In contrast to *distinguish*, *differentiate* suggests subtle differences that must be compared in some detail (*the color of the first paint sample was difficult to differentiate from the third sample*).

Ten Tips to Improve Your Vocabulary

1. Decide why you need new words. Do you need new words in a particular area or subject, so that you can learn more about that subject? Do you want to improve your writing, or your speaking, or both? Do you want to replace overused words in your vocabulary? Make a plan first, so that you can get the most out of your new words.

2. READ! You will learn more new words, faster, by seeing them in their natural habitats, rather than in dull lists. Choose subjects that interest you or ones you aren't already familiar with. When you see an unfamiliar word, guess what it means from its context. If it still doesn't make sense, look it up in a dictionary. Keep a list of words you find and might like to use.

3. Use your new words right away. When you find one you like, make a point of using it in writing or in conversation that very day. If you don't use it, you'll lose it. Even if you have to write it in an e-mail to yourself, make sure to use it that day.

4. Subscribe to a word-a-day e-mail list. The biggest and best-known is A Word A Day, at www.wordsmith.org. Many dictionary sites have their own word-a-day lists or pages as well, including the Oxford English Dictionary

---

(www.oed.com). Print out or write down the words you especially like—and use them.

5. Buy and use a good dictionary. Look up a word every day. You can even look up words you think you know the meaning of already. You might be surprised to find that the word you think you know has additional meanings you aren't familiar with. Then you can make that word do twice the work in your vocabulary.

6. Ask your friends and family to help you by using new words with you. Ask them to tell you words they use in their work, or their favorite words. When you associate those new words with the people who told them to you, they will be easier to remember.

7. Set little word-hunt goals for yourself. Decide that you will find a word that you don't know that rhymes with "mellow," or a word that has to do with buildings, for instance, and keep looking for them until you find them. Then you can cross them off your list and add them to your vocabulary.

8. Buy and use a good thesaurus. Look up a word that you use too often and memorize the first five synonyms, and any antonyms. Be sure to look them up in a dictionary so that you know exactly what they mean. Then use them to replace the word you use too often. Some good words to replace: very, great, good, beautiful.

9. Watch TV, especially TV news programs, with the closed-captioning on. This will show you how words you may have only heard are spelled. (Caution: Often captioning has typographical errors. Check words in a dictionary before you use them.)

10. Don't forget to check the pronunciation of new and difficult words in your dictionary. While you're there, check out the etymology of the word, too. A good word history will often help you to remember the meaning of your new word.

Commonly Confused Words

Certain words in the English language are commonly confused with other words that are in some way similar. Some of the most frequently confused terms are listed here, accompanied by brief usage notes.

CONFUSED TERMS	PROPER USAGE
accept	*Accept* is a verb, meaning "consent to receive" or "agree to undertake." I am pleased to accept your generous offer.
except	*Except* is usually a preposition, meaning "not including" or "other than." Everyone <u>except</u> Ursula has made reservations.
advice	*Advice* is a noun meaning "guidance" or "recommendations." May I ask your <u>advice</u> on a personal matter?
advise	*Advise* is a verb meaning "offer suggestions," "give an opinion," or "warn." We were <u>advised</u> to take an alternate route.
affect	*Affect* is a verb meaning "influence" or "produce an effect on." The rise in gas prices has <u>affected</u> our travel plans.
effect	*Effect*, as a noun, means "the result or consequence of an action." The rise in gas prices has had an <u>effect</u> on our travel plans. *Effect*, as a verb, means "bring about" or "cause to occur." Exactly what circumstances have <u>effected</u> these rising gas prices?

CONFUSED TERMS	PROPER USAGE
already	*Already* means "before now" or "by now." Evelyn <u>already</u> fixed the leak.
all ready	*All ready* means "completely ready." Are you <u>all ready</u> to leave?
all together	*All together* means "all in one place" or "all at once." For the first time in years, we were <u>all together</u>.
altogether	*Altogether* means "in total." <u>Altogether</u>, there are six bedrooms.
allusion	*Allusion* is used to refer indirectly to someone or something. The <u>allusion</u> to Jesus in his poetry is fairly obvious.
illusion	*Illusion* means "a false or misleading appearance or impression." His mother created the <u>illusion</u> of a happy family.
adverse	*Adverse* means "unfavorable" or "harmful." Drought has had an <u>adverse</u> effect on the crops.
averse	*Averse* means "having a strong dislike of or opposition to." I am not <u>averse</u> to the idea of moving.
as	*As* is sometimes a preposition, used to refer to function or character. He landed a job <u>as</u> an editor. *As* is sometimes a conjunction, used to indicate the concurrence of events. The fans went wild <u>as</u> Elvis walked onto the stage.

CONFUSED TERMS	PROPER USAGE
like	*Like*, as a preposition, takes an object. It means "similar to."
	That dog looks <u>like</u> a bear.
	Like is not a conjunction, yet it is frequently used as one. Especially in formal speech or writing, be careful to avoid this incorrect usage:
	I don't have a big kitchen <u>like</u> you do. [incorrect]
	I don't have a big kitchen <u>like</u> yours. [correct]
	Sammy goes to bed by eight, just <u>like</u> children should. [incorrect]
	Sammy goes to bed by eight, just <u>as</u> children should. [correct]
beside	*Beside* is a preposition meaning "next to" or "alongside."
	Please put the tray on the table <u>beside</u> my bed.
besides	*Besides*, as a preposition, means "in addition to."
	<u>Besides</u> the free room, we were given a lavish breakfast.
	Besides, as an adverb, means "furthermore."
	I'm too tired to go to a restaurant. <u>Besides</u>, I'm not hungry.
can	*Can* expresses ability
	Cheetahs <u>can</u> run at a remarkable speed.
may	*May* expresses permission or possibility.
	The children <u>may</u> have more pizza. [permission]
	I <u>may</u> join you later. [possibility]
	Note: In most informal contexts, the use of can to express permission is generally accepted as standard usage.
	The children <u>can</u> have more pizza.

CONFUSED TERMS	PROPER USAGE
capital	*Capital* refers to uppercase letters, money, administrative cities, or crimes punishable by death. 　　The first word should begin with a <u>capital</u> Q. [letters] 　　The <u>capital</u> expenditures exceeded our budget. [money] 　　Vilnius is the <u>capital</u> of Lithuania. [cities] 　　Treason is a <u>capital</u> offense. [crimes]
capitol	*Capitol* refers only to a building that houses a legislature. The proper name *the Capitol* refers specifically to the building that houses the U.S. Congress in Washington, D.C. 　　We met on the steps of the Virginia state <u>capitol</u>.
could have/	*Could have* and *should have* are grammatically correct should have verb forms. 　　I <u>could have</u> gone to Harvard.
could of/	*Could of* and *should of* are meaningless forms that should should of never be used. They are mistakenly used because they sound like *could have* and *should have*.
elicit	*Elicit* is a verb meaning "draw out (a response, answer, or fact) from someone." 　　The police were unable to <u>elicit</u> a confession from the suspect.
illicit	*Illicit* is an adjective meaning "forbidden by law" or "improper." 　　Ray's <u>illicit</u> use of the funds led to his dismissal.

CONFUSED TERMS	PROPER USAGE
emigrate	*Emigrate* means "move out of a country." Her grandfather <u>emigrated</u> from Poland in 1926.
immigrate	*Immigrate* means "move into a country." Gerda <u>immigrated</u> to Australia with her second husband.
good	*Good* is an adjective meaning "favorable" or "appropriate" or "pleasing." The dance performance was <u>good</u>.
well	*Well* is an adverb meaning "in a good or satisfactory way." She dances <u>well</u>.
lend	*Lend* is a verb meaning "grant the temporary use of." *Lend* is always a verb. I will <u>lend</u> my car to you.
loan	*Loan*, as a verb, means "grant the temporary use of." Hence, it can be a synonym of *lend*. I will <u>loan</u> my car to you. *Loan*, as a noun, means "a thing that is borrowed" or "an act of lending something." He thanked me for the <u>loan</u> of my car.
lay, laid	*Lay* is a verb meaning "put (something) down." The past tense of lay is *laid*. Let's <u>lay</u> our towels in a sunny spot. We are <u>laying</u> our towels in a sunny spot. We <u>laid</u> our towels in a sunny spot.
lie, lay	*Lie* is a verb meaning "assume a horizontal or resting position." The past tense of *lie* is *lay*. Let's <u>lie</u> on our towels. We are <u>lying</u> on our towels. Earlier today, we <u>lay</u> on our towels. Note: The base *lay* and the past tense *lay* are two different words with distinctly different usages.

CONFUSED TERMS	PROPER USAGE
personal	*Personal* is an adjective that refers to a person's private or individual affairs. I will give this matter my <u>personal</u> attention.
personnel	*Personnel* is a plural noun that refers to the people employed by an organization. All <u>personnel</u> are invited to attend the reception. *Personnel* is often used as a shortened form of *personnel department*. Ask someone in <u>personnel</u> for a copy of the form.
principal	*Principal,* as an adjective, means "most important." Our <u>principal</u> concerns are food and shelter. *Principal,* as a noun, refers to a person in charge or to a sum of money on which interest is paid. The <u>principal</u> of Franklin High School is Mr. Barnes. [person] I still owe most of the <u>principal</u> on my student loan. [money]
principle	*Principle* is a noun meaning "rule" or "basis for conduct." He strictly adhered to the <u>principles</u> of his faith.
real	*Real* is an adjective meaning "actual" or "genuine." Is that painting a <u>real</u> Picasso?
really	*Really* is an adverb used to mean "in actual fact" or as an emphasis to a statement. She and I are not <u>really</u> related. ["in actual fact"] Do you <u>really</u> want to go? [emphasis] Note: The word *real* is sometimes used adverbially for emphasis, in place of the adverb *really*. In informal contexts, such usage may be acceptable, but it should be strictly avoided in formal contexts. He is a <u>real</u> nice salesman. [informal] He is a <u>really</u> nice salesman.[formal]

CONFUSED TERMS	PROPER USAGE
than	*Than* is used in comparisons. The original movie was much better <u>than</u> the sequel.
then	*Then* is usually used to indicate a relative time. We saw the movie, and <u>then</u> we went home. *Then* sometimes means "also" or "in that case." The hours are great, and <u>then</u> there's the overtime. ["also"] You don't want salad? <u>Then</u> don't stop at the store. ["in that case"]
there	*There* is an adverb meaning "at that place." The tomatoes are over <u>there</u>.
their	*Their* is a possessive pronoun meaning "belonging to them." I wonder if they still have tomatoes in <u>their</u> garden.
they're	*They're* is the contracted form of "they are." I wonder if <u>they're</u> going to grow tomatoes this year.
to	*To* is a preposition that expresses motion in a particular direction or indicates a point reached. I've never been <u>to</u> Japan. *To* is also used as the mark of an infinitive. Would you like me <u>to</u> help?
too	*Too* is an adverb meaning "also" or "excessively." Is Arlene coming <u>too</u>? ["also"] He's driving <u>too</u> fast. ["excessively"]
two	*Two* is a number. There are <u>two</u> candles in the drawer.

CONFUSED TERMS	PROPER USAGE
waive	*Waive* is a verb meaning "give up (a right or claim)" or "refrain from enforcing." Sidney refused to <u>waive</u> his parental rights.
wave	*Wave*, as a verb, means "move one's hands to and fro, especially to signal a message such as a greeting." Sidney <u>waved</u> to reporters as he left the courthouse.
we	*We* is a subjective pronoun. It is used as a subject of a verb, either by itself or with a noun that expresses the category to which the *we* belongs. <u>We</u> received our schedules on Monday. <u>We</u> <u>teachers</u> received our schedules on Monday.
us	*Us* is an objective pronoun. It is used as an object of a verb. The schedules were distributed to <u>us</u> on Monday. Note: Especially in informal speech, the pronoun *us* is frequently used subjectively, but such usage is never correct. When Dr. Wilson retired, <u>us students</u> gave her a party. [incorrect] When Dr. Wilson retired, <u>we students</u> gave her a party. [correct]
who	*Who* is used as a subject. This is the woman <u>who</u> found your wallet.
whom	*Whom* is used as the object of a verb or preposition. For <u>whom</u> did you make the card?
whose	*Whose* is the possessive form of *who*. We're not sure <u>whose</u> money this is.
who's	*Who's* is the contracted form of *who is* and *who has*. <u>Who's</u> the new accountant? [*who is*] <u>Who's</u> got change for a ten? [*who has*]

CONFUSED TERMS	PROPER USAGE
your	*Your* is the possessive form of *you*. Why is Owen wearing <u>your</u> coat?
you're	*You're* is the contracted form of *you are*. If <u>you're</u> going home now, I'll lock up.

Clichés

A **cliché** is a worn-out expression. It was once fresh and meaningful, but it has lost its original impact through overuse. Numerous clichés have become so familiar that it would be virtually impossible to eradicate them from one's vocabulary. However, writers and speakers should make the effort to avoid using them, especially in formal material.

Common clichés to avoid:

above and beyond the call
 of duty
accident waiting to happen
acid test
add insult to injury
after all is said and done
all hands on deck
all in all
all wet
all's well that ends well
almighty dollar
along the same lines
A-OK
as luck would have it
at a loss for words
at arm's length
avoid like the plague

back in the saddle
back on track
backseat driver
ball is in your court
barking up the wrong tree
be your own worst enemy
beat a dead horse
beat around the bush
been there, done that
beggars can't be choosers
be an open book
believe me
better late than never
between a rock and hard
 place
between you, me, and the
 lamppost

big picture
big spender
bigger fish to fry
bird's-eye view
bitter end
bone of contention
born and bred
both sides of the coin
brain trust
bring home the bacon
broad spectrum
broaden one's horizons
bundle of nerves
bury the hatchet
busy as a bee
buy into
by leaps and bounds
by the skin of one's teeth
call her bluff
can't judge a book by its
    cover
can't take a joke
cast the net
catbird seat
catch as catch can
center of attention
cheat death
chew the fat
clear as a bell
clear as mud
cloak and dagger
coast is clear
cold as ice
cold shoulder

come full circle
come to no good
come up for air
conspicuous by their
    absence
cool it
cop out
could eat a horse
counting on you
count your blessings
cover all the bases
crazy like a fox
cream of the crop
creature of habit
crossing the line
cut me some slack
cut to the chase
dead in the water
dead wrong
dog-eat-dog
done deal
done to death
don't know him from Adam
down and dirty
down and out
down in the dumps
down in the mouth
dressed to the nines
due in large measure to
duly noted
dumb luck
easier said than done
easy come, easy go
easy mark

easy target

eat crow

end of discussion

every fiber of my being

face the music

fair and square

fall from grace

fall through the cracks

far and away

feast or famine

few and far between

fighting the tide

fill the bill

find it in your heart

fit as a fiddle

fit to be tied

fits like an old shoe

flat as a pancake

fly in the ointment

fly off the handle

for all intents and purposes

for love or money

for your information

fork it over

free as a bird

from the frying pan into the fire

from time immemorial

game plan

get behind the eight ball

get down to brass tacks

get off scot-free

get our ducks in a row

get the lead out

get the show on the road

get to the bottom of it

give a damn

give rise to

go for the kill

go it alone

go the distance

go the extra mile

go to pieces

go with the flow

goes without saying

good for nothing

goodly number

grass is always greener

green with envy

grist for the mill

hammer out the details

handwriting on the wall

hang in there

has a screw loose

have your heart in your mouth

head over heels

heated argument

his bark is worse than his bite

hit or miss

hit the ceiling

hit the ground running

hit the nail on the head

hold that thought

holding back the tide

hook, line, and sinker

hour of need

I wasn't born yesterday
icing on the cake
if looks could kill
if the price is right
I'm all over it
I'm speechless
in a nutshell
in due course
in hot water
in layman's terms
in one fell swoop
in over their heads
in seventh heaven
in the bag
in the ballpark
in the driver's seat
in the event that
in the final analysis
in the groove
in the near future
in the neighborhood of
in the nick of time
in the same boat
in the zone
in this day and age
irons in the fire
it could be worse
it stands to reason
it takes all kinds
it takes guts
it's your baby
join the club
keep your fingers crossed
keep the home fires burning

keeping score
kill the fatted calf
kiss of death
knock on wood
knock the socks off of
know the ropes
last but not least
last straw
lay an egg
learning curve
leave no stone unturned
left to his own devices
lend me an ear
let the cat out of the bag
let your hair down
letter perfect
lie low
light of day
like a bull in a china shop
like a bump on a log
like greased lightning
like rolling off a log
little does he know
live it up
lock, stock, and barrel
look like a million bucks
low man on the totem pole
make ends meet
make tracks
makes her blood boil
method in (or to) my
    madness
millstone around your neck
mince words

misery loves company
moment of truth
Monday-morning quarter-
back
monkey on your back
more money than God
more than meets the eye
more than you could shake
a stick at
nail to the wall
naked truth
nearing the finish line
needle in a haystack
needs no introduction
never a dull moment
nip and tuck
nip in the bud
no harm, no foul
no skin off my nose
no strings attached
no-brainer
none the worse for wear
nose to the grindstone
not one red cent
nothing new under the sun
off the cuff
old as the hills
old hat
old soldiers never die
older than dirt
on cloud nine
on the one hand/on the
other hand
on the road

on the same page
on the same track
on the wagon
on top of the world
out of my league
out of the woods
over a barrel
pan out
par for the course
pass the buck
pay the piper
perish the thought
piece of cake
playing for keeps
powers that be
practice makes perfect
proud as a peacock
pulling my leg
pulling no punches
put faces to names
put on hold
put the bite on
put words in one's mouth
put your money where your
mouth is
quick and dirty
rags to riches
rant and rave
reading me like a book
real McCoy
red as a beet
regret to inform you
reign supreme
rings a bell

ripe old age
rise and shine
rolling over in his grave
rub elbows
rule the roost
run circles around
run it up the flagpole
run off at the mouth
sadder but wiser
safe to say
salt of the earth
scarce as hen's teeth
sea of faces
see the forest for the trees
sell like hotcakes
set in stone
shake a leg
sharp as a tack
ships that pass in the night
shoot the breeze
shooting himself in the foot
shot in the arm
shot to hell
sight for sore eyes
sitting duck
skeleton in the closet
skin alive
sleep on it
smells fishy
smooth sailing
snake in the grass
spill the beans
stay in the loop
steal the limelight

stem the tide
stick to your guns
stick your neck out
straight from the horse's
    mouth
strange bedfellows
strike a balance
strong as an ox
stubborn as a mule
sturdy as an oak
suffice it to say
sweating bullets
take a breather
take into consideration
take on board
take one's word for
take pleasure in
take the bitter with the
    sweet
take the easy way out
take the liberty of
talk shop
talk the talk
talk through your hat
talk your ear off
that's all she wrote
the die is cast
they'll be sorry
thick as thieves
thin as a rail
think outside the box
think tank
those are the breaks
through thick and thin

throw caution to the wind
thrown to the wolves
tighten our belts
time is money
time marches on
time waits for no man
to each his own
to your heart's content
too funny for words
took the words right out of
   my mouth
touch base
turn the other cheek
turn up your nose
two peas in a pod
ugly as sin
under the wire
up a creek
upset the applecart
venture a guess
vicious circle
waiting for the other shoe to
   drop

walk the walk
walking encyclopedia
walking on air
welcome with open arms
when the cows come home
where angels fear to tread
where there's smoke,
   there's fire
whole nine yards
wild-goose chase
wipe the slate clean
wishful thinking
with bated breath
without further ado
without further delay
wonders never cease
words fail me
wreak havoc
yada, yada, yada
you said a mouthful
you'll never know if you
   don't try

Redundant Expressions

A redundant expression is a group of words (usually a pair) in
which at least one word is superfluous—that is, unnecessary.
The superfluous element can be removed without affecting
the meaning of the expression. In formal speech or writing,
redundant expressions should be strictly avoided.

In the following list of common redundant expressions, the superfluous elements have been crossed out.

absolute guarantee

absolutely certain

absolutely essential

absolutely necessary

AC current

actual fact

actual truth

add an additional

adding together

advance reservations

advance warning

after the end of

all meet together

alongside of

already existing

and moreover

annoying pest

ATM machine

awkward predicament

bald-headed

basic essentials

basic fundamentals

blend together

brief moment

but however

but nevertheless

came at a time when

cancel out

chief protagonist

clearly obvious

climb up

close proximity

close scrutiny

collaborate together

combine into one

commute back and forth

complete monopoly

completely destroyed

completely eliminated

completely empty

completely filled

completely random

consensus of opinion

continue on

continue to remain

cooperate together

currently today

DC current

decorative garnish

deep chasm

definitely decided

descend down

different varieties

difficult dilemma

direct confrontation

drop down

during the course of

dwindled down

each and every

earlier in time

empty space

end result

enter in

equal to one another

~~established~~ fact

estimated ~~at about~~

estimated ~~roughly at~~

~~every~~ now and then

~~evil~~ fiend

~~exact~~ duplicate

~~exact~~ opposites

~~fake~~ copy

~~false~~ pretenses

~~fellow~~ classmates

~~fellow~~ teammates

few ~~in number~~

filled ~~to capacity~~

~~final~~ conclusion

~~final~~ outcome

first ~~and foremost~~

~~first~~ began

~~first~~ introduction

first ~~of all~~

~~first~~ started

follow ~~after~~

for ~~a period of~~ six months

for ~~the purpose of~~

~~foreign~~ exports

~~foreign~~ imports

forever ~~and ever~~

foundered ~~and sank~~

~~free~~ gift

~~free~~ pass

~~future~~ prospects

gather ~~together~~

gave birth to a ~~baby~~ girl

~~glowing~~ ember

~~good~~ bargain

~~good~~ benefits

had done ~~previously~~

~~harmful~~ injury

HIV ~~virus~~

~~honest~~ truth

~~hopeful~~ optimism

~~hot~~ water heater

I ~~myself personally~~

if ~~and when~~

~~important~~ breakthrough

in ~~close~~ proximity

~~intense~~ fury

introduced ~~for the first time~~

~~invited~~ guests

ISBN ~~number~~

joined ~~together~~

~~just~~ recently

kneel ~~down~~

last ~~of all~~

lift ~~up~~

look back ~~in retrospect~~

~~major~~ breakthrough

may ~~possibly~~

~~mental~~ telepathy

merged ~~together~~

meshed ~~together~~

~~midway~~ between

might ~~possibly~~

mix ~~together~~

~~mutual~~ cooperation

~~natural~~ instinct

never ~~at any time~~

~~new~~ beginning

~~new~~ bride

new innovation

new recruit

nine A.M. in the morning

no trespassing allowed

none at all

now pending

null and void

old cliché

old proverb

opening introduction

originally created

over and done with

overexaggerate

pair of twins

parched dry

passing fad

past experiences

past history

past memories

past records

penetrate into

perfect ideal

permeate throughout

personal friend

personal opinion

personally believes

PIN number

plan in advance

poisonous venom

positively true

possibly might

postponed until a later time

prerecorded

present incumbent

probed into

proceed ahead

protest against

protrude out

proven facts

raise up

reason why

refer back

reflect back

repeat again

reply back

revert back

Rio Grande River

sad tragedy

same identical

seemed to be

share together

short in length

since the time when

sincerely mean it

skipped over

solemn vow

spelled out in detail

stacked on top of each other

still continues

still persists

still remains

strangled to death

stupid fool

suddenly exploded

sufficient enough

sum total

summer season

sworn affidavit

~~temporary~~ recess

~~temporary~~ reprieve

~~terrible~~ tragedy

~~thoughtful~~ contemplation

~~thoughtful~~ deliberation

~~totally~~ eliminated

~~true~~ fact

~~twelve~~ midnight

~~twelve~~ noon

~~two~~ twins

~~ultimate~~ conclusion

~~unexpected~~ surprise

~~unintentional~~ mistake

~~uninvited~~ party crashers

UPC ~~code~~

~~usual~~ custom

~~utter~~ annihilation

~~very~~ unique

ways ~~and means~~

~~well-known old~~ adage

when ~~and if~~

whether ~~or not~~

widow ~~woman~~

written ~~down~~

CHAPTER 8

Correspondence

In business, there are many reasons for writing letters, even in the age of almost instantaneous communication. One of the important reasons for written communication is the need to have notifications, plans, contracts, and agreements in writing for legal purposes. How you present yourself through correspondence says much about you and your business, and people will often judge your ability on the basis of your presentation. Unlike a phone call, a letter gives you the opportunity to choose your words wisely, determining the intent of your message, and executing that intent at your own pace. Your tone, grammar, neatness, and layout play an important role in this process. While e-mails have offered the businessperson the opportunity to communicate on a more casual level, traditional forms of communication are not out of the picture and should be handled professionally. Taking the time to be concise, courteous, and neat can leave a lasting impression. In this case, your actions (choosing attractive stationery) and words (how you construct your correspondence) speak equally loudly.

STATIONERY

A business letter is typed on one side of white, unlined paper that measures 8½ x 11 inches. The letter should be mailed in a standard business envelope (usually about 4 x 10 inches) unless it is accompanied by documents (enclosures) that cannot or should not be folded. If your company has letterhead stationery and envelopes, of course that is what you should use. (In no case is it acceptable to send a handwritten business letter or to use lined paper.) It is important to keep in mind that most, if not all, letters are composed on a computer and, therefore, must be printed on the commonly used company ink-jet or laser printer. The standard copy paper used in most printers is 20-pound weight. Letterhead is usually slightly heavier and may even be textured, but printer requirements must be taken into account before choosing the stock. While textured or woven stock is more attractive and impressive, ask the paper supplier how characters will print on it. Bleeding or fuzzy letters will not convey the image you want to project on your letterhead. Crisp, clean print is the ideal. White and off-white stock is the preferred color choice, but very light pastels occasionally may be acceptable. Avoid dark paper. The print is difficult to read and it is too showy in the business world.

COMMON FORMATS

Find out whether your company prefers a specific letter format. Some companies specify whether a full block, modified block, or simplified block format is to be used for your correspondence.

> *Block style* features all elements of the letter keyed
> flush left. It has a neat and simple appearance.
> Paragraphs are separated by a double space.
> *Modified block* is the more traditional style of letter
> formatting. It differs from block style in that the date,
> complimentary close, and signature lines begin at

the center point of the line length. The beginning of
each paragraph is indented five spaces, along with
the subject line, if used. Depending on the length of
the letter, paragraphs may be separated by a single or
double space.

Simplified block is similar to block but has a more
informal appearance. All elements are flush left, as in
block, but the salutation and complimentary close
are omitted. The addressee's name is usually
mentioned in the beginning paragraph, as a way of
personalizing the letter, but in keeping with a very
informal style.

If you choose to use mixed punctuation, the
salutation is followed by a colon and the complimentary close is followed by a comma. Or you may
choose to have no punctuation after these two lines.
But you must be consistent: either both lines receive
punctuation, or both do not.

PARTS OF A LETTER

The basic components of a letter are:

- date
- inside address, including recipient's name, company
  name, street address, and city/state/ZIP code
- attention line
- salutation
- subject line
- body of the letter
- complimentary close
- signature, name, and title of sender
- closing notations such as keyer's initials, enclosure
  notation, copy notation, postscript, and file name
  notation (for computer filing reference)

Date

The date is keyed two or more lines below the letterhead, depending on the length of the letter, and includes the month, date, and year: March 19, 2002. Military (and European) style reverses the month and date and uses no punctuation: 19 March 2002. Do not abbreviate the month. Also, avoid using numerals only, as it can be confusing to some, especially if you're preparing an international letter. They are interpreted differently, depending on where the addressee is from. For example, 6/8/02 usually means June 8, 2002 in the United States, but it could also be read as August 6, 2002.

Inside Address

No matter what style of letter you use, the inside address is keyed flush left, three or more lines below the date, depending on the length of the letter. It includes the name of the addressee, title (if applicable), company name, street address (and suite number if applicable) or post office box, city, state, and ZIP or postal code. In the case of international mail, the country name is keyed in all caps on a separate line. If any particular line is too long and runs to the next line, indent the second line two or three spaces.

Name

Abbreviate Mr., Mrs., Ms., Messrs., and Dr., but spell out Miss, Professor, Father, Reverend, Captain, and so on. When addressing a letter to an individual using initials or a name common to both men and women (For example, L. M. Roberts or Robin Jackson.) and you're unsure of the addressee's sex, omit the gender reference (Mr., Ms., etc.). If you don't know the name of the person you are writing to, use a job title—for example, Managing Editor. In the case of a titled individual, such as a doctor, use only one title: Dr. Mary Evans, not Dr. Mary Evans, M.D. The same applies to an attorney: Ralph Stevens, Esq., not Mr. Ralph Stevens, Esq. If you are including a job title, it is keyed after the name, separated by a comma, or it goes on a separate line, flush left, for example,

D. G. Marshall, Managing Editor
or
D. G. Marshall
Managing Editor

Company Name

The company name should be keyed as it appears on the company's letterhead, including all punctuation.

Street Address, Suite, or Post Office Box

Spell out numerical street and avenue names ten and under: Seventh Avenue; 42nd Street. Use numerals for house and building numbers but spell out number one: 301 Hubble Road; One Mulberry Street. Spell out *Street, Avenue, Boulevard, Circle, Road,* and so on. Room and suite numbers should be on the same line as the street address, separated by a comma. A post office box number is keyed on a separate line below the street address (use no punctuation for "PO"):

12 Main Street
PO Box 1234

City, State, and ZIP

The city, state, and ZIP code should be keyed on one line. Do not abbreviate the city. Use the approved USPS two-letter abbreviation for the state or province. Always include a ZIP code + the 4-digit code after, if known. If correspondence is being mailed to another country, key the country name in all caps on a separate line, below the city and postal code:

Oxford, OX2 6DP
UNITED KINGDOM

Salutation

The salutation is keyed two lines below the inside address, flush left, in block and modified block style. It is omitted in the simplified block style. The salutation often begins with "Dear," followed by the formal address such as Mrs. Johnson, Dr. Hansen, Professor Michaels.

Dear Mayor Jensen: Dear Dr. Lewis:
Dear Ms. Hilliard: Dear Mr. Ngu:

Use a first name only if you are well acquainted with the recipient: "Dear Ann,". When addressing a woman, Ms. is acceptable if her marital status is not known, or if it is known to be the recipient's preference. The salutation is followed by a colon, if using mixed punctuation.

If you do not have a name to address your correspondence to, use a general salutation:

Dear Ladies and Gentlemen: Dear Human Resources Director:
Dear Board Members: Dear Sir or Madam:

If the name is available but the person's sex is unknown, you may address the individual using both first and last name:

Dear Robin Garvey: Dear A. S. Anderson:

While the very basic "To whom it may concern" is still acceptable, it is advantageous to take the time to research the name of the person to whom you should direct your letter. Often a single phone call will be sufficient to obtain such information. It avoids the probability that your letter will be passed from one in-box to another. If you are writing to someone in the U.S. government (a senator or representative, an officer in the military, etc.)

Subject

While a subject line is not necessary, it can be a welcome addition to a letter, especially when the recipient receives volumes of correspondence. It is eye-catching and spells out the purpose of the letter, eliminating the need to expound on the purpose of your letter in the first paragraph. It may be keyed as follows:

Block style: two lines below the salutation, flush left.
Modified block style: two lines below the salutation, indented.
Simplified block style: three lines below the inside address, no salutation.

The subject line may be preceded by the word *Subject*, followed by a colon. In the simplified block style, do not use the word *Subject*.

Body of the Letter

The body of the letter begins two lines below the salutation in block style and modified block style, and three lines below the subject line in simplified block style. The letter is single-spaced with a line space between paragraphs. Modified block style features indented paragraphs, about one-half inch (or five spaces) from the left margin.

Regardless of the specific purpose of a letter—whether it's a cover letter for a résumé or manuscript, a response to a customer's complaint or praise for an employee, or a request for payment—a business letter should seldom be longer than one page. The tone should be formal (without sounding too distant or patronizing), polite, and to the point. Avoid slang, clichés, colloquialisms, harsh or rude language, and repeating information that is contained in enclosures or attachments. It is appropriate, however, to provide a summary of the information available in additional documents, or to emphasize those points you regard as most important.

Always consider your audience when preparing a business letter. Do not say something in a letter that you would not say to the person in a face-to-face situation, and do not put in writing anything that might later embarrass you or your company, commit you or your company to something that you might not be able to fulfill, or be used against you (or your company) in the future. Explain technical terms and procedures that the recipient may not understand or know about, but provide only as much information as the individual will find useful. Whether you are writing to your immediate superior, an officer of the company you work for, or a disgruntled employee, be respectful and professional.

The content (body) of a business letter has five basic parts: (1) a reference, (2) the reason for writing, (3) a description of enclosed documents (if appropriate), (4) closing remarks, (5) and some reference to future contact. The first element tells the recipient what your letter refers to: "With reference to your classified advertisement in . . .," "your letter of June 19th . . .," "our phone conversation yesterday afternoon. . . ." This element is important as a beginning because several days (or weeks) may go by before your letter is delivered, and it provides the recipient with the context of your letter or refreshes his or her mind.

Next, state your reason for writing: "I am writing to apply for the position . . .," "to inquire about your offer . . .," "to confirm delivery of . . . ." If you want to ask for something, be specific and humble: "Could you possibly extend my deadline . . .?" or "I would be grateful if you could send me a review copy of your new video." If you are agreeing to a request, be specific and gracious: "I would be delighted to speak to your organization about . . . ." If you must decline, be appreciative: "Thank you for the invitation to speak, but . . . ." "Bad news" letters are among the most difficult to write, and it is important that you use the right tone: "Unfortunately, I am the bearer of sad news . . ." or "I am afraid that my news isn't good." If you are writing to someone within your company, using the "Re:" line at the top of your letter is also appropriate.

Having given whatever information is required, state explicitly that you are enclosing documents (if you are), tell the recipient how many separate documents you are sending, explain what they are, and how they are relevant to the subject of your letter: "I am enclosing my résumé, which details . . ." or, more formally, "Please find enclosed a copy of your letter . . . ."

In your closing remarks, it is appropriate to thank the recipient in advance for help, offer to be of further service if it is necessary, or summarize the important points of your letter: "Thank you in advance for your help with . . ., "If I can provide additional information, please don't hesitate . . .," or "I hope this information will help you . . . ."

If you expect the recipient to initiate the next contact, say so: "I look forward to hearing from you soon," ". . . our meeting next week . . .," ". . . seeing you next Friday." At this point, if you expect the recipient to respond to you in a particular way (for example, if you are asking the person to fax you a document), specify in your letter how you expect him or her to respond. If you want the person to telephone you and are using company letterhead, the company telephone number will probably be on the stationery, but also provide your extension number or direct office number if you have one. If you want a document sent to you by fax, you should also provide that number. Both numbers, when necessary, should be part of the heading (as shown in the sample letter). If you definitely need an answer from the recipient, you might enclose a self-addressed, stamped envelope for his or her convenience and mention this fact. This shows both your consideration and your desire for a response.

Complimentary Close

In full-block style, your closing should be typed flush with the left-hand margin. If your company uses a modified block or indented format, the closing should be aligned with the heading on the right side of the letter. The closing consists of three or four elements: (1) a complimentary close, (2) your signature, (3) your typed name, and, if you are acting in an official capacity, (4) your title.

The complimentary close is typed two line spaces below the end of the body of the letter and must be followed by a comma. Several formal closes are acceptable, depending on the degree of formality:

Formal	Less Formal
Very truly yours,	Sincerely,
Sincerely yours,	Cordially,

Formal closings are formulaic and don't require any thought on the writer's part. When appropriate, friendlier, more informal closings may be used:

All best wishes,
With my best (*or* warmest) wishes,
Best wishes (for your future),
Warmest greetings,

Your recipient will notice whether you've taken the time to close your letter in an unusual way. (But don't end up saying something inappropriate. Use good judgment.)

Signature, Name, and Title of Sender

Leave three or four lines under the close for your signature, and type your name, aligned with the beginning of the close.

If you are acting or responding in an official capacity, type your title, followed by a comma, and your department or committee, aligned with your typed name.

Cary D'Amato

Vice President, Sales

Closing Notations

Notations are the last elements of a business letter, and they should be typed flush with the left margin. There are three kinds of notation: (1) a reference to documents enclosed with or attached to the letter (enclosures/enc. or attachments/att.), (2) the names of people who are receiving copies of the letter (cc:), and, if someone else has typed the letter, (3) the initials of the writer and the typist—for example, KM/mds (KM is the writer; mds is the typist).

Reread your letter, checking for typographical errors, misspelled words, grammatical problems, and for elements or information you omitted. If you have typed the letter on a computer and have used the software's spell-checker (as you should), be sure to look for omitted words (especially grammatical elements) and typographical or spelling errors that have resulted in a legitimate, but wrong, word. English has numerous homonyms (words that sound alike but have different meanings or functions)—for example, *to, too, two*; *their, there, they're*; *its* (possessive), *it's* (contraction of *it is*); *your* (possessive), *you're* (contraction of *you are*). No software program can alert you to such problems, and inadvertently leaving them in a formal letter is sloppy. Many people believe they are experts on grammatical correctness and are critical of the writing of others. For such people, errors can raise questions about your ability. Once you are satisfied that your letter is clean in every respect, sign it, in ink.

SAMPLE BUSINESS LETTERS

Just as there is a standard form for business letters, which sets out the information that should be included in virtually every business letter, so there are also formulas that govern the content of specific business letters. Some types of business letter are more difficult to write than others, but as you gain experience in writing letters you'll find that knowing what to say and how to phrase it is largely a matter of common sense. To help you get started as a business correspondent, sample letters for some of the most commonly occurring situations are provided here.

Letter of Resignation

Writing a letter of resignation can be difficult, depending on the circumstances. For one thing, it's hard to strike just the right tone. Even if you're leaving a position because you're not happy or making enough money, you don't want to risk alienating your superiors or coworkers. You never know when you might want to ask one of them for a reference or recommendation.

The best tactic is to keep your resignation letter simple. Use company letterhead (this is an official act) and state only the barest facts and leave it at that. Date your letter, state the date on which your resignation is official and the position you're resigning, sign it, and hand (or send) it to the appropriate person.

February 3, 2003

Miriam Selznik, Personnel Manager
Acme Plumbing & Heating

12366 Industrial Parkway
Atlanta, GA 30094

Dear Ms. Selznik:

I am writing to let you know that I am resigning my position
as Administrative Assistant to the Vice President for Marketing, effective February 17, 2003.

It's been a pleasure working for Acme.

Sincerely,
Joseph Clayhurst

[signature]

Administrative Assistant
Marketing

It is also appropriate for Ms. Selznik to acknowledge receipt of Mr. Clayhurst's letter of resignation.

February 5, 2003
Joseph Clayhurst, Administrative Assistant Marketing
Acme Plumbing & Heating
12366 Industrial Parkway
Atlanta, GA 30094

Dear Mr. Clayhurst:

It is with deep regret that I accept your resignation as
Administrative Assistant to Acme's Vice President for
Marketing, effective February 17th of this year.

We here at Acme are aware of the demands that this position
has placed on you, and we appreciate the fine work you have
done as an administrative assistant.

I wish you success in your new position.

Best wishes,

[signature]

Miriam Selznik
Personnel Manager

First Reminder of an Unpaid Invoice or Bill

Writing a dunning letter is never a pleasure, but it may become a necessary task. When a nonpayer forces you to resort to second and third requests for payment, you are losing valuable time as well as money in your efforts to collect the debt. You have to maintain a delicate balance between firmly stating your request and still retaining the recipient's goodwill. This is especially true for the first letter regarding an unpaid bill. The individual may have innocently forgotten to pay you, or the payment may be in the mail.

The letter can be brief without being rude. In a first notice, you should: (1) give a gentle reminder that payment is due; (2) state a relevant details regarding the invoice (invoice number, amount due, and due date); (3) make it clear to your customer that you assume this is a mistake or oversight; (4) affirm your confidence that nonpayment is a mistake or oversight and state that you look forward to receiving payment in a few days.

> [Company letterhead]
> [Date]
> [Recipient's Name, Position]
> [Company]
> [Street Address]
> [City, State ZIP code]
>
> Dear [Name]:
>
> I am writing to remind you that we have not yet received payment for invoice [number] for [amount], due on [date]. I am enclosing a full statement of your account as of [date] and a copy of the invoice.
>
> We're sure that this is an oversight on your part, and would appreciate your prompt attention to this matter.
>
> If your payment is already in the mail, please disregard this letter. Should you have any questions about your account, please do not hesitate to contact me.

Yours Sincerely,

[signature]

[Your name]
[Your title]
[ID initials: UC/lc]
Enclosures: 2

Introduction of New Colleague

If you have been asked to write a letter introducing a new
colleague, your letter should be warm and friendly, at the
same time maintaining a concise, businesslike tone. Be sure
to include sufficient details so there is no confusion about
who you're introducing, his or her last position and place of
employment, and the details of the position for which he or
she has been hired.

Start your letter by announcing the name of the new colleague and providing a few brief, relevant details of his or
her previous position. Next, include a warm compliment
that welcomes the new colleague and supply some initial
details about his or her new role in the company. Finally, say
that the new person is eager to meet all the members of the
staff and looks forward to their help and assistance in carrying out the duties of his or her new position.

[Company letterhead]
[Date]

[Name]
[Address]

Dear [Name]:

I want to take this opportunity to inform you that [Name] will
soon be joining us as the [Title] in the [Department]. [He or
She] will be taking over from [Name] and will begin work on
[Date].

[Name] has been the [Title] of the [Department] at
[Company] for [number] years and we are delighted that [he

or she] has decided to join our company at this stage of our development.

[He or She] is a person of [one or two qualities] and I have no doubt [he or she] will contribute significantly to all aspects of our work here.

I hope all of you will try to make [Name] feel welcome here as [he or she] becomes accustomed to [his or her] new position.

Yours Sincerely,

[signature]

[Your name]
[Your title]

Announcing or Acknowledging the Death of an Employee

Informing others of another person's death is not an easy task, but it is one you may be called on to perform at some point in your career. Keep your letter short and to the point. Express your sympathy for the individual's family, friends, and coworkers without exaggerated emotion. In this kind of letter, do not say more than is absolutely necessary. The fact that you have written it is the most genuine sign of your feelings.

[Company letterhead]
[Date]

[Name]
[Address]

Dear [Name],

I am writing to express the sadness all of us at [Company name] feel on hearing of [Name's] death.

[Name] was a much liked and respected employee. [He or She] will certainly be missed by everyone who worked with [him or her].

All of us send our deepest sympathies to you. If there is anything we can do, please do not hesitate to contact us.

Yours Sincerely,

[signature]

[Your name]
[Your title]

Apology for an Employee's Conduct

Having to apologize to a customer who was treated rudely by an employee is difficult, but it is among the most important communications you will ever undertake. An angry or offended customer is one who may never do business with your company again. Your goal is to convey a sincere apology to the customer. The more effectively you do this, the more inclined that individual may be to continue doing business with you.

This is a letter that must be written as soon as you have been informed that an employee has somehow alienated a customer. You cannot delay. First, assure the customer that your company does not tolerate such behavior from its employees and, second, that appropriate action will be taken. Finally, finish your letter with a full apology.

[Company letterhead]
[Date]

[Name]
[Address]

Dear [Name]:

Thank you for your [letter or call] of [date] detailing the offensive behavior of one of our employees. Please be assured that such conduct is not, and never will be, tolerated in this company.

After investigating your complaint, we severely reprimanded the individual involved. Please accept our sincere apology for any distress this situation may have caused you, and be assured that it will not happen again.

Thank you for bringing this matter to our attention. We place great importance on the conduct of our employees, and your complaint has given us the opportunity to remedy the problem.

Yours Sincerely,

[signature]

[Your Name]
[Your Title]

WRITING A MEMO

If you can write a good business letter, you can write a good memo (short for *memorandum*, 'a brief reminder'). In fact, many office memos are "brief reminders" about an upcoming meeting or taking up a collection to send a card to a colleague who's in the hospital, but the office setting also requires more complex memos. Think of a memo as an "in-house business letter," somewhere between a note and a brief report in length, to be read and passed on quickly. Now that most businesses of any size have individual computer work stations for employees, most memos are now sent as e-mail messages.

Like a business letter, memos provide needed information in an effective and efficient way without a time-consuming meeting and they are written in a somewhat formal style— no misspellings, slang, or sentence fragments. Because memos are written to be widely distributed and posted, they reach numerous people very quickly and the effects of careless errors multiply, resulting in more memos (requesting clarification or drawing attention to the errors).

There are three basic ways to organize office memos, each suited to providing information in the most effective format:

1. The *direct approach* states the most important information first and then goes on to supporting or supplementary information. This approach works well if you need to convey routine information or pass on organizational news.
2. The *indirect approach* first makes an appeal to the reader or points out the factual elements of a situation or issue and then states a conclusion based on the evidence provided. This approach is especially effective when you want to get the reader's attention before describing your proposed plan of action.
3. The *balanced approach* combines the direct and the indirect approaches, and is particularly effective when the information you are providing is "bad news."

Parts of a Memo

A good memo organizes the information to be conveyed both for the reader's convenience and ease of understanding and to achieve the writer's purpose in the most effective way.

HEADING.

The heading for every memo follows the same basic format:

> TO: [Reader's name and job title]
> cc: [List others who are receiving copies]
> FROM: [Your name and job title]
> DATE: [Month, day, and year, spelled out]
> SUBJECT: [Topic of the memo]

Some memo pads, in fact, already have this format printed at the top of each page. If your group or organization uses a slightly different format for the heading, use it. Be sure that you have the name of each recipient spelled correctly and his or her job title accurate. In general, some titles (for example, "Professor" or "Ms." are unnecessary), nor do you need the salutation required in a formal business letter. Next to your name, hand-write your initials (on a memo, a closing signature is not necessary).

Your subject line should be brief, no more than a few words, but explicit, so that there is no chance for misunderstanding. "Ordering Pizza" as a subject line, for example, might lead your readers to think that your memo will provide instructions on the correct procedure for ordering in pizza on late nights at the office when, in fact, you're passing on complaints from the cleaning staff about the tomato sauce on the carpet and the boxes strewn all over the floor. Something like, "Clean up your mess before leaving," announces the main point of the memo.

OPENING.

The opening sentences or paragraphs of a memo tell readers the context of the issue, the suggested assignment or task, and the purpose of the memo.

Context. The context you describe is the event, situation, or background of the problem or issue you are addressing. Whether it takes a sentence or a paragraph will depend on the complexity of the situation. For example, the context may begin with "The cleaning company has complained that it takes too long to clean our floors . . . ." Be clear and direct, providing only as much information as your readers need.

Task. Your task or assignment statement describes what you are doing to solve the problem, issue, or situation. If your reader asked that you act, you might say, "You asked me to look at . . . ." If you want to present alternatives for employees to consider, you might say, "We need to consider alternatives that will satisfy the cleaning company without . . . ."

Purpose. Your purpose statement explains why you are writing the memo and leads in to the remainder of it. You need to be direct, and avoid trying to downplay the information. Your statement might begin with: "This memo describes my understanding of the cleaning company's complaint, proposes several ways of accommodating these people, and my own recommendations for resolving the problem." If the memo will be so long that adding section headings will make it easier to follow the organization of the information, by all means, do so.

When the purpose of a memo is to convince your readers that there is a real problem, avoid going into more detail than the situation requires. If you discover that you're having difficulty describing the task, you may need to do more thinking before you write the memo. If you decide to break your memo into segments, be sure that they the most important points.

SUMMARY.

Wait until you've written the main body of your memo to write a summary section. If your memo is one page or less, a summary may not be necessary. If, however, you've covered several important issues or events, or your analysis is fairly detailed, a summary paragraph is appropriate. If the memo is a short report on research you've done on an issue or for a project, this is a good place to sum up methods and sources you've used so far. Remember, though, that this is a summation. Keep it brief and don't needlessly repeat detailed information.

DISCUSSION PARAGRAPH(S).

After you've adequately covered the basic presentation of your topic, here is where you lay out all the details—facts, statistics, hypotheses—that support the ideas you've discussed. In this section you demonstrate your ability to think creatively and critically by presenting your ideas.

Begin with the most important or most "telling" information, proceeding from your strongest fact to the weakest (or, if you're providing historical background, from oldest to newest information). These paragraphs are also the place where you make your recommendations, acknowledge others' recommendations, and describe future problems that might occur and how your suggestions will ensure that such problems they simply don't happen. It often helps to put important facts or details into numbered or bulleted lists, again going from strongest point to weakest. (Caution: The items included in such lists must all be grammatically parallel. This means that each item must have the same grammatical form as all the others. That is, if your first list item is a noun phrase, every list item has to be a noun phrase; if one item begins with an –ing verb form, every item must begin with an –ing verb; if one item is a complete sentence, all the items must be complete sentences.)

YOUR CLOSING.

Once you've given your readers all the information relevant to the subject of your memo, use a courteous closing that describes the actions you want them to take, and point out how those actions will benefit everyone. This one-paragraph closing might begin with, "We can discuss my recommendations in greater detail at our next meeting . . . ." or "Should you need more information, I'll be glad to . . . ."

ATTACHMENTS.

Provide whatever documentation or additional information your readers will need to come to their own understanding of the event, issue, or problem you've described, and list such attachments at the end. For example, if there has been an exchange of letters regarding your subject, include copies of them (if doing so will not breach confidentiality or if they contain information that your readers need to know). If you've created graphs of facts or statistics or diagrams that illustrate physical relationships, attach those. You can also refer to such graphs, diagrams, or illustrations at appropriate points in your memo. Do not attach materials that do not bear directly on the subject of the memo.

CHAPTER 9

Making Speeches and Presentations

PUBLIC SPEAKING

There are many contexts in which public speaking is called for. One may think of a politician standing in front of hundreds of people and millions more on TV. Public speaking, of course, is not only a political speech; it is also the sales rep presenting a product to potential customers. It is the human relations manager explaining benefits to a group of new employees. It is the project manager discussing schedule changes with a project team. In everyday business, public speaking is an integral part of operations and effective communications.

Is Public Speaking Science or Art?

For some, public speaking is a science. It has forms and rules that must be followed and, as with most endeavors, practice makes perfect. For others, public speaking is an art that is guided more by inspiration than preparation. In reality, both views are correct. Public speaking has forms and rules that work best when coupled with inspiration and extemporaneous thought. We all know people who speak better "off the cuff," as well as those who require many hours of practice. Depending on the person, the topic, and/or the situation, a speech or presentation might be best done with hours of preparation and several practice "run-throughs," or it may lose its freshness with too much rehearsal. Only the speaker knows how best to prepare.

This chapter enumerates the steps it takes to create an effective public speech, no matter the speaker, audience, or topic. It assumes a level of preparation that should go into any presentation or speech, but it does not assume the level of expertise, comfort, or extemporaneous speaking ability of the speaker. As with any recipe, you should adjust the ingredients to your taste.

Selecting a Topic

The most important part of public speaking is having a clear and concise topic. No matter your audience, people in business expect that you will respect their time. This is as true for a speaker in front of 300 people as it is for a presentation to three people in your department.

Selecting your topic may come easy, or it may take some thinking. It all depends on the event or assignment at hand. No matter how challenging, it is important that you answer the following questions as you consider your topic selection:

• To whom are you speaking?
• Can you speak confidently on the topic?
• Why were you asked to make the presentation?
• How much time is allotted for your speech?

Audience

Knowing the audience is the first step in planning a speech or presentation. Without an understanding of why people are there to hear you speak, it is impossible to plan for an effective presentation. Assess the audience to determine what they are expecting. An audience expecting to be sold a product has different assumptions than an audience expecting to learn how to use a software product. A management team learning about a quarterly sales performance requires a different approach than a group of interns learning the voice- and e-mail systems. By knowing your audience and their expectations, you can better plan your approach.

Knowledge

It is imperative that you feel comfortable discussing the topic you have chosen (or have had chosen for you). However, comfort isn't measured by how nervous you are, but by how much you know compared to what your audience knows. You may feel that you can easily demonstrate how to use a particular software program to anyone in your company but would not feel comfortable speaking about that same software to a group of programmers. Your level of comfort is in direct relation to the audience's expertise. Ask yourself if you can reasonably answer the needs of the audience at hand and try to determine why you were asked to make the presentation. If you feel that you can "fake your way through it," you probably can.

Goals

You are speaking or presenting for a reason. You know that your audience has expectations, but what about those who asked you to speak? Find out exactly what both the audience and those who asked you to present expect. Understanding what they want out of your presentation is a must because you can waste everyone's time if you do not satisfy the audience's expectations. By ignoring the goals of the audience, you may find that your presentation is either way over their heads or is too remedial to be useful to them. If you can find out what your audience expects and needs, you can better serve those needs.

Time

Not having enough or having too much time is one of the most common problems in public speaking; giving yourself enough time to present is not only important for you but also for your audience. Busy professionals will not sit idly by as you ramble on into their next appointment. Nor will people look too kindly on a fifteen-minute speech when they are expecting an hour's worth of your information. Make sure you know how much time you have and that you know exactly how much time you will need.

Preparation

Preparation for a presentation or speech is extremely important. Whether you are speaking on a topic that you are the world's foremost expert on or giving a presentation on something you have just learned, good preparation will make the difference between a fair and an outstanding performance.

WRITTEN OUTLINE.

Outlining what you will say in your speech is usually associated with presentation software. While it is important to have a clear outline to show your audience, charting the subtleties and nuances of your speech in notes to yourself is even more important. An outline that only you see (in note cards, on paper, or via a teleprompter) helps you prepare for and deliver your speech. Some people believe that you should write out everything that you will say in a speech. While this helps with judging time, there is a real danger that you will start reading off the page, and reading a prepared statement is usually stiff and unengaging.

An outline helps you formulate your thoughts, create clever asides, and embed the presentation plan in your head. Your outline should have one or two levels of detail more than what you hand out or show to your audience. If, for example, a slide shown while you are speaking says "Year-to-Date Sales $2.3 million," your outline may give you salient details to mention such as "Int'l $1.1mm, Domestic $1.8mm, Special Sales $400K."

Your outline, like a third-grade teacher during the class play, should feed you the first words of your lines, but not the entire script. Its function is both to help you prepare and to help you through the presentation in an ordered and logical fashion.

PRACTICE.

Practice may be in the form of actual run-throughs in real time or a mental walk through your written outline. The simple rule for most is that the more you practice, the better your speech or presentation. Ideally, practicing should be done in the room or hall you will be using, so that you can learn the subtleties of the room. Think like a professional golfer and go out and learn the course.

If you cannot practice in the place where you will be presenting, try practicing in front of peers, friends, or family. Seeing how people react to what you are saying is important because you may learn that you need to stress certain words or concepts differently from what you had assumed.

Time your practice sessions and figure out how to stretch or cut your material if you need to. The more you practice, the more flexible you will become with your presentation. If something occurs that delays your speech (fire alarms, late attendees, etc.), all your practice will help you figure out the best way to edit on the spot and still get your point across.

SETTING UP: FACILITIES AND EQUIPMENT

Setting up the facility is the presenter's responsibility. That is how you must look at things because, when you go in to give a speech or presentation, you are the one everyone thinks poorly of when the presentation facilities are inadequate or the equipment does not work.

There are many memorable examples in the world of business presentations when equipment has sabotaged an otherwise excellent presentation and caused a speaker extreme embarrassment. A notable example happened to Bill Gates, CEO of Microsoft. While giving a speech demonstrating the latest and most stable version of the Microsoft Office Suite software, the PowerPoint presentation froze the PC he was using.

With this in mind, make sure that you arrive well in advance of the presentation time to check out the facilities. Here is a quick checklist to run through:

- Is there a podium, lectern, or special place for your notes?
- Is there a projector hooked up to a computer?
- Is your presentation loaded up and ready to go?
- Is there enough seating in the room?
- Will everyone be able to see and hear you?
- Is there a PA system and is it working?

Starting off with everything under control is the best way to start any presentation. By advance planning and preparation, your speech will stand on the merits of what you say, not how you say it. Planning and preparing reduces the risk of a harried or disjointed presentation.

GIVING A SPEECH AND MAKING A PRESENTATION

Most presentations and speeches should have the following structure:

- Introduction
- Warm Up
- Speech or Presentation
- Q & A
- Follow-Up/Action Items
- Thanks

Introduction

Whether you are being introduced to a room full of strangers, or you are standing in front of five peers, it is imperative that

---

Tips for the Nervous

Does speaking in front of people make you nervous? Relax; it makes everyone nervous. It's how individuals deal with it that makes some seem cooler and more collected than others. Here are some things you can do to quiet your nerves:

1. Drink plenty of fluids so you don't get dry-mouthed and mumble. Make sure there is water nearby while you speak.
2. Take deep, long breaths before speaking. Make your exhalation breaths last three times as long as your inhalation breaths.
3. Find a friendly face in the room and speak to that individual.
4. If you are speaking to a large group, pick a point in the middle of the audience and imagine your mom or your little brother sitting there. Talk directly to that person.

your audience knows exactly who you are and why you are there. Managing the expectations of the audience is your job. Make sure they are clear about what your goals are.

Warm-Up

Depending on the setting, the audience, and the topic, almost every presentation or speech is helped by some form of warm-up or decompression exercise. The setting dictates the kind of warm-up you select.

When speaking in front of a large group, again depending on the topic and audience, a joke or personal anecdote is often the perfect way to set up your talk. The context of the joke or anecdote should match your topic in some way. For a smaller, more intimate setting, a good exercise is to go around the room and let everyone introduce themselves and state

---

Jokes

Relaxing yourself and your audience can make a big difference in a presentation, but one individual's humor may be another's insult. Making any assumptions about the people in your audience is always a bad idea. Humor is very much bound to ethnic and cultural experience, and you should avoid any jokes that rely on stereotypes of any group of people. A joke can be a great way to begin a speech if its humor does not come at someone else's expense. When choosing an appropriate joke to share with your audience, remember to keep the message lighthearted.

1. Never tell an ethnic, religious, or sexual joke. Your career may depend on someone's sensitivity to insult.
2. Try to find an amusing story or joke that you can connect to the speech or presentation in some way. The best speakers use jokes like the Bible uses parables (stories that illustrate deeper moral lessons).

Toastmasters International and Other Speakers' Organizations

If you're not comfortable speaking in front of a crowd, there are several organizations you can turn to for help and encouragement. One of the longest-established and best-known is Toastmasters International, which has clubs all over the world. Toastmasters International encourages leadership and speaking skills by providing a supportive environment in which to learn those skills. Members join small clubs where they learn to give both impromptu and prepared speeches and accept and give feedback and criticism. More information can be found at www.toastmasters.org.

If it's not just nervousness but an actual speech impediment that's holding you back, you might want to check out the National Stuttering Association (www.nsastutter.org) for more information and help. Another excellent organization is the Stuttering Foundation of America (www.stuttersfa.org). You can find information about and help for other speech disorders at the Web site of the American Speech-Language-Hearing Association (www.asha.org).

Once you're comfortable with public speaking, you might be ready to take the next step and become a professional. The National Speakers Association (www.nsaspeaker.org) is the leading organization for experts who speak professionally. Membership requirements are strict, but they provide certification and marketing help to professional speakers.

what they hope to get out of the presentation. (This also helps you double-check the expectations of your audience.)

The warm-up should be designed to help both you and the audience focus on the topic at hand. Furthermore, the best warm-up sets up your presentation, so everyone is ready to listen and learn.

The Speech or Presentation

You have practiced, prepared, been introduced, warmed the audience up, and now you launch into the meat of your speech or presentation. Follow a few guidelines and you will be successful:

- Look around often, trying to make as much eye contact as possible. Don't stare at the PowerPoint slide or bury your face in your index cards. Smile!
- Use vocabulary you are comfortable with. Do not try to "sound smart." Be yourself!
- Breathe. The first few seconds can sometimes take your breath away. Breathe slowly and deeply and do not rush. Speak clearly!
- Be aware of the time. Don't get so caught up in your topic or pace that you lose track of time. Wear a watch!
- If possible, walk around the room. If not, use your hands, your shoulders, and your face to show expression. Be engaging!
- Watch your audience. Make sure they are following what you say. Slow down if they look lost, speed up if they look bored. Be aware!

Q & A (Questions and Answers)

Depending on the time, the appropriateness, or the purpose of your presentation, you may need to offer a Q & A session following it. If so, consider the following:

- Make sure you understand the question by stating it back to the audience. You do not want to answer something that wasn't asked.
- Answer a question only if you feel you can or should.
- Guessing, speculating, and answering for others is generally bad form.

- If a question is posed that goes beyond your scope, write it down and offer to provide an answer later.
- Look at the person who asked the question when answering, but also look around at the rest of the audience.

(Note: Follow-up/Action Items and Thanks are discussed later in the chapter.)

MAKING A MULTIMEDIA PRESENTATION

Good presentations have nothing to do with technical slickness. Remember those great IBM commercials from 1999 and 2000 in which executives are looking at Web-site designs and one asks, quizzically, "The logo, it's on fire?" The designer answers enthusiastically, "Yeah, it's on fire!" The commercial was illustrating the limitations of modern design software. You can do a lot of cool things, 99 percent of which are annoying.

Presentation software presents a similar challenge to the user. With all the bells and whistles that come with Power-Point and other presentation software, it is easy to get carried away. So, before you go and set the corporate logo ablaze, read the rest of this chapter.

Do You Really Need a Multimedia Presentation?

With most presentation software programs such as Power-Point you can animate letters and words, stream video, play background audio, and do many other things impossible with a paper presentation. Before you run off to get the digital camcorder, ask yourself this simple question: Do you really need a multimedia presentation?

Old-school thinking will say "no." The merits of what you present will stand on its own whether people are reading it on paper or as a projected image. However, there are many benefits, especially in a sales situation, to controlling the flow of information.

Multimedia presentations offer you the opportunity to control what people see and when they see it. By using presentation software and not giving out hard copies until the presentation is over, you have control over what the people in the room see.

If you decide that you need to do a multimedia presentation, here are a few things to consider:

- appropriateness
- facility capabilities
- creation time
- platform
- design rules
- plan B (*or* what if it doesn't work?)

APPROPRIATENESS.

The appropriateness of a multimedia presentation depends on the topic, the audience, and the facilities. You must ask yourself whether the topic is appropriate for a multimedia presentation. For example, a CPA wouldn't be wise to project a family's tax return on a conference room wall while reviewing it at a meeting. Nor would it be appropriate for a funeral director to show slides of other funerals to a grieving family there to bury a loved one. While both presentations would certainly make the process simpler, they lack tact and sensitivity.

FACILITY CAPABILITIES.

With your topic selected and deemed appropriate for a dazzling multimedia presentation, you work for hours finding video clips, editing background music, and animating the slides so they dramatically spell out the key points as you cue them. Then you find out that the conference room with all the technical gizmos is booked and you will be presenting in the reception waiting area. No computer, no network ports, no screen, no speakers . . . no presentation. This is why it is imperative that you first determine the capabilities of the facility where you will be working and, expecting the worst, always have a backup presentation in case there is a change of venue (more on that later).

CREATION TIME.

The last factor in determining whether to do a multimedia presentation is time. Typing up a list of key points in the form of an outline to hand out to an audience doesn't require much time or effort. However, taking that same outline, styling it, adding music, video, and animation is a sizable task.

Be sure that you have the time to create your presentation. Be wary if your plans include creating a presentation with elements that you have never used before. While software today makes an amazing amount of razzle-dazzle possible, you will often find yourself spending hours trying to figure out how to get an image to paste where you want it, as opposed to where it insists on being placed.

Staying up until 4 a.m. to finish a presentation that you will be making at 9 that morning is not the best use of your time, nor does it allow you to prepare properly. Do not underestimate the importance of creation time.

PLATFORM.

The most popular presentation software is PowerPoint, which is part of the Microsoft Office suite. However, Power-Point is hardly the only player out there. For example, Mac users have their own presentation software, AppleWorks. Furthermore, depending on the topic, one might only require a spreadsheet program such as Excel or Lotus, a word-processing program such as Word or WordPerfect, or Web-presentation software such as Flash.

Whatever you choose to use, be sure that the computer you are using to present has the software installed and that it has the processing power to handle your presentation. Multimedia presentations have crashed more computers during key presentations due to lack of RAM or processing power than any other factor. Also be sure that you are platform conscious. Creating in a Mac environment may be easiest, but will you be able to run it on a PC?

DESIGN RULES.

It is likely that somewhere in your company is a document that outlines design rules. This document, perhaps called *design specs*, *design rules*, or *design bible*, is usually found in the marketing or advertising department and details the corporate color scheme, the rules of logo placement, and a list of approved fonts.

If you are making a presentation on behalf of your company, it is not acceptable to use random colors, a logo scanned off a catalog, and your sixteen favorite gothic fonts.

Before you begin building your presentation, find out if there is a PowerPoint (or other program) template already created. Chances are that many others in your organization have needed this before you. If there isn't such a template, ask for the design specs and an electronic copy of the corporate logo.

If your organization does not have either a template or a design spec, you are on your own . . . to a degree. Your company's Web site can provide you with the color scheme, the logo, and the corporate fonts. While this is hardly the best method, approximating by using the Web site is far better than making up your own design.

PLAN B (OR WHAT IF IT DOESN'T WORK?)

You have done everything right. You chose an appropriate topic. Your audience and facilities are perfect for a full-blown multimedia presentation. You and/or your design department have created a perfect presentation that runs perfectly during practice sessions. Then, as you turn down the lights and start up the projector, the bulb in the machine dies and your presentation is ruined.

Or is it? Being smart, you expect that technology will fail, and you have a backup plan. You ask that the lights be put back on and you reach into a box that you carried in with you and voilà! You hand out hard copies (preferably in color) of the presentation that you printed out the day before.

This kind of planning should be part of every presentation you make. Sure, you would rather control the pace of the show and not let attendees read ahead, but, all things considered, it is better to be able to go ahead with your presentation and have people follow in print. If you do not have copies, look for a white board or tear-away meeting note sheets and write the highlights of each PowerPoint slide as you speak. *Always have one hard copy of your speech with you.* Continue on as if your presentation hinged only on what you say, not how the message is delivered. Never let technology ruin what you have to say.

What Makes a Good Multimedia Presentation?

A good presentation is akin to telling a good story. There is a beginning, middle, and end. It needs to be clear. It needs to energize and excite the audience. It cannot be burdened with extraneous details, sounds, or visual effects.

A good presentation starts with a premise, describes the

premise, and then reviews the premise. This elliptical approach is a proven pedagogy. Look at any textbook or learning aid you have ever used. They always outline the topic, then teach the topic, then review what was just taught. All presentations should be conceived with similar objectives and should have the following characteristics:

- clear topic
- repeated statement of ideas
- good information flow
- energizing style
- no gratuitous graphics, sounds, or animation
- follow-up/action items
- thanks

CLEAR TOPIC.

Without a clear topic, your presentation will not be successful. It will be difficult to create as you will find yourself looking to replace focus with fluff, substance with style. Most poor presentations are the result of a lack of clarity of topic. Example of a good topic: "Our Sales Goals and Selling Points for 2004"; bad topic: "Sales 2004."

REPEATED STATEMENT OF IDEAS.

Explain what you will be presenting. Clearly state the topic. Review what you just presented. Structure your presentation like a textbook chapter. You are teaching your audience.

GOOD INFORMATION FLOW.

Every presentation should have a logical flow of information. You must build an argument from the ground up. Make sure that you don't jump around haphazardly. Your audience must perceive a progression of thought. For example, if you were presenting the company benefits package to new employees, you wouldn't start with the 401K plan, then jump to the medical plan, then go on to discuss the profit-sharing plan, and finish with health-insurance payroll deductions. Though you may have covered all the broad topics, you didn't organize the process for your audience.

The more logical approach for such a presentation would be to start with Financial Benefits (401K, profit sharing) then move on to Health Benefits (medical plan, health-insurance payroll deductions). Information that is related works best together.

ENERGIZING STYLE.

Look around often, trying to make as much eye contact as possible (don't stare at the PowerPoint slide or bury your face in your index cards). If possible, walk around the room. If not, use your hands, your shoulders, and your face to show expression. Watch your audience. Make sure they are following you. Slow down if they look lost, speed up if they look bored.

NO GRATUITOUS GRAPHICS, SOUNDS, OR ANIMATION.

The importance of *substance over style* cannot be stressed too much. Just because you have the technical wherewithal to create elaborate effects does not mean you should go overboard. Don't create cartoon characters to dance across your slides. Don't program machine-gun sounds to accompany type as it flies onto a screen. Don't get "creative" with gaudy background colors or intrusive music.

Multimedia should be appropriate to the message. If you are presenting the new baby-care center to employees, you can get away with certain well-chosen cute graphics and sound effects. However, when presenting bad financial results or imminent layoffs, no sound or graphic effects are appropriate.

FOLLOW-UP/ACTION ITEMS.

Presentations, especially in sales situations, often have follow-up or action items. Before you end your presentation or speech, be sure to list aloud your follow-up or action items. It is always a good idea to bring hard copies of your presentation for those who wish to see it and for those who couldn't attend. Ask your host how many you should bring.

THANKS.

Thank your audience. Thank those who introduced you. Thank those who asked you to speak and present. No speech or presentation is complete without thanks to everyone who organized and participated in it.

Being Considerate of People with Disabilities

If you work with people who have readily apparent disabilities, you may already be sensitive to their needs and will have modified your presentations to make sure that they can get the most benefit from them. However, there are many 'silent' disabilities, including color-blindness and minor hearing loss, that you should take into consideration when planning a presentation. Here are some things to keep in mind:

Visual:

Is the room set up so that people can choose how close or far they sit from any screens?

Are you using readable type? Avoid light type on light backgrounds, or odd combinations of colors, especially red on green and vice-versa.

Avoid flashing animation and type set along curves.

Auditory:

Avoid background music.

Can you be heard clearly from every seat in the room?

Is there noise from fans or vents that might *(continued)*

interfere with hearing your talk? Arrange to have chairs moved away from them or have the vents shut during your presentation.

During Q&A sessions, repeat the question that was asked of you before answering it.

Other:

Be aware of the length of your presentation. It's considerate to build in breaks for any presentation longer than an hour. Consider taking a five-minute break before taking questions if you've already spoken for an hour.

Have copies of your presentation available for people who may not have been able to get all the information they needed during the session.

Offer to answer questions by phone or e-mail as well. Some people may not feel comfortable asking questions in an open session.

One last thing: ask for feedback. If possible, ask your listeners to give you anonymous feedback about your style, your manner, and the presentation as a whole. Ask specifically about whether your listeners felt they comprehended what you had to say. It will help you, and your listeners, in future presentations.

Using Design Specs from the Corporate Web Site

Your corporate Web site can be a treasure trove of design elements if your marketing department cannot or will not give you assistance. There you will find the corporate logo as well as approved fonts and color schemes. Here is how to apply them to your presentation:

1. **Logo:** Go to the site and find your company logo. Using Windows, place the cursor or arrow on the logo and right-click your mouse. Select "Save Picture As" and save it to your computer's desktop. In your presentation, set up the page or slide and insert by using the Insert menu and selecting "Insert Picture." The logo will appear on the page where you can move it, resize it, or rotate it.

2. **Font:** This is a less scientific process. Here you must use your judgment as to what font will work best. Look at the company's Web site, note the font used there, and find a font on your computer that most closely matches it.

3. **Colors:** Look at the corporate site and figure out the colors used there. Go to your presentation software and go to Format, then Colors, and select "Custom Colors." From there you can play with the mix of colors to match your company's.

PowerPoint Mistakes to Avoid

1. Background music: Why would you ever need this?
2. Zooming type or other annoying effects: Business presentations rarely need this kind of effect.
3. Non-sanctioned colors and fonts: Make sure you represent your company appropriately.
4. Streaming video: This is rarely useful and very tough to pull off successfully.
5. Each slide having its own design: Every slide should have the identical background color, font, and logo placement. Create a template if there isn't one already, and work from that template.
6. Presenting in the edit mode: Make sure your slides are taking up the full screen (F5 in Windows).
7. Reading from the slide: Everyone in the room can read. Talk from the slide, don't read it.
8. Too much information on a slide: Slides should contain outline information, not your entire discussion.
9. Too little information on a slide: "Introduction" is not sufficient information for a slide.
10. Spelling: Make sure the spell-check in your word-processing program is on and that you triple-check your work!

CHAPTER 10

Managing Information

RECORDS MANAGEMENT

The managing of records, whether on paper, as microfilm, or as electronic files, entails the retention, protection, preservation, and organization of those records. Some records must be kept for legal purposes for a specified number of years, or even permanently, which may require considerable space for storage, depending on the size of the company.

Larger companies may have a centralized records department, with a full-time staff to handle the filing and maintaining of these records, along with handling retrieval or copy requests. Smaller companies would depend on the office professional for such a task. Records must be filed efficiently and concisely, whatever the size of the company. A misfiled record is as good as gone, and the consequences could be dire.

Consideration must also be placed on the type of storage units used for filing. If records are of a sensitive nature, is the storage adequately locked and secure? If records are valuable or irreplaceable, are they in a fireproof or waterproof cabinet?

Periodic disposal of outdated or unnecessary records is helpful in the maintenance of office files. Records that must be retained for legal or documentation purposes but are not necessary in the everyday workings of the business may be transferred to another location such as a warehouse or storage facility. The records must be labeled and dated for easy retrieval.

When more than one person works on a project, each participant may maintain a personal file for that project, adding to the accumulation of correspondence and records. It is advisable to maintain an official file for each project and keep it in the hands of one person. It should contain the original of every piece of correspondence and other documentation related to the project.

REMINDER AND FOLLOW-UP SYSTEMS

Organizational skills are best implemented with the help of daily reminder calendars and follow-up files. An efficiently run office depends on such tools to keep track of important meetings, appointments, and special occasions.

Calendar Management

It is imperative that the executive and assistant keep lines of communication open at all times regarding appointments. An appointment change written on the executive's calendar but not relayed to the assistant can result in embarrassment or even irate clients. It is a good idea for the assistant to check the executive's calendar each morning to be sure both calendars coincide.

CALENDAR ENTRIES.

Some activities require notation on only the office professional's calendar—those of a more personal nature or those that do not involve the executive in any way. Others require notation on both calendars, with possible reminders a few days in advance, such as special anniversaries, which would give the office professional time to send a letter or card for the occasion.

Some activities occur regularly, such as staff meetings. While it may seem unnecessary to mark such an item on the calendar, do it anyway. In the course of a busy day or week, it's easy to overlook something routine. Having it penciled in will avoid the need for changes in appointments later. Use the previous year's calendar to mark annually occurring events. If the exact date is unknown but the general time of year is always the same, make such a notation in pencil on the calendar, which can later be permanently noted when the exact date is known.

TYPES OF CALENDARS.

Calendars come in all shapes and sizes, from pocket to desk to wall. The traditional write-in types never go out of style and are a great visual reminder, and software programs are now available that give executives and office professionals the ability to schedule and keep track of appointments at the push of a button. Electronic schedulers may allow both the executive and the office professional to log into one calendar, so any additions or changes in appointments will be obvious at a glance, avoiding any confusion or missed dates.

Hand-held organizers, called personal digital assistants (PDAs) or personal information managers (PIMs), can store names, addresses, notes, and appointments, but it is important that any appointments made or cancelled be transferred to the office calendar as soon as possible. (See "Do You Need A PDA?" on pages 4–5.)

Follow-Up Files

A follow-up filing system may be as simple as an expandable letter file with pockets labeled Monday through Friday.

Each transaction that requires some type of follow-up action should be placed in the corresponding day on which that action is supposed to take place. If an executive writes a memo stating that a client is requesting a phone call on Wednesday to confirm a luncheon meeting the following week, that memo is placed in the Wednesday pocket. On Wednesday, the memo will be acted upon when all the paperwork is pulled out of that day's pocket. Larger expanding files are also available, with such pocket designations as A to Z, January to December, and 1 to 31.

More complex versions of this system would require file cabinets or desk drawers. A common system uses twelve monthly files, with each month having numbered daily folders according to how many days there are in that month. As each day's follow-up transactions are taken care of, the reminders can be thrown away or correspondence can be filed in the appropriate regular file, such as a client's folder or a project folder.

A card file can also be set up in a similar way, taking up much less space. Notes may be written on cards, as reminders of actions to be taken on each day. Whatever system is chosen, it should be designed to give the office professional the means to handle each day in an organized, efficient manner.

CHAPTER 11

Meetings and Conferences

TYPES OF MEETINGS

Informal

Most in-house staff, departmental, or executive meetings are informal. An informal meeting is not firmly structured and can generate spontaneity and creativity. No matter the size or type, though, all meetings require planning. In larger companies, reservation of a meeting room may be called for, along with audiovisual equipment. Well in advance of the meeting, preferably at least a week before, all those expected to attend must be notified (usually by memo, phone, or e-mail). The notification should make clear the meeting time, place, and agenda. Whoever requests the meeting is considered the leader or facilitator. It is that person's responsibility not only to make up the agenda, but to keep the meeting on track and orderly. If minutes are not taken at a meeting, it is advisable that an appointed person jot down notes throughout the meeting. The leader can later have these notes summarized and sent to participants as a reminder of what was accomplished. The summary will be particularly useful should follow-up action be required. Whether the meeting is called to resolve a problem, discuss progress, or enact a plan, it must be conducted respectfully. It is important to listen to all ideas and agree or disagree on a professional level, not a personal one. All meetings should end with a sense of accomplishment or plans for a follow-up meeting.

Formal

A formal meeting may involve shareholders, board members, directors, or executives. Often there are bylaws, certain guidelines, or protocol to be followed, depending on the organization involved. The meetings are conducted usually by following parliamentary procedure, with officers assuming certain roles. For example, the meeting is announced formally, usually in an advanced mailing, and is headed by a chairperson or president. A secretary takes the minutes of the meeting, which will later be distributed to the appropriate people. Often, presentations are made by the officers or invited speakers. Formal meetings are structured and well-organized, offering few distractions. The agenda is detailed, listing allotted time frames for speakers and subject matter.

Off-Site

Off-site meetings require much advance planning that should be done in a number of steps: (1) reserve a hall or meeting room; (2) once you know the layout and size of the space, consider a seating plan; (3) notify participants of the meeting date and place and any aspects of the agenda they are responsible for; (4) make out the agenda; (5) book speakers; (6) secure transportation, accommodations, and meal plans; (7) plan before- or after-meeting entertainment; (8) find out if speakers will require special equipment for their presentations and secure it; (9) if audiovisual equipment will be used, be sure it is in good working order; (10) order necessary business supplies.

Whether using a formal or informal format, it is important to have a specific goal in mind. Individuals often invest

Tips for Better Videoconferencing

Telecommunications has made it possible to see and be seen while talking to others from a distance. As this technology becomes more commonplace, it will be increasingly more important for users to follow certain rules of protocol and procedure.

1. Always identify yourself and your location when you begin speaking to another site.
2. The name on top of your video window should identify your site (its name and/or location) so that others can identify your image on their screens.
3. Do not use facial expressions and gestures that other participants might find inappropriate. Monitor the image you are showing to others.
4. If you don't know the person you are addressing in the video window, specify the individual's site (at the top of his or her window) before commenting or asking a question. Doing so also informs other participants to whom your comment or question is addressed.
5. Listen to verbal cues (falling intonation for a statement, followed by a pause) indicating that the person talking is finished before making a comment or asking a question. If someone has asked you a question, that person is usually waiting for your response.
6. If you must leave while actively involved in a conversation, inform the other participants before disconnecting. Indicate verbally (or by typing) that you must leave, just as you would when ending a telephone conversation.
7. If you join a reflector site where there is already an ongoing conversation, do not just start talking. Wait until someone speaks to you or there is a pause in the conversation. Respect the right of others to "hold the floor," just as you would in a face-to-face conversation.

(continued)

8. If you plan to have a private conversation with a specific site or do not want to be interrupted by all participating sites, click on the necessary microphone or speaker buttons.

9. Conserving bandwidth is important, so check the area under your video window or your preferences menu for the transmission send-and-receive rates to be sure that they conform to the reflector's standards.

10. For the same reason, do not leave a message moving across the screen.

11. Unless you have been asked to do so, do not remain connected for hours, especially if you will not be in front of the camera and participating in the conversation.

12. Above all, keep your questions and comments relevant and to the point.

much time, effort, and expense to attend an off-site meeting, so a purposeful experience is a prime objective. No one wants to walk away feeling nothing was gained or accomplished.

PARLIAMENTARY PROCEDURE

When conducting a formal meeting, parliamentary procedure is usually followed. At such a meeting, each officer has specific tasks: The president (or chairperson) calls the meeting to order and follows the written agenda. Often, voting is required on certain issues, at which time "motions" will be called. The vice president acts as an assistant to the president but may also fill in as president at formal meetings if the president is unavailable. The secretary's most important task is the recording of the minutes, which become the official record of what occurred during the meeting. He or she may also be called on to fill in for an absent president or vice president by calling the meeting to order, at which time the assembled group elects a chair pro tem. The treasurer keeps the financial records and reports on them at certain meetings. He or she is also responsible for paying bills and making deposits.

Motions

When a topic is introduced for discussion, it is then opened up to the members of the meeting. The chairperson recognizes one of the members who then "moves" that the appointed topic be resolved. It might be stated as:

> I move that we cancel all ties with XYZ Company and go with UVW Company.

The chairperson asks the members at the meeting for a second to the motion. Any member can answer by saying "I second the motion" or simply "Second." The chairperson then opens the meeting up for discussion on the topic by stating something like: "It has been moved by Li-yu Roberts and seconded by Brenton Josephs that we cancel all ties with XYZ Company and go with UVW Company. Is there any discussion?"

The floor is then opened for discussion. When all discussion is over, the chairperson calls for a vote on the matter. If discussion on a topic goes on and on, the chairperson (or someone else) may suggest that those in attendance agree on a time limit for discussion. Votes can be taken by voice ("aye" for yes and "nay" for no), a show of hands, ballot, or any method approved of in advance. The chairperson may say:

> Any further discussion on this matter? [*If all is quiet, chair proceeds.*] All those in favor of going with UVW Company, say "aye" [*waits for response*]; those opposed? [*waits for responses of "nay"*]. [*After tallying votes, chairperson responds:*] The "ayes" [*or* "nays"] have it.

The secretary is responsible for recording into the minutes every motion, who made it, who seconded it, and the outcome of the vote.

Minutes

The secretary is responsible for recording all minutes of the meeting, beginning with the time, place, and date, and listing all members present (even recording who came late and who left early) and those who are not present, and identifying the person chairing the meeting and what type of meeting it is (shareholders, executive, board members, etc.). The minutes are not a word-for-word accounting of the proceedings, but they must be accurate, concise, and unbiased. The minutes cover the agenda, point-by-point, recording who is responsible for each recorded statement. Sometimes minutes are used in legal proceedings, so accuracy and degree of detail can be critical. The time the meeting was adjourned must be recorded as well.

The minutes are typed, double-spaced to make corrections easier to mark, then checked for accuracy by the meeting secretary. The minutes are then typed in final draft form, single-spaced if company policy allows, following previous minutes format. The minutes are then distributed to the appropriate participants as soon as possible after the meeting. A master copy is always kept on file, along with copies of motions and resolutions and any reports or documents that were passed around during the meeting.

Note: The standard source for learning the basics and specifics of parliamentary procedure is *Robert's Rules of Order.* For information on the most recent version, visit www. robertsrules.com.

CHAPTER 12

International and Domestic Travel

GUIDE TO MAKING TRAVEL ARRANGEMENTS

Travel has been a necessity of "doing business" since our ancestors dropped out of trees and became bipedal. Even with telecommunications and videoconferencing, travel remains the only way of meeting your customers (and competitors) face-to-face. Now, however, instead of joining a caravan and riding a camel across Asia for a few months, it is possible to be anywhere in the world in a matter of hours. Domestic airplane travel carries us anywhere in the continental United States quickly. How long a trip will take, however, depends on how much you can spend and how well you plan ahead.

Planning the Trip

Before you make a reservation with an airline, you will need to know at least three things: your destination, the dates of your departure and return (assuming you're purchasing a round-trip ticket), and the preferred times of your departure and return. In addition, a good travel agent will also ask you whether you want a first-class, business, or coach ticket; your seating preference (aisle or window; over the wing or near the tail); whether you'll accept a flight with one or two inter-vening stops, how long you want layovers to be (if changing planes); whether you will require assistance boarding, leav-ing the plane, and changing flights; and, if a meal will be served, whether you have special dietary needs (diabetic, low-salt, vegetarian, kosher, etc.). If the agent fails to ask you any of these questions, you should make your needs and pref-erences known. Failing to do so may mean redoing your travel plans later, which translates into a loss of time and, per-haps, money. You may also choose to have your agent handle the reservations for hotel rooms and leased vehicles.

Making a Reservation

Most businesses, whatever their size, use a travel agency to book flights, and, regularly request the services of a specific travel agent who is familiar with the company and the travel requirements of its employees. An agent who has handled several travel arrangements for a company comes to know the company's preferred airlines, method of ticket and itin-erary distribution, and various employee particulars, such as dietary restrictions and the need for handicapped access.

An agent who knows your company keeps reminders of special travel needs and preferences and will often see to such details automatically when making a reservation. But it is always the traveler's ultimate responsibility to confirm that all desired conditions have been satisfied.

Preparing to Fly

When you pack, you should be mindful of airport security precautions. Airlines recommend that passengers be at the airport two hours prior to takeoff to allow ample time for security searches (which may include the baggage you are checking through). Passengers are no longer allowed to have anything sharp in their carry-on baggage (only one carry-on bag is allowed) that might serve as a weapon, including nail files, razors (safety razors are allowed), box cutters, tweezers, scissors, plastic knives, and so forth. In order to avoid unnecessary problems, be sure to call the airline about which items and materials could be problematic, especially if you must have them for your trip. Anything that might be perceived as strange or threatening could cost you valuable time.

You should also check to find out whether the airport you're using has curbside check-ins. If you will have to stand in line at the ticket counter to check your baggage, allow more time. Finally, if someone takes you to the airport and plans to park the vehicle, security guards, police officers, or a member of the National Guard may want to check the undercarriage of the vehicle and the trunk as well. Again, allow time for this procedure because you will probably have to wait in line to enter the parking area. Because no one is allowed beyond the security checkpoint, tearful goodbyes at the gate are a thing of the past. Take a taxi, drive yourself and use long-term parking, or use a limousine service (available at many hotels). Also, you may want to carry more than one form of picture ID.

Online Reservations

Many businesspeople use one of the many online travel services to book travel, instead of a traditional travel agent. If you do so, be sure to print out your receipts and itineraries, and make sure you have a toll-free number to call in case of problems with your tickets or reservations. If you are using an e-ticket, you must carry a copy of your printed itinerary.

TRIP FOLLOW-UP

When the executive has returned from a trip, it is important to get pertinent information right away, while details are fresh in mind and receipts are easily retrievable. Thank yous may have to be written for courtesies shown while traveling, and expenses will have to be accounted for.

Expense Reports

All receipts must be collected after a trip in order to make out the expense report. Many of the expenses are reimbursable and some are even tax deductible. Most companies have a specific form that must be filled out. It is a good idea to have the executive fill in pertinent information on receipts that are generic in nature—for example, writing on a restaurant receipt, telling who was present and what business was discussed.

If the trip involved dealing with foreign currency, the exchange rate will have to be figured into the expense. Tips, sometimes paid in cash, will have to be accounted for as well. Most expenses, though, are paid for with a credit card, so submitting a completed expense report will be delayed until the credit card bill is received. Having the report filled in up to that point will save time in the completion process later.

Correspondence

Collect any business cards accumulated during the trip and log them onto card or computer files. Any courtesies shown during the trip should be acknowledged with thank-you letters. Arranged business deals should also be acknowledged, and pertinent delivery dates for products or services sold should be confirmed in writing.

Reports

Any office communication received from the executive during the trip should be organized and typed in an outline form for the executive to use as a guide for writing a follow-up report. If you have no specific format for reports, you may choose to follow a chronological order when typing the final report, listing daily events from the trip. Or you may use a summary format, listing topics discussed and progress made. A single-spaced format is acceptable, with double spacing between paragraphs for easy reading.

COUNTRY PROFILES

Argentina

Best time to visit: Southern: November–February; Northern: May–September.

Times to avoid: Easter and Christmas; January–February (vacations).

Before you go: Start to adapt your body clock for long evening business engagements.

Etiquette tip: Leave the complex ritual of wine-pouring to your host.

Visa for U.S. citizens: No.

Australia

Best time to visit: Any, except as noted.

Times to avoid: December and January (vacations).

Before you go: Get permission for business samples in advance; they may be hard to bring in.

Etiquette tip: Men sit in the front with the taxi driver; women sit in the back on the passenger side.

Visa for U.S. citizens: Check with ticket vendor.

Belgium

Best time to visit: Late spring; early autumn.

Times to avoid: Midwinter (dismal weather); August (vacations).

Before you go: Pack an umbrella and something warm; leave room for chocolate!

Etiquette tip: Don't play divide and conquer with the Flemings and the Walloons.

Visa for U.S. citizens: No.

Brazil

Best time to visit: Any, except as noted.

Times to avoid: Carnival; December–February (vacations).

Before you go: Prepare high-quality, clear visual aids for your presentation.

Etiquette tip: Don't touch food with your hands; use utensils or napkins for everything.

Visa for US: Yes, if you will transact business.

Canada

Best time to visit: Any, except as noted.

Times to avoid: Weather can disrupt winter travel.

Before you go: Find out if a French interpreter is needed.

Etiquette tip: Modesty in Americans is unexpected and therefore appreciated.

Visa for U.S. citizens: No.

China

Best time to visit: Spring and autumn.

Times to avoid: Chinese New Year; July and August (very muggy).

Before you go: Get bilingual business cards printed with simplified PRC Chinese characters.

Etiquette tip: If you get applauded when introduced to a group, applaud back.

Visa for U.S. citizens: Yes.

Colombia

Best time to visit: December–March (dry season).

Times to avoid: December to mid-January (holidays and vacations).

Before you go: Pack cheap jewelry and accessories; leave the good stuff at home.

Etiquette tip: Don't neglect to shake everyone's hand when parting from them.

Visa for U.S. citizens: Yes.

France

Best time to visit: Any, except as noted.

Times to avoid: August (vacations); Christmas and Easter.

Before you go: Upgrade the wardrobe to the height of conservative fashion.

Etiquette tip: Learn and use peoples' titles, or use "Madame" and "Monsieur" at the very least.

Visa for US: No.

Germany

Best time to visit: Any, except as noted.

Times to avoid: July and August (vacations); May (five public holidays).

Before you go: Send your credentials and company information ahead if you want to be credible.

Etiquette tip: Use your sense of humor discreetly until you see if it works.

Visa for U.S. citizens: No.

Hong Kong

Best time to visit: November–April.

Times to avoid: Chinese New Year (late January).

Before you go: Pack a handful of hospitality gifts; they're useful everywhere.

Etiquette tip: Avoid physical contact except shaking hands.

Visa for U.S. citizens: No.

India

Best time to visit: November–March.

Times to avoid: June–August (monsoon season).

Before you go: Make sure you are carrying nothing made of gold.

Etiquette tip: Don't point at or touch anyone with your feet or shoes.

Visa for U.S. citizens: Yes.

Ireland

Best time to visit: Late spring; early autumn.

Times to avoid: July and August (vacations); Christmas through New Year's.

Before you go: Pack the golf clubs; they may be required for business success.

Etiquette tip: Buy a round of drinks if everyone else is doing this.

Visa for U.S. citizens: No.

Israel

Best time to visit: Spring and autumn.

Times to avoid: Major Jewish holidays.

Before you go: Print up engraved business cards; adding Hebrew is a plus.

Etiquette tip: Give and receive gifts with the right hand, not the left.

Visa for U.S. citizens: Yes, issued in-country.

Italy

Best time to visit: Any, except as noted.

Times to avoid: August; Christmas through New Year's.

Before you go: Have a designer go over your presentation materials to spruce them up.

Etiquette tip: Start out formally in business dealings and let the natives set the pace.

Visa for U.S. citizens: No.

Japan

Best time to visit: Spring and autumn.

Times to avoid: New Year's; Golden Week (late April–early May).

Before you go: Pack company-logo gifts to pass out liberally.

Etiquette tip: Bow frequently; don't blow your nose in public.

Visa for U.S. citizens: No.

Malaysia
Best time to visit: Any, except as noted.
Times to avoid: December–February (holidays); Chinese New Year; Ramadan.
Before you go: Send ahead an official-looking third-party letter of introduction.
Etiquette tip: Don't touch anyone on the head.
Visa for U.S. citizens: No.

Mexico
Best time to visit: Spring and late autumn.
Times to avoid: Holy Week and the Christmas season.
Before you go: Print up loads of bilingual business cards, and be generous with them.
Etiquette tip: All comparisons of Mexico with the United States are invidious.
Visa for US: No.

Netherlands
Best time to visit: Spring and summer.
Times to avoid: Easter and Christmas.
Before you go: Pack books and objets d'arts for business and hospitality gifts.
Etiquette tip: Repeat your last name while shaking hands with new acquaintances.
Visa for U.S. citizens: No.

Norway
Best time to visit: May–September.
Times to avoid: Easter; Christmas; winter holiday (February).
Before you go: Pack warm clothing; take simple and modest gifts.
Etiquette tip: Don't lump Norwegians with other Scandinavians.
Visa for U.S. citizens: No.

Philippines

Best time to visit: October–March.

Times to avoid: Christmas and Easter; midsummer (vacations).

Before you go: Make sure you have a dependable intermediary to make introductions.

Etiquette tip: Don't raise your voice in conversation; quiet repetition is better.

Visa for U.S. citizens: No.

Russia

Best time to visit: Mid-May–June; September–October.

Times to avoid: Early January; early May (many public holidays).

Before you go: Pack business and hospitality gifts that are not available in Russia.

Etiquette tip: Don't refer to a Russian as your "comrade," even jokingly.

Visa for U.S. citizens: Yes.

Saudi Arabia

Best time to visit: November–February.

Times to avoid: Ramadan and pilgrimage time.

Before you go: Forget travelers' checks, but take ATM cards.

Etiquette tip: Don't touch food or people with your left hand.

Visa for U.S. citizens: Yes.

Singapore

Best time to visit: Any, except as noted.

Times to avoid: Christmas; Easter; Chinese New Year.

Before you go: Divest yourself of all chewing gum.

Etiquette tip: Don't point, touch people on the head, or jaywalk.

Visa for U.S. citizens: Yes; issued on arrival.

South Korea
Best time to visit: Any, except as noted.

Times to avoid: New Year and Chusok (September).

Before you go: Tune up! Good karaoke may be your key to business success.

Etiquette tip: Always show deference and respect to senior citizens.

Visa for U.S. citizens: No, unless staying more than two weeks.

South Africa
Best time to visit: Spring and autumn (opposite times from N hemisphere).

Times to avoid: December and January (vacations).

Before you go: Brush up on cricket, soccer, and rugby; spectating is a common business entertainment.

Etiquette tip: Don't shrink from friendly physical contact.

Visa for U.S. citizens: No.

Spain
Best time to visit: Spring and autumn.

Times to avoid: Holy Week; Christmas; August (vacations).

Before you go: Pack American crafts, books, and CDs for gifts.

Etiquette tip: Let the natives set the pace for friendly physical contact.

Visa for U.S. citizens: No.

Sweden
Best time to visit: September–early December; spring.

Times to avoid: July and the long Christmas period (early December–early January).

Before you go: Prepare to deal with women on terms of 100% equality.

Etiquette tip: Avoid glib compliments; make only the ones you really mean.

Visa for U.S. citizens: No.

Switzerland
Best time to visit: April–May; September–October.
Times to avoid: Christmas week.
Before you go: Get plenty of business cards with your name, degrees, and founding date of your company.
Etiquette tip: Wait for someone to introduce you rather than introducing yourself.
Visa for U.S. citizens: No.

Taiwan
Best time to visit: April–September.
Times to avoid: Chinese New Year, late October (public holidays).
Before you go: Practice tiny sips in order to endure lengthy toasting sessions.
Etiquette tip: Save the handshake till you become friendly, then expect only a limp one.
Visa for U.S. citizens: No.

Thailand
Best time to visit: November–February.
Times to avoid: Christmas; April and May (vacations).
Before you go: Pack reading material to keep you amused in taxis during long traffic jams.
Etiquette tip: Your hands should be visible at all times in social situations.
Visa for U.S. citizens: No, unless staying longer than two weeks.

United Kingdom
Best time to visit: May–October.
Times to avoid: Easter; Christmas through New Year's; August (holidays).
Before you go: Work up your repertoire of droll and ironic jokes for use at business lunches.

Etiquette tip: Be sensitive to national divisions within the UK, especially between Scotland and England.

Visa for U.S. citizens: No.

Venezuela

Best time to visit: December–April (dry season)

Times to avoid: Holy Week; Christmas.

Before you go: Pick up some *New York Times* best-sellers as business gifts.

Etiquette tip: Don't back away from "in-your-face" conversations; this is the cultural norm.

Visa for U.S. citizens: No. (Tourist card issued en route.)

Common Financial Equations

Ratio, etc.	How determined	Definition and use
accounts receivable days	(accounts receivable ÷ sales) × 365	average length of time between credit sales and payment receipts
accounts receivable turnover	net credit sales ÷ average accounts receivable	a short-term solvency ratio that measures how efficiently a company grants credit to produce revenue
acid test ratio	(current assets - inventories) ÷ current liabilities	a short-term solvency ratio that gives an indication of a company's liquidity and its ability to meet obligations. Also called **quick ratio** or **current ratio**.
asset/equity ratio	total assets ÷ stockholder equity	a ratio used to compare the revenue-producing abilities of companies within the same industry
asset turnover	net sales ÷ total assets	a ratio that measures the efficiency of a company's use of its assets. It is typically inversely related to the profit margin.
Average rate of return (ARR)	Average net earnings ÷ average investment	a percentage figure used to compare different investment vehicles over the long term
bid-to-cover ratio	bids received ÷ bids accepted	a rough measure of the success of a treasury security auction

Ratio, etc.	How determined	Definition and use
bond ratio	par value of bonds ÷ (this figure + all other equity)	a figure that represents the percent-age of a company's capitalization in bonds
book-to-bill	orders taken ÷ orders filled (within the same period, e.g. one month)	a measure of supply and demand in a market or for a company's products, used especially in evaluating high-technology companies. Figures >1 indicate an expanding market.
cash flow coverage	EBITDA ÷ interest expense	a measure of a company's ability to service debt payments from operating cash flow
cash flow leverage	Total liabilities ÷ EBITDA	a measure of a company's ability to repay debt obligations from operating cash flow
debt/asset ratio	total liabilities ÷ total assets	a ratio used on companies within the same industry to compare their ability to manage their long-term debt
debt/equity ratio	long-term debt ÷ stockholder equity	a ratio that compares the assets of a company that are held by creditors to those held by owners. High ratios indicate aggressive use of debt to manage growth.
debt-service coverage ratio	net operating income ÷ total debt service (in the same period, e.g. one year)	a ratio used to determine a company's or property's ability to remain viable.
earnings yield	yearly earnings per share ÷ share market price	a figure that essentially gives the percentage of earnings that one dollar of equity buys. It is the inverse of the price-earnings ratio.
EBITDA	revenues - expenses (excluding tax, interest, depreciation and amortization)	earnings before interest, tax, depreciation, and amortization
fixed-charge coverage ratio	(net earnings + interest paid + lease expense) ÷ (interest paid + lease expense)	a measure of a company's ability to meet its fixed-charge obligations

Ratio, etc.	How determined	Definition and use
inventory days	(inventory ÷ cost of goods sold) × 365	a measure of the value of inventory on hand, sometimes used as an indication of a company's ability to respond to market changes
inventory turnover	annual sales ÷ average inventory	a measure of the speed at which inventory is produced and sold. Higher figures normally indicate strong sales and good turnover.
loan-to-value (LTV) ratio	value of loan ÷ market value of property	a general indication of the risk involved in a mortgage. Banks usually require a ratio of at least 75%.
loss ratio	claims paid ÷ premiums collected (in a similar period, e.g. one year)	a factor in the profitability and efficiency of an insurance company or insurance market.
management expense ratio (MRE)	total of all fees ÷ total value of portfolio	a percentage figure that expresses the amount of a mutual fund's value that is consumed by the expenses of managing it
member short sale ratio	total number of shares sold short ÷ total short sales	a tool used to anticipate bullish or bearish trends on the New York Stock Exchange
Macaulay duration	weighted average term to maturity ÷ bond price	an indicator of the volatility of a bond's price to a change in its yield
market to book ratio	share market price ÷ book value per share	a figure used in estimating the cost of capital of an enterprise
net operating margin	net operating income ÷ net sales	a performance indicator used on companies within the same industry or historically of the same company
operating cycle	accounts receivable days + inventory days	the time that elapses from when a product is added to inventory to receipt of the income from its sale

Ratio, etc.	How determined	Definition and use
operating profit margin	operating profit ÷ net sales	a tool for measuring effective pricing strategy and operating efficiency
payout ratio	total dividend ÷ total earnings	a measure of how much profit a company is returning to stockholders in dividends, often used to mark historical trends
price-earnings (P/E) ratio	current share price ÷ per share in the past 12 months	an often-quoted figure that earnings is usually an indication of growth expectations. Useful only for comparisons within the same industry, or historically for the same company (also called **multiple**).
price-to-book ratio	current share price ÷ last quarter's book value per share	a tool used for speculating on the accuracy of the valuation of a company's stock. A low ratio could mean that the company is undervalued, or that there is something fundamentally wrong with it.
price-to-sales ratio	current share price ÷ revenue per share in the year to date	a tool for comparing a stock's valuation relative to its own history, to its industry peers, or to the market generally.
profit margin	net income ÷ revenue (in the same period)	a percentage that expresses profitability, most often used in comparisons within the same industry.
prospective earnings growth (PEG) ratio	P/E ratio ÷ projected earnings growth rate	an indicator of a stock's potential value that is favored by some over the P/E ratio because it takes growth into account. Projected earnings growth rate is determined from proprietary sources.
Q ratio	market asset value ÷ asset replacement value	a figure used as an indication of the success of a company's investment strategy (also called **Tobin's Q ratio** after its inventor James Tobin)

Ratio, etc.	How determined	Definition and use
receivables turnover ratio	total operating revenues ÷ average receivables	a figure that indicates efficiency in managing accounts receivable
retention rate	1 - payout ratio	the percentage of earnings retained by a company, which may be a factor in its investment and growth strategy
return on assets (ROA)	net income ÷ total assets	a percentage figure that indicates how profitable a company is relative to its assets
return on equity (ROE)	net income ÷ stockholder equity	a comparative indicator of profitability within the same industry, expressed as a percentage.
return on investment (ROI)	total income ÷ total capital	the percentage of income derived from the amount invested, used as a measure of a company's performance
return on net assets (RONA)	net income ÷ (fixed assets + net working capital)	a percentage figure used as a measure of the profitability of a company
return on sales (ROS)	net profit ÷ net sales	a percentage figure widely used as an indicator of operational efficiency
risk-reward ratio	expected return on an investment ÷ standard deviation of an index	a figure that roughly indicates the amount of risk in an investment relative to comparable investments
relative strength	(current share price ÷ year-ago share price) ÷ (current S&P 500 ÷ year-ago S&P 500)	a measure of the strength of a stock relative to the market; values >1 show relative strength (does not take risk into account)
rule of 72	72 ÷ rate of interest	a figure that tells how many years it will take to double your money at a given rate of compound interest
Sharpe ratio	(ROI - T-bill rate) ÷ standard deviation of a portfolio	a measure of a portfolio's excess return relative to its total variability. It may indicate whether returns are due to wise investment or excess risk (see also **Treynor ratio**)

Ratio, etc.	How determined	Definition and use
times-interest-earned ratio	earnings before interest and tax ÷ interest payments	a measure of a company's debtservicing ability
total debt-service (TDS) ratio	Total obligations ÷ gross income (calculated for the period)	the percentage of gross income required to cover all payments for same housing and all other debts such as car payments; used typically to calculate creditworthiness of a household borrower
Treynor ratio	excess return ÷ portfolio standard deviation	a measure of the return on an investment in excess of what could have been earned on a riskless investment (also called **reward-to-volatility ratio**)
working capital ratio	(current assets - current liabilities) ÷ total sales	a percentage figure used for comparing operating efficiency within the same industry.

Glossary of Business and Finance Terms

ab•so•lute ad•van•tage ▸ n. the ability of an individual or group to carry out a particular economic activity more efficiently than another individual or group.

ab•sorp•tion cost•ing ▸ n. [mass noun] a method of calculating the cost of a product or enterprise by taking into account indirect expenses (overheads) as well as direct costs.

ac•cept ▸ v. agree to meet (a draft or bill of exchange) by signing it.

ac•cept•ance ▸ n. agreement to meet a draft or bill of exchange, effected by signing it. ■ a draft or bill so accepted.

ac•cep•tor ▸ n. a person or bank that accepts a draft or bill of exchange.

ac•count ▸ n. (abbr.: **acct.**) a record or statement of financial expenditure or receipts relating to a particular period or purpose. ■ an arrangement by which a body holds funds on behalf of a client or supplies goods or services to the client on credit: *a bank account | I began buying things on account.* ■ the balance of funds held under such an arrangement. ■ a client having such an arrangement with a supplier. ■ a contract to do work periodically for a client.

ac•count•ant (abbr.: **acct.**) ▸ n. a person whose job is to keep or inspect financial accounts.

ac•count ex•ec•u•tive ▸ n. a business executive who manages the interests of a particular client, typically in advertising.

ac•count•ing ▸ n. the action or process of keeping financial accounts.

ac•counts pay•a•ble ▸ plural n. money owed by a company to its creditors.

ac•counts re•ceiv•a•ble ▸ plural n. money owed to a company by its debtors.

ac•crue ▸ v. (accrues, accrued, accruing) (of sums of money or benefits) be received by someone in regular or increasing amounts over time. ■ accumulate or receive (such payments or benefits). ■ make provision for (a charge) at the end of a financial period for work that has been done but not yet invoiced.

ac•cu•mu•la•tion ▸ n. the growth of a sum of money by the regular addition of interest.

ac•quire ▸ v. buy or obtain (an asset or object) for oneself.

ac•qui•si•tion ▸ n. an act of purchase of one company by another. ■ buying or obtaining an asset or object.

ac•qui•si•tion ac•count•ing ▸ n. a procedure in accounting in which the value of the assets of a company is changed from book to fair market level, after a takeover.

ac•tu•ar•y ▸ n. (pl. **-ies**) a person who compiles and analyzes statistics and uses them to calculate insurance risks and premiums.

ADR ▸ abbr. American depositary receipt.

ad va•lo•rem ▸ adv. & adj. (of the levying of tax or customs duties) in proportion to the estimated value of the goods or transaction concerned.

ad•vice ▸ n. a formal notice of a financial transaction: *remittance advices.*

af•fin•i•ty card ▸ n. a credit card carrying the name of an organization to which a portion of the money spent using the card is paid.

af•ter•mar•ket ▸ n. the market for shares and bonds after their original issue.

a•gainst ▸ prep. in relation to (an amount of money owed or due) so as to reduce or cancel it.

A•mer•i•can de•pos•i•tar•y re•ceipt (also **American depositary share**) ▸ n. (in the US) a negotiable certificate of title to a number of shares in a non-US company that are deposited in an overseas bank.

Amex ▸ abbr. American Stock Exchange.

am•or•tize ▸ v. reduce or extinguish (a debt) by money regularly put aside: *loan fees can be amortized over the life of the mortgage.*
▪ gradually write off the initial cost of (an asset).

AMT ▸ abbr. alternative minimum tax, introduced to prevent companies and individuals using deductions andcredits to pay no tax.

an•nu•al•ized ▸ adj. (of a rate of interest, inflation, or return on an investment) recalculated as an annual rate: *an annualized yield of about 11.5%.*

an•nu•i•tant ▸ n. formal a person who receives an annuity.

an•nu•i•ty ▸ n. (pl. **-ies**) a fixed sum of money paid to someone each year, typically for the rest of their life.
▪ a form of insurance or investment entitling the investor to a series of annual sums.

an•swer•ing serv•ice ▸ n. a business that receives and answers telephone calls for its clients.

an•ti•trust ▸ adj. of or relating to legislation preventing or controlling trusts or other monopolies, with the intention of promoting competition in business.

APR ▸ abbr. annual or annualized percentage rate, typically of interest on loans or credit.

ar•bi•trage ▸ n. the simultaneous buying and selling of securities, currency, or commodities in different markets or in derivative forms in order to take advantage of differing prices for the same asset.

ar•bi•tra•geur (also **arbitrager**) ▸ n. a person who engages in arbitrage.

ask ▸ v. request (a specified amount) as a price for selling something.
▸ n. the price at which an item, esp. a financial security, is offered for sale.

ask•ing price ▸ n. the price at which something is offered for sale.

as•sess ▸ v. (usu. **be assessed**) calculate or estimate the price or value of.
▪ (often **be assessed**) set the value of a tax, fine, etc., for (a person or property) at a specified level.

as•ses•sor ▸ n. a person who calculates or estimates the value of something or an amount to be paid, chiefly for tax or insurance purposes.

as•set ▸ n. (usu. **assets**) property owned by a person or company, regarded as having value and available to meet debts, commitments, or legacies: *growth in net assets.*

as•set-backed ▸ adj. denoting securities having as collateral the return on a series of mortgages, credit agreements, or other forms of lending.

as•set-strip•ping ▸ n. the practice of taking over a company in financial difficulties and selling each of its assets separately at a profit without regard for the company's future.

ATM ▸ abbr. automated (or automatic) teller machine.

au•dit ▸ n. an official inspection of an individual's or organization's accounts, typically by an independent body.
▸ v. (**audited, auditing**) conduct an official financial examination of (an individual's or organization's accounts): *companies must have their accounts audited.*

au•di•tor ▸ n. a person who conducts an audit.

aus•ter•i•ty ▸ n. (pl. -ies)
- difficult economic conditions created by government measures to reduce a budget deficit, esp. by reducing public expenditure.

av•er•age (abbr.: **avg.**) ▸ n. the apportionment of financial liability resulting from loss of or damage to a ship or its cargo.
- reduction in the amount payable under an insurance policy, e.g., in respect of partial loss.

back end ▸ adj. relating to the end or outcome of a project, process, or investment: *many annuities have back-end surrender charges.*

back•load ▸ v. (usu. **be backloaded**) place more charges at the later stages of (a financial agreement) than at the earlier stages.

bad debt ▸ n. a debt that cannot be recovered.

bail•out ▸ n. informal an act of giving financial assistance to a failing business or economy to save it from collapse.

bait-and-switch ▸ n. the action (generally illegal) of advertising goods that are an apparent bargain, with the intention of substituting inferior or more expensive goods.

bal•ance ▸ n. a figure representing the difference between credits and debits in an account; the amount of money held in an account.
- the difference between an amount due and an amount paid: *unpaid credit-card balances.* ▪ an amount left over.

▸ v. compare debits and credits in (an account), typically to ensure that they are equal.
- (of an account) have credits and debits equal.

–PHRASES **balance of payments** the difference in total value between payments into and out of a country over a period. **balance of trade** the difference in value between a country's imports and exports.

bal•ance sheet ▸ n. a statement of the assets, liabilities, and capital of a business or other organization at a particular point in time, detailing the balance of income and expenditure over the preceding period.

bal•loon pay•ment ▸ n. a repayment of the outstanding principal sum made at the end of a loan period, interest only having been paid hitherto.

bank draft ▸ n. a check drawn by a bank on its own funds in another bank.

bank•note (also **bank note**) ▸ n. a piece of paper money, constituting a central bank's promissory note to pay a stated sum to the bearer on demand.

bank•rupt ▸ adj. (of a person or organization) declared in law unable to pay outstanding debts: *the company was declared bankrupt* | *he committed suicide after going bankrupt.*
▸ n. a person judged by a court to be insolvent, whose property is taken and disposed of for the benefit of creditors.
▸ v. reduce (a person or organization) to bankruptcy: *the strike nearly bankrupted the union.*

ba•sis point ▸ n. one hundredth of one percent, used chiefly in expressing differences of interest rates.

bas•ket ▸ n. a group or range of currencies or investments: *the European currency unit is made up of a basket of ten currencies.*

bean count•er ▸ n. informal, derogatory a person, typically an accountant or bureaucrat, perceived as placing excessive emphasis on controlling expenditure and budgets.

bear ▸ n. a person who forecasts that prices of stocks or commodities will fall, esp. a person who sells shares hoping to buy them back later at a lower price.

bear•er ▸ n. a person who presents a check or other order to pay money.
- payable to the possessor: *bearer bonds.*

bear•ish ▸ adj. characterized by falling share prices.
- (of a dealer) inclined to sell because of an anticipated fall in prices.

bear mar•ket ▸ n. a market in which prices are falling, encouraging selling.

bid price ▸ n. the price that a dealer or other prospective buyer is prepared to pay for securities or other assets.

Big Board n. informal term for the New York Stock Exchange.

bill•ing ▸ n. the process of making out or sending invoices.
■ the total amount of business conducted in a given time, esp. that of an advertising agency.

bill of ex•change ▸ n. a written order to a person requiring the person to make a specified payment to the signatory or to a named payee; a promissory note.

bill of goods ▸ n. a consignment of merchandise.

bill of sale ▸ n. a certificate of transfer of personal property.

black mon•ey ▸ n. income illegally obtained or not declared for tax purposes.

blank check ▸ n. a bank check with the amount left for the payee to fill in.

block ▸ v. restrict the use or conversion of (currency or any other asset).

blue-chip ▸ adj. denoting companies or their shares considered to be a reliable investment, though less secure than gilt-edged stock.

Board of Trade ▸ n. (also **Chicago Board of Trade**) the Chicago futures exchange.

boil•er room ▸ n.
■ a room used for intensive telephone selling.

bond ▸ n. a certificate issued by a government or a public company promising to repay borrowed money at a fixed rate of interest at a specified time. ■ (of dutiable goods) a state of storage in a bonded warehouse until the importer pays the duty owing. ■ an insurance policy held by a company, which protects against losses resulting from circumstances such as bankruptcy or misconduct by employees.

bond•ed ▸ adj. (of a person or company) bound by a legal agreement, in particular:
■ (of a debt) secured by bonds. ■ (of dutiable goods) placed in bond.

bond•ed ware•house ▸ n. a customs-controlled warehouse for the retention of imported goods until the duty owed is paid.

bo•nus is•sue ▸ n. an issue of additional shares to shareholders instead of a dividend, in proportion to the shares already held.

book•keep•ing ▸ n. the activity or occupation of keeping records of the financial affairs of a business.

book val•ue ▸ n. the value of a security or asset as entered in a company's books.

bounce ▸ v. informal (of a check) be returned by a bank when there are insufficient funds to meet it. ■ informal write (a check) on insufficient funds: *I've never bounced a check.*

bourse ▸ n. a stock market in a non-English-speaking country, esp. France.
■ (**Bourse**) the Paris stock exchange.

bp ▸ abbr. basis point(s).

BPR ▸ abbr. business process reengineering.

brand a•ware•ness ▸ n. the extent to which consumers are familiar with the distinctive qualities or image of a particular brand of goods or services.

brand ex•ten•sion ▸ n. an instance of using an established brand name or trademark on new products, so as to increase sales.

brand im•age ▸ n. the impression of a product held by real or potential consumers.

brand lead•er ▸ n. the best-selling or most highly regarded product or brand of its type.

brand loy•al•ty ▸ n. the tendency of some consumers to continue buying the same brand of goods despite the availability of competing brands.

brand man•age•ment ▸ n. the activity of supervising the promotion of a particular brand of goods.

brand name ▸ n. a name given by the maker to a product or range of products, esp. a trademark.

Brand X ▸ n. a name used for an unidentified brand contrasted unfavorably with a product of the same type being promoted.

break ▸ v. (past **broke**; past part. **broken**) (of prices on the stock exchange) fall sharply.

break-e•ven ▸ n. the point or state at which a person or company breaks even.

bridge loan ▸ n. a sum of money lent by a bank to cover an interval between two transactions, typically the buying of one house and the selling of another.

bro•ker ▸ n. a person who buys and sells goods or assets for others.
▸v. arrange or negotiate (a settlement, deal, or plan): *fighting continued despite attempts to broker a cease-fire.*

bro•ker•age ▸ n. the business or service of acting as a broker.
▪ a fee or commission charged by a broker: *a revenue of $1,400 less a sales brokerage of $12.50.* ▪ a company that buys or sells goods or assets for clients.

bro•ker-deal•er ▸ n. a brokerage firm that buys and sells securities on its own account as a principal before selling the securities to customers.

BS ▸ abbr. balance sheet.

bub•ble e•con•o•my ▸ n. an unstable expanding economy; in particular, a period of heightened prosperity and increased commercial activity in Japan in the late 1980s brought about by artificially adjusted interest rates.

buck•et shop ▸ n. informal, derogatory an unauthorized office for speculating in stocks or currency using the funds of unwitting investors.

budg•et ▸ n. an estimate of income and expenditure for a set period of time.
▪ an annual or other regular estimate of national revenue and expenditure put forward by the government, often including details of changes in taxation.

bulk buy•ing ▸ n. the purchase of goods in large amounts, typically at a discount.

bull ▸ n. a person who buys shares hoping to sell them at a higher price later.

bull•ish ▸ adj. characterized by rising share prices.
▪ (of a dealer) inclined to buy because of an anticipated rise in prices.

bull mar•ket ▸ n. a market in which share prices are rising, encouraging buying.

buoy•an•cy ▸ n. figurative a high level of activity in an economy or stock market.

busi•ness cy•cle ▸ n. a cycle or series of cycles of economic expansion and contraction.

busi•ness proc•ess re•en•gi•neer•ing (abbr.: BPR) ▸ n. the process or activity of restructuring a company's organization and methods, esp. to exploit the capabilities of computers.

busi•ness stud•ies ▸ plural n. [treated as sing.] the study of economics and management, esp. as an educational topic.

buy-back ▸ n. the buying back of goods by the original seller.
▪ the buying back by a company of its own shares. ▪ a form of borrowing in which shares or bonds are sold with an agreement to repurchase them at a later date.

buy•er ▸ n. a person who makes a purchase.
▪ a person employed to select and purchase stock or materials for a large retail or manufacturing business, etc.
–PHRASES **a buyer's market** an economic situation in which goods or shares are plentiful and buyers can keep prices down.

buy-in ▸ n. a purchase of shares by a broker after a seller has failed to deliver similar shares, the original seller being charged any difference in cost.

buy•out ▸ n. the purchase of a controlling share in a company, esp. by its own managers.

ca•das•tral ▸ adj. (of a map or survey) showing the extent, value, and ownership of land, esp. for taxation.

ca•das•tre ▸ n. a register of property showing the extent, value, and ownership of land for taxation.

CAF ▸ abbr. cost and freight.

call ▸ n. a demand for payment of lent or unpaid capital. ▪ short for CALL OPTION.

call mon•ey ▸ n. money lent by a bank or other institutions that is repayable on demand.

call op•tion ▸ n. an option to buy assets at an agreed price on or before a particular date.

cap ▸ n. an upper limit imposed on spending or other activities.

▸v. (**capped, capping**) (often **be capped**) place a limit or restriction on (prices, expenditure, or other activity): *council budgets will be capped.*

cap•i•tal ▸ n. wealth in the form of money or other assets owned by a person or organization or available or contributed for a particular purpose such as starting a company or investing.
■ the excess of a company's assets over its liabilities.

cap•i•tal ad•e•qua•cy ▸ n. the statutory minimum reserves of capital that a bank or other financial institution must have available.

cap•i•tal gain ▸ n. (often **capital gains**) a profit from the sale of property or of an investment.

cap•i•tal gains tax ▸ n. a tax levied on profit from the sale of property or of an investment.

cap•i•tal goods ▸ plural n. goods that are used in producing other goods, rather than being bought by consumers.

cap•i•tal-in•ten•sive ▸ adj. (of a business or industrial process) requiring the investment of large sums of money.

cap•i•tal•ize ▸ v. provide (a company or industry) with capital. realize (the present value of an income); convert into capital.
■ reckon (the value of an asset) by setting future benefits against the cost of maintenance.

cap•i•tal mar•ket ▸ n. the part of a financial system concerned with raising capital by dealing in shares, bonds, and other long-term investments.

cap•i•tal sum ▸ n. a lump sum of money payable to an insured person or paid as an initial fee or investment.

cap•i•ta•tion ▸ n. the payment of a fee or grant to a doctor, school, or other person or body providing services to a number of people, such that the amount paid is determined by the number of patients, pupils, or customers.

cap•tive ▸ adj. (of a facility or service) controlled by, and typically for the sole use of, an establishment or company: *a captive power plant.*

car•bon tax ▸ n. a tax on fossil fuels, esp. those used by motor vehicles, intended to reduce the emission of carbon dioxide.

card•hold•er ▸ n. a person who has a credit card or debit card.

car•ry ▸ n. (pl. **-ies**) [usu. in sing.] the maintenance of an investment position in a securities market, esp. with regard to the costs or profits accruing.

car•ry•ing charge ▸ n. an expense or effective cost arising from unproductive assets such as stored goods or unoccupied premises. a sum payable for the conveying of goods.

car•tel ▸ n. an association of manufacturers or suppliers with the purpose of maintaining prices at a high level and restricting competition.

car•tel•ize ▸ v. (of manufacturers or suppliers) form a cartel in (an industry or trade).

cash and car•ry ▸ n. a system of wholesale trading whereby goods are paid for in full at the time of purchase and taken away by the purchaser.
■ a wholesale store operating this system.

cash cow ▸ n. informal a business, investment, or product that provides a steady income or profit.

cash flow ▸ n. the total amount of money being transferred into and out of a business, esp. as affecting liquidity.

cash•ier ▸ n. a person handling payments and receipts in a store, bank, or other business.

cash nex•us ▸ n. the relationship constituted by monetary transactions.

cash on de•liv•er•y (abbr.: **COD**) ▸ n. the system of paying for goods when they are delivered.

cash reg•is•ter ▸ n. a machine used in places of business for regulating money transactions with customers. It typically has a compartmental drawer for cash and totals, displays, and records the amount of each sale.

cen•tral bank ▸ n. a national bank that provides financial and banking services for its country's government and commercial banking system, as well as implementing the government's monetary policy and issuing currency.

cer•tif•i•cate of de•pos•it (abbr.: **CD**) ▸ n. a certificate issued by a bank to a person depositing money for a specified length of time.

cer•ti•fied check ▸ n. a check that is guaranteed by a bank.

cer•ti•fied pub•lic ac•count•ant (abbr.: **CPA**) ▸ n. a member of an officially accredited professional body of accountants.

c.f. ▸ abbr. carried forward (used to refer to figures transferred to a new page or account).

CGT ▸ abbr. capital gains tax.

chae•bol ▸ n. (pl. same or **chaebols**) (in South Korea) a large business conglomerate, typically a family-owned one.

cham•ber of com•merce (abbr.: **C. of C.**) ▸ n. a local association to promote and protect the interests of the business community in a particular place.

change man•age•ment ▸ n. the management of change and development within a business or similar organization, esp. the personal management of those having to adapt to new conditions.

Chap•ter 11 ▸ n. protection from creditors given to a company in financial difficulties for a limited period to allow it to reorganize.

charge ▸ n. a price asked for goods or services: *an admission charge.*
∎ a financial liability or commitment: *an asset of $550,000 should have been taken as a charge on earnings.*

charge ac•count ▸ n. an account to which goods and services may be charged on credit.

charge card ▸ n. a credit card for use with an account that must be paid when a statement is issued.

char•tist ▸ n. a person who uses charts of financial data to predict future trends and to guide investment strategies.

churn ▸ v. (of a broker) encourage frequent turnover of (investments) in order to generate commission.

cir•cu•la•tion (abbr.: **cir.** or **circ.**) ▸ n. the movement, exchange, or availability of money in a country: *the new coins go into circulation today.*

claim ▸ n. an application for compensation under the terms of an insurance policy: ∎ a right or title to something: *they have first claim on the assets of the trust.*

clear ▸ adj. (of a sum of money) net: *a clear profit of $1,100.*
▸ v. pass (a check) through a clearinghouse so that the money goes into the payee's account. ∎ (of a check) pass through a clearinghouse in such a way. ∎ earn or gain (an amount of money) as a net profit.

clear•ing•house (also **clearing house**) (abbr.: **c.h.** or **C.H.**) ▸ n. a bankers' establishment where checks and bills from member banks are exchanged, so that only the balances need be paid in cash.

closed-end ▸ adj. denoting an investment trust or company that issues a fixed number of shares.

closed shop ▸ n. a place of work where membership in a union is a condition for being hired and for continued employment.
∎ [in sing.] a system whereby such an arrangement applies: *the outlawing of the closed shop.*

clos•ing price ▸ n. the price of a security at the end of the day's business in a financial market.

Co. ▸ abbr. company: *the Consett Iron Co.*
–PHRASES **and Co.** used as part of the titles of commercial businesses to designate the partner or partners not named.

co•de•ter•mi•na•tion ▸ n. cooperation between management and workers in decision-making, esp. by the representation of workers on management boards.

COLA ▸ abbr. cost-of-living adjustment, an increase made to wages or Social Security benefits to keep them in line with inflation.

col•lat•er•al•ize ▸ v. provide something as collateral for (a loan).

col•lec•tive a•gree•ment ▸ n. an agreement about pay and working conditions reached collectively by management and the workforce.

col•lec•tive own•er•ship ▸ n. ownership of something, typically land or industrial assets, by all members of a group for the mutual benefit of all.

com•mand e•con•o•my ▸ n. an economy in which production, investment, prices, and incomes are determined centrally by a government.

com•mer•cial bank ▸ n. a bank that offers services to the general public and to companies.

com•mer•cial pa•per ▸ n. short-term unsecured promissory notes issued by companies.

com•mod•i•ty ▸ n. (pl. **-ies**) a raw material or primary agricultural product that can be bought and sold, such as copper or coffee.

com•mon car•ri•er ▸ n. a person or company that transports goods or passengers on regular routes at rates made available to the public.
■ a company providing public telecommunications facilities.

com•mon mar•ket ▸ n. a group of countries imposing few or no duties on trade with one another and a common tariff on trade with other countries.

com•mon stock ▸ plural n. (also **common stocks**) shares entitling their holder to dividends that vary in amount and may even be missed, depending on the fortunes of the company.

com•mu•ta•tion ▸ n. the conversion of a legal obligation or entitlement into another form, e.g., the replacement of an annuity or series of payments by a single payment.

com•mute ▸ v. (**commute something for/into**) change one kind of payment or obligation for (another). ■ replace (an annuity or other series of payments) with a single payment: *he commuted his pension and got $50,000.*

com•par•a•tive ad•van•tage ▸ n. the ability of an individual or group to carry out a particular economic activity (such as making a specific product) more efficiently than another activity.

com•pound ▸ adj. (of interest) payable on both capital and the accumulated interest.
▸ v. calculate (interest) on previously accumulated interest: *the yield at which the interest is compounded.*

■ (of a sum of money invested) increase by compound interest.

comp•trol•ler ▸ n. a controller (used in the title of some financial officers).

con•ces•sion ▸ n. the right to use land or other property for a specified purpose, granted by a government, company, or other controlling body. *new logging concessions.*
■ a commercial operation within the premises of a larger concern, typically selling refreshments.

con•ces•sion•aire (also **concessioner**) ▸ n. the holder of a concession or grant, esp. for the use of land or commercial premises.

con•glom•er•ate ▸ n. a large corporation formed by the merging of separate and diverse firms.
▸ adj. of or relating to a conglomerate, esp. a large corporation: *conglomerate businesses.*
▸ v. form a conglomerate by merging diverse businesses.

con•sign•ment ▸ n. a batch of goods destined for or delivered to someone: *a consignment of beef.*
■ agreement to pay a supplier of goods after the goods are sold: *new and used children's clothing on consignment.*

con•sol•i•date ▸ v. combine (a number of financial accounts or funds) into a single overall account or set of accounts.

con•sor•ti•um ▸ n. (pl. **consortia** or **consortiums**) an association, typically of several business companies.

con•sum•er ▸ n. a person who purchases goods and services for personal use.

con•sum•er dur•a•ble ▸ n. (usu. **consumer durables**) a manufactured item, typically a car or household appliance, that is expected to have a relatively long useful life after purchase.

con•sum•er goods ▸ plural n. goods bought and used by consumers, rather than by manufacturers for producing other goods.

con•sum•er•ism ▸ n. the protection or promotion of the interests of consumers. ■ often derogatory the preoccupation of society with the acquisition of consumer goods.

con•sum•er price in•dex (abbr.: **CPI**) ▸ n. an index of the variation in prices paid by typical consumers for retail goods and other items.

con•sum•er re•search ▸ n. the investigation of the needs and opinions of consumers, esp. with regard to a particular product or service.

con•sum•er so•ci•e•ty ▸ n. chiefly derogatory a society in which the buying and selling of goods and services is the most important social and economic activity.

con•sum•er sov•er•eign•ty ▸ n. the situation in an economy where the desires and needs of consumers control the output of producers.

con•sump•tion ▸ n. the purchase and use of goods and services by the public.

con•tin•gen•cy fund ▸ n. a reserve of money set aside to cover possible unforeseen future expenses.

con•tin•gent ▸ adj. (of losses, liabilities, etc.) that can be anticipated to arise if a particular event occurs.

con•trar•i•an ▸ n. a person who opposes or rejects popular opinion, esp. in stock exchange dealing.

con•trol ac•count ▸ n. an account used to record the balances on a number of subsidiary accounts and to provide a cross-check on them.

con•trol•ling in•ter•est ▸ n. the holding by one person or group of a majority of the stock of a business, giving the holder a means of exercising control.

con•ver•sion fac•tor ▸ n. the manufacturing cost of a product relative to the cost of raw materials.

con•vert ▸ v. change (money, stocks, or units in which a quantity is expressed) into others of a different kind.

con•vert•i•ble ▸ adj. (of currency) able to be converted into other forms, esp. into gold or US dollars. ◼ (of a bond or stock) able to be converted into ordinary or preference shares.
▸ n. (usu. **convertibles**) a convertible security.

co-op ▸ n. informal a cooperative society, business, or enterprise.

co•op•er•a•tion (also **co-operation**) ▸ n. the formation and operation of cooperatives.

co•op•er•a•tive (also **co-operative**) ▸ adj. ◼ (of a farm, business, etc.) owned and run jointly by its members, with profits or benefits shared among them.
▸ n. a farm, business, or other organization that is owned and run jointly by its members, who share the profits or benefits.

cor•ner ▸ n. a position in which one dominates the supply of a particular commodity.
▸ v. control (a market) by dominating the supply of a particular commodity. ◼ establish a corner in (a commodity).

Corp. ▸ abbr. corporation: *IBM Corp.*

cor•po•rate ▸ adj. of or relating to a corporation, esp. a large company or group: *airlines are very keen on their corporate identity.*
◼ (of a company or group of people) authorized to act as a single entity and recognized as such in law.
▸ n. a corporate company or group.

cor•po•rate raid•er ▸ n. a financier who makes a practice of making hostile takeover bids for companies, either to control their policies or to resell them for a profit.

cor•po•ra•tion ▸ n. a company or group of people authorized to act as a single entity (legally as a person) and recognized as such in law.

cor•po•ra•tize ▸ v. convert (a state organization) into an independent commercial company.

cor•rec•tion ▸ n. a temporary reversal in an overall trend of stock market prices, esp. a brief fall during an overall increase.

cost ac•count•ing ▸ n. the recording of all the costs incurred in a business in a way that can be used to improve its management.

cost-ben•e•fit ▸ adj. relating to or denoting a process that assesses the relation between the cost of an undertaking and the value of the resulting benefits: *a cost-benefit analysis.*

cost-ef•fec•tive ▸ adj. effective or productive in relation to its cost.

cost of liv•ing ▶ n. the level of prices relating to a range of everyday items.

cost-of-liv•ing in•dex (abbr.: CLI) ▶ n. former term for CONSUMER PRICE IN-DEX.

cost-plus ▶ adj. relating to or denoting a method of pricing a service or product in which a fixed profit factor is added to the costs.

cot•tage in•dus•try ▶ n. a business or manufacturing activity carried on in a person's home.

coun•ter•of•fer ▶ n. an offer made in response to another.

coun•ter•trade ▶ n. international trade by exchange of goods rather than by currency purchase.

coun•ter•vail•ing du•ty ▶ n. an import tax imposed on certain goods in order to prevent dumping or counter export subsidies.

cou•pon ▶ n. a voucher entitling the holder to a discount off a particular product.
■ a detachable portion of a bond that is given up in return for a payment of interest.

cou•pon bond ▶ n. an investment bond on which interest is paid by coupons.

cov•er•age ▶ n. the amount of protection given by an insurance policy.

CP ▶ abbr. commercial paper.

CPA ▶ abbr. certified public accountant.

cr ▶ abbr. credit. ■ creditor.

cre•a•tive ac•count•an•cy (also cre•ative accounting) ▶ n. informal the exploitation of loopholes in financial regulation in order to gain advantage or present figures in a misleadingly favorable light.

cred•it ▶ n. the ability of a customer to obtain goods or services before payment, based on the trust that payment will be made in the future.
■ the money lent or made available under such an arrangement: *the bank refused to extend their credit.* ■ an entry recording a sum received, listed on the right-hand side or column of an account. The opposite of DEBIT.
■ a payment received.
▶ v. (**credited, crediting**) (often **be credited**) add (an amount of money) to an account: *this deferred tax can be credited to the profit and loss account.*

cred•it an•a•lyst ▶ n. a person employed to assess the credit rating of people or companies.

cred•it bu•reau ▶ n. a company that collects information relating to the credit ratings of individuals and makes it available to credit card companies, financial institutions, etc.

cred•it card ▶ n. a small plastic card issued by a bank, business, etc., allowing the holder to purchase goods or services on credit.

cred•i•tor ▶ n. a person or company to whom money is owed.

cred•it rat•ing ▶ n. an estimate of the ability of a person or organization to fulfill their financial commitments, based on previous dealings.
■ the process of assessing this.

cred•it un•ion ▶ n. a nonprofit-making money cooperative whose members can borrow from pooled deposits at low interest rates.

cred•it•worth•y ▶ adj. (of a person or company) considered suitable to receive credit, esp. because of being reliable in paying money back in the past.

cross own•er•ship ▶ n. the ownership by one corporation of different companies with related interests or commercial aims.

cross-rate ▶ n. an exchange rate between two currencies computed by reference to a third currency, usually the US dollar.

cross-sell ▶ v. sell (a different product or service) to an existing customer: *their database is used to cross-sell financial services.*

cross-sub•si•dize ▶ v. subsidize (a business or activity) out of the profits of another business or activity.

cru•el•ty-free ▶ adj. (of cosmetics or other commercial products) manufactured or developed by methods that do not involve experimentation on animals.

crunch ▶ n. a severe shortage of money or credit.

ct. ▶ abbr. cent.

CTT ▶ abbr. capital transfer tax.

cum div•i•dend ▶ adv. (of share purchases) with a dividend about to be paid.

cu•mu•la•tive pre•ferred stock ▶ n. a preferred stock whose annual fixed-rate dividend, if it cannot be paid in any year, accrues until it can and is paid before common dividends.

curb mar•ket ▶ n. a market for selling shares not dealt with on the normal stock exchange.

cur•rent as•sets ▶ plural n. cash and other assets that are expected to be converted to cash within a year.

cur•rent cost ac•count•ing ▶ n. a method of accounting in which assets are valued on the basis of their current replacement cost, and increases in their value as a result of inflation are excluded from calculations of profit.

cur•rent li•a•bil•i•ties ▶ plural n. amounts due to be paid to creditors within twelve months.

cut•back ▶ n. an act or instance of reducing something, typically expenditures.

cut•o•ver ▶ n. a rapid transition from one phase of a business enterprise or project to another.

c.w.o. ▶ abbr. cash with order.

day•book ▶ n. an account book in which a day's transactions are entered for later transfer to a ledger.

day shift ▶ n. a period of time worked during the daylight hours in a hospital, factory, etc., as opposed to the night shift.
■ [treated as sing. or pl.] the employees who work during this period.

day•work ▶ n. casual work paid for on a daily basis.

dead ▶ adj. (of money) not financially productive.

dead cat bounce ▶ n. a temporary recovery in share prices after a substantial fall, caused by speculators buying in order to cover their positions.

dead weight (also **deadweight**) ▶ n. losses incurred because of the inefficient allocation of resources, esp. through taxation or restriction.

deal•er ▶ n. a person or business that buys and sells goods: *a car dealer.*
■ a person who buys and sells shares, securities, or other financial assets

as a principal (rather than as a broker or agent).

dear ▶ adj. (of money) available as a loan only at a high rate of interest.

death tax ▶ n. another term for ESTATE TAX.

de•ben•ture ▶ n. (also **debenture bond**) an unsecured loan certificate issued by a company, backed by general credit rather than by speciifed assets.

deb•it ▶ n. an entry recording an amount owed, listed on the left-hand side or column of an account. The opposite of CREDIT.
■ a payment made or owed.
▶ v. (**debited, debiting**) (usu. **be debited**) (of a bank or other financial organization) remove (an amount of money) from a customer's account, typically as payment for services or goods: *$10,000 was debited from their account.*
■ remove an amount of money from (a bank account).

deb•it card ▶ n. a card issued by a bank allowing the holder to transfer money electronically to another bank account when making a purchase.

debt coun•se•lor ▶ n. a person who offers professional advice on methods of debt repayment.

debt•or ▶ n. a person or institution that owes a sum of money.

debt se•cu•ri•ty ▶ n. a negotiable or tradable liability or loan.

debt swap (also **debt-for-na•ture swap**) ▶ n. a transaction in which a foreign exchange debt owed by a developing country is transferred to another organization on the condition that the country use local currency for a designated purpose, usually environmental protection.

dec•i•mal•ize ▶ v. convert (a system of coinage or weights and measures) to a decimal system.

dec•la•ra•tion ▶ n. a listing of goods, property, income, etc., subject to duty or tax.

de•con•trol ▶ v. (**decontrolled, decontrolling**) release (a commodity, market, etc.) from controls or restrictions.

de•duct•i•ble ▶ adj. able to be deducted, esp. from taxable income or tax to be paid: *child-care vouchers will be deductible expenses for employers.*

▸n. (in an insurance policy) a specified amount of money that the insured must pay before an insurance company will pay a claim: *a traditional insurance policy with a low deductible.*

de•duc•tion ▸ n. the action of deducting or subtracting something.

■ an amount that is or may be deducted from something, esp. from taxable income or tax to be paid: *tax deductions.*

deep-dis•count ▸ adj. denoting financial securities carrying a low rate of interest relative to prevailing market rates and issued at a discount to their redemption value, thus mainly providing capital gain rather than income.

■ heavily discounted; greatly reduced in price.

de•ferred an•nu•i•ty ▸ n. an annuity that commences only after a lapse of some specified time after the final purchase premium has been paid.

de•fi•cien•cy pay•ment ▸ n. a payment made, typically by a government body, to cover a financial deficit incurred in the course of an activity such as farming or education.

def•i•cit ▸ n. the amount by which something, esp. a sum of money, is too small.

■ an excess of expenditure or liabilities over income or assets in a given period.

def•i•cit fi•nanc•ing ▸ n. government funding of spending by borrowing.

def•i•cit spend•ing ▸ n. government spending, in excess of revenue, of funds raised by borrowing rather than from taxation.

de•flate ▸ v. bring about a general reduction of price levels in (an economy).

de•fla•tion ▸ n. reduction of the general level of prices in an economy.

de•fla•tion•ar•y ▸ adj. of, characterized by, or tending to cause economic deflation.

de•gres•sive ▸ adj. (of taxation) at successively lower rates on lower amounts.

de-in•dex ▸ v. end the indexation to inflation of (pensions or other benefits).

de•in•dus•tri•al•i•za•tion ▸ n. decline in industrial activity in a region or economy: *severe deindustrialization with substantial job losses.*

de•lin•quen•cy ▸ n. (pl. **-ies**) a failure to pay an outstanding debt.

de•lin•quent ▸ adj. in arrears: *delinquent accounts.*

de•list ▸ v. remove (a security) from the official register of a stock exchange: *the stock collapsed and was delisted.* ■ remove (a product) from the list of those sold by a particular retailer.

de•liv•er•a•ble ▸ n. (usu. **deliverables**) a thing able to be provided, esp. as a product of a development process.

de•mand ▸ n. the desire of purchasers, consumers, clients, employers, etc., for a particular commodity, service, or other item: *a recent slump in demand.*

de•mand curve ▸ n. a graph showing how the demand for a commodity or service varies with changes in its price.

de•mand de•pos•it ▸ n. a deposit of money that can be withdrawn without prior notice.

de•mand draft ▸ n. a financial draft payable on demand.

de•mand-led (also **demand-driven**) ▸ adj. caused or determined by demand from consumers or clients.

de•mand note ▸ n. a formal request for payment.

■ another term for DEMAND DRAFT.

de•mand pull ▸ adj. relating .to or denoting inflation caused by an excess of demand over supply.

de•ma•te•ri•al•ize ▸ v. (**dematerialized**) replace (physical records or certificates) with a paperless computerized system.

dem•o•graph•ics ▸ plural n. statistical data relating to the population and particular groups within it: *the demographics of book buyers.*

de•mon•e•tize ▸ v. (usu. **be demonetized**) deprive (a coin or precious metal) of its status as money.

de•mo•nop•o•lize ▸ v. introduce competition into (a market or economy) by privatizing previously nationalized assets.

de•mu•tu•al•ize ▸ v. change (a mutual

organization such as a savings and loan association) to one of a different kind.

de•nom•i•nate ▸ v. (**be denominated**) (of sums of money) be expressed in a specified monetary unit.

de•ple•tion al•low•ance ▸ n. a tax concession allowable to a company whose normal business activities (in particular oil extraction) reduce the value of its own assets.

de•pos•it ▸ n. a sum of money placed or kept in a bank account, usually to gain interest.
■ an act of placing money in a bank account: *I'd like to **make a deposit**.*
■ a sum payable as a first installment on the purchase of something or as a pledge for a contract, the balance being payable later.
■ a returnable sum payable on the rental of something, to cover any possible loss or damage.
▸v. (**deposited, depositing**) pay (a sum of money) into a bank account: *the money is deposited with a bank.* ■ pay (a sum) as a first installment or as a pledge for a contract.

de•pos•i•tar•y (also **depository**) ▸ adj. (of a share or receipt) representing a share in a foreign company. The depositary share or receipt is traded on the stock exchange of the investor's country rather than the actual share, which is deposited in a foreign bank.

de•pos•i•tor ▸ n. a person who keeps money in a bank account.

de•pre•ci•ate ▸ v. diminish in value over a period of time: *the pound is expected to depreciate against the dollar.*
■ reduce the recorded value in a company's books of (an asset) each year over a predetermined period.

de•pre•ci•a•tion ▸ n. a reduction in the value of an asset with the passage of time, due in particular to wear and tear.
■ decrease in the value of a currency relative to other currencies.

de•press ▸ v. reduce the level or strength of activity in (something, esp. an economic or biological system): *fear of inflation in America depressed bond markets*

de•pres•sant ▸ n. an influence that depresses economic or other activity.

de•pres•sion ▸ n. a long and severe recession in an economy or market: *the depression in the housing market.* ■ (**the Depression** or **the Great Depression**) the financial and industrial slump of 1929 and subsequent years.

de•riv•a•tive ▸ adj. (of a financial product) having a value deriving from an underlying variable asset: *equity-based derivative products.*
▸n. (often **derivatives**) an arrangement or instrument (such as a future, option, or warrant) whose value derives from and is dependent on the value of an underlying asset.

de•rived de•mand ▸ n. a demand for a commodity, service, etc., that is a consequence of the demand for something else.

de•skill ▸ v. reduce the level of skill required to carry out (a job).
■ make the skills of (a worker) obsolete.

de•val•ue ▸ v. (**devalues, devalued, devaluing**) (often **be devalued**) reduce the official value of (a currency) in relation to other currencies.

de•vel•op•ing coun•try ▸ n. a poor agricultural country that is seeking to become more advanced economically and socially.

dig•it•al cash (also **digital money**) ▸ n. money that may be transferred electronically from one party to another during a transaction.

di•lute ▸ v. (often **be diluted**) reduce the value of (a shareholding) by issuing more shares in a company without increasing the values of its assets.

di•lu•tion ▸ n. a reduction in the value of a shareholding due to the issue of additional shares in a company without an increase in assets.

di•rect la•bor ▸ n. labor involved in production rather than administration, maintenance, and other support services. labor employed by the authority commissioning the work, not by a contractor.

di•rect mail ▸ n. unsolicited advertising sent to prospective customers through the mail.

di•rect mar•ket•ing ▶ n. the business of selling products or services directly to the public, e.g., by mail order or telephone selling, rather than through retailers.

di•rec•tor (abbr.: **dir.**) ▶ n. a member of the board of people that manages or oversees the affairs of a business.

di•rec•to•rate ▶ n. [treated as sing. or pl.] the board of directors of a company.

di•rect tax ▶ n. a tax, such as income tax, that is levied on the income or profits of the person who pays it, rather than on goods or services.

dirt•y mon•ey ▶ n. money obtained unlawfully or immorally.

dis•count ▶ n. a deduction from the usual cost of something, typically given for prompt or advance payment or to a special category of buyers: *many stores will offer a discount on bulk purchases.*
  ■ a percentage deducted from the face value of a bill of exchange or promissory note when it changes hands before the due date.
▶ v. deduct an amount from (the usual price of something).
  ■ reduce (a product or service) in price. ■ buy or sell (a bill of exchange) before its due date at less than its maturity value.
▶ adj. (of a store or business) offering goods for sale at discounted prices: *a discount drugstore chain.*
  ■ at a price lower than the usual one.
– PHRASES **at a discount** below the nominal or usual price.

dis•count•ed cash flow ▶ n. a method of assessing investments taking into account the expected accumulation of interest.

dis•count house ▶ n. another term for DISCOUNT STORE.

dis•count rate ▶ n. the minimum interest rate set by the Federal Reserve for lending to other banks. a rate used for discounting bills of exchange.

dis•count store ▶ n. a store that sells goods at less than the normal retail price.

dis•cre•tion•ar•y ▶ adj. denoting or relating to investment funds placed with a broker or manager who has dis-

cretion to invest them on the client's behalf: *discretionary portfolios.*

dis•cre•tion•ar•y in•come ▶ n. income remaining after deduction of taxes, other mandatory charges, and expenditure on necessary items.

dis•e•con•o•my ▶ n. (pl. **-ies**) an economic disadvantage such as an increase in cost arising from an increase in the size of an organization: *in an ideal world, these diseconomies of scale would be minimized.*

dis•e•qui•lib•ri•um ▶ n. a loss or lack of equilibrium in relation to supply, demand, and prices.

dis•hon•or ▶ v. refuse to accept or pay (a check or a promissory note).

dis•in•cor•po•rate ▶ v. dissolve (a corporate body).

dis•in•fla•tion ▶ n. reduction in the rate of inflation.

dis•in•ter•me•di•a•tion ▶ n. reduction in the use of banks and savings institutions as intermediaries in the borrowing and investment of money, in favor of direct involvement in the securities market.

dis•in•vest ▶ v. withdraw or reduce an investment.

dis•pos•a•ble ▶ adj. (chiefly of financial assets) readily available for the owner's use as required.

dis•pos•a•ble in•come ▶ n. income remaining after deduction of taxes and other mandatory charges, available to be spent or saved as one wishes.

dis•sav•ing ▶ n. the action of spending more than one has earned in a given period.
  ■ (**dissavings**) the excess amount spent.

dis•tressed ▶ adj. ■ (of property) for sale, esp. below market value, due to mortgage foreclosure or because it is part of an insolvent estate. ■ (of goods) for sale at unusually low prices or at a loss because of damage or previous use.

dis•tri•bu•tion (abbr.: **distr.**) ▶ n. the action or process of supplying goods to stores and other businesses that sell to consumers: *a manager has the choice of four types of distribution.*

dis•tri•bu•tive ▶ adj. concerned with the supply of goods to stores and other businesses that sell to consumers: *transportation and distributive industries.*

dis•trib•u•tor (abbr.: **distr.**) ▸ n. an agent who supplies goods to stores and other businesses that sell to consumers: *a wholesale liquor distributor | the movie's distributor booked the film into theaters.*

dis•u•til•i•ty ▸ n. the adverse or harmful effects associated with a particular activity or process, esp. when carried out over a long period.

di•ver•si•fy ▸ v. (**-ies, -ied**) (of a company) enlarge or vary its range of products or field of operation.
 ■ (**diversified**) enlarge or vary the range of products or the field of operation of (a company): *the rise of the diversified corporation.* ■ spread (investment) over several enterprises or products in order to reduce the risk of loss.

di•vest ▸ v. rid oneself of something that one no longer wants or requires, such as a business interest or investment: *it appears easier to carry on in the business than to divest | the government's policy of **divesting itself of** state holdings.*

di•vest•i•ture (also **divesture**) ▸ n. the action or process of selling off subsidiary business interests or investments: *the divestiture of state-owned assets.*

di•vest•ment ▸ n. another term for DI-VESTITURE.

div•i•dend ▸ n. a sum of money paid regularly (typically quarterly) by a company to its shareholders out of its profits (or reserves).
 ■ a payment divided among a number of people, e.g., members of a cooperative or creditors of an insolvent estate. ■ an individual's share of a dividend.

div•i•dend cov•er•age ▸ n. the ratio of a company's dividends to its net income.

div•i•dend yield ▸ n. a dividend expressed as a percentage of a current share price.

di•vi•sion•al•ize ▸ v. subdivide (a company or other organization) into a number of separate divisions: *a large divisionalized Western corporation.*
 ■ undergo this process.

dock•et ▸ n. a document or label listing the contents of a package or delivery.
 ▸ v. (**docketed, docketing**) (usu. **be docketed**) mark (goods or a package) with a document or label listing the contents.

dol•lar ▸ n. the basic monetary unit of the US, Canada, Australia, and certain countries in the Pacific, Caribbean, Southeast Asia, Africa, and South America.

dol•lar ar•e•a ▸ n. the area of the world in which currency is linked to the US dollar.

dol•lar gap ▸ n. the amount by which a country's import trade with the dollar area exceeds the corresponding export trade.

dol•lar•i•za•tion (also **-sation**) ▸ n. the process of aligning a country's currency with the US dollar.

dom•i•cile (also **domicil**) ▸ n. formal or Law the place at which a company or other body is registered, esp. for tax purposes.

dou•ble-en•try ▸ adj. denoting a system of bookkeeping in which each transaction is entered as a debit in one account and a credit in another.

dou•ble in•dem•ni•ty ▸ n. provision for payment of double the face amount of an insurance policy under certain conditions, e.g., when death occurs as a result of an accident.

dou•ble time ▸ n. a rate of pay equal to double the standard rate, sometimes paid for working on holidays or outside normal working hours.

Dow short for DOW JONES INDUSTRIAL AVERAGE.

Dow Jones In•dus•tri•al Av•er•age (also **Dow Jones Average**) an index of figures indicating the relative price of shares on the New York Stock Exchange, based on the average price of selected stocks.

down pay•ment ▸ n. an initial payment made when something is bought on credit.

down•side ▸ n. a downward movement of share prices.

down•swing ▸ n. another term for DOWNTURN.

down•turn ▸ n. a decline in economic, business, or other activity: *a downturn in the housing market.*

dr. ▸ abbr. debit.

draft ▸ n. a written order to pay a specified sum; a check.

draw•back ▸ n. an amount of excise or import duty remitted on imported goods that the importer reexports rather than sell domestically.

draw•down ▸ n. a withdrawal of oil or other commodity from stocks.

draw•ee ▸ n. the person or organization, typically a bank, who must pay a draft or bill.

draw•er ▸ n. a person who writes a check.

due date ▸ n. the date on which something falls due, esp. the payment of a bill or the expected birth of a baby.

dump ▸ v. send (goods unsalable in the home market) to a foreign market for sale at a low price.
■ informal sell off (assets) rapidly.

du•op•o•ly ▸ n. (pl. **-ies**) a situation in which two suppliers dominate the market for a commodity or service.

Dutch auc•tion ▸ n. a method of selling in which the price is reduced until a buyer is found.

du•ti•a•ble ▸ adj. liable to customs or other duties.

du•ty ▸ n. (pl. **-ies**) a payment due and enforced by law or custom, in particular:
■ a payment levied on the import, export, manufacture, or sale of goods.

ear•ly re•tire•ment ▸ n. the practice of leaving employment before the statutory age, esp. on favorable financial terms.

earn ▸ v. (of a person) obtain (money) in return for labor or services: *they earn $35 per hour | he now **earns his living** as a truck driver.*
■ (of capital invested) gain (money) as interest or profit.

earned in•come ▸ n. money derived from paid work.

ease ▸ v. (of share prices, interest rates, etc.) decrease in value or amount.

eas•y mon•ey ▸ n. money available at relatively low interest.

e-cash ▸ n. electronic financial transac-

tions conducted in cyberspace via computer networks.

e•con•o•met•rics ▸ plural n. [treated as sing.] the branch of economics concerned with the use of mathematical methods (esp. statistics) in describing economic systems.

ec•o•nom•ic ▸ adj. of or relating to economics or the economy: *the government's economic policy.*
■ justified in terms of profitability: *many organizations must become larger if they are to remain economic.* ■ requiring fewer resources or costing less money: *solar power may provide a more economic solution.* ■ (of a subject) considered in relation to trade, industry, and the creation of wealth: *economic history.*

ec•o•nom•i•cal•ly ▸ adv. in a way that involves careful use of money or resources: *the new building was erected as economically as possible.*

ec•o•nom•ic good ▸ n. a product or service that can command a price when sold.

ec•o•nom•ic rent ▸ n. the extra amount earned by a resource (e.g., land, capital, or labor) by virtue of its present use.

ec•o•nom•ics ▸ plural n. [often treated as sing.] the branch of knowledge concerned with the production, consumption, and transfer of wealth.
■ the condition of a region or group as regards material prosperity.

e•con•o•mist ▸ n. an expert in economics.

e•con•o•my ▸ n. (pl. **-ies**) the wealth and resources of a country or region, esp. in terms of the production and consumption of goods and services.
■ a particular system or stage of an economy.
▸ adj. (of a product) offering the best value for the money: [in comb.] *an economy pack.*
■ designed to be economical to use: *an economy car.*
– PHRASES **economy of scale** a proportionate saving in costs gained by an increased level of production. **economy of scope** a proportionate saving gained by producing two or more distinct goods, when the cost of doing so

is less than that of producing each separately.

ef•fec•tive ▸ adj. assessed according to
actual rather than face value: *an effective price of $176 million.*

ef•fec•tive de•mand ▸ n. the level of
demand that represents a real intention to purchase by people with the
means to pay.

EFTPOS ▸ abbr. electronic funds transfer at point of sale.

e•las•tic ▸ adj. (of demand or supply)
sensitive to changes in price or income.

em•bar•go ▸ n. (pl. -oes) an official ban
on trade or other commercial activity
with a particular country: *an em-
bargo on grain sales.*

▸ v. (-oes, -oed) (usu. **be embargoed**)
impose an official ban on (trade or a
country or commodity): *the country
has been virtually embargoed by most of
the noncommunist world.*

e•mol•u•ment ▸ n. (usu. **emoluments**)
formal a salary, fee, or profit from employment or office: *the directors' emoluments.*

en•dorse ▸ v. sign (a check or bill of exchange) on the back to make it payable to someone other than the stated
payee or to accept responsibility for
paying it.

en•dorse•ment ▸ n. a clause in an insurance policy detailing an exemption
from or change in coverage. the action
of endorsing a check or bill of exchange.

en•dow•ment ▸ n. an income or form
of property given or bequeathed to
someone.
■ a form of life insurance involving
payment of a fixed sum to the insured person on a specified date, or
to their estate should they die before
this date: *an endowment policy.*

end us•er (also **end-user**) ▸ n. the person who actually uses a particular
product.

en•ter•prise zone ▸ n. an impover-
ished area in which incentives such as
tax concessions are offered to encourage business investment and provide
jobs for the residents.

en•tre•pre•neur ▸ n. a person who
organizes and operates a business or

businesses, taking on greater than
normal financial risks in order to
do so.

en•try-lev•el ▸ adj. at the lowest level in
an employment hierarchy.

EPOS ▸ abbr. electronic point of sale
(used to describe retail outlets that
record information electronically).

eps ▸ abbr. earnings per share.

e•qui•lib•ri•um ▸ n. (pl. **equilibria**) a
situation in which supply and demand
are matched and prices stable.

eq•ui•ty ▸ n. (pl. **-ies**) the value of the
shares issued by a company: *he owns
62% of the group's equity.*
■ **(equities)** stocks and shares that
carry no fixed interest. the value of a
mortgaged property after deduction
of charges against it.

es•ca•la•tor clause ▸ n. a clause in a
contract that allows for an increase or
a decrease in wages or prices under
certain conditions.

es•crow ▸ n. a bond, deed, or other
document kept in the custody of a
third party, taking effect only when a
specified condition has been fulfilled.
■ a deposit or fund held in trust or as
a security. ■ the state of being kept
in custody or trust in this way: *the
board holds funds in escrow.*

▸ v. place in custody or trust in this way.

es•tate tax ▸ n. a tax levied on the net
value of the estate of a deceased person before distribution to the heirs.

eu•ro ▸ n. (also **Euro**) the single European currency introduced into some
of the states of the European Union
countries in 1999 as an alternative
currency in noncash transactions and
scheduled to replace national currencies in 2002.

Eu•ro•bond ▸ n. an international bond
issued in Europe or elsewhere outside
the country in whose currency its
value is stated (usually the US or
Japan).

Eu•ro•cheque ▸ n. a check issued
under an arrangement between European banks that enables account-
holders from one country to use their
checks in another.

Eu•ro•cur•ren•cy ▸ n. a form of money
held or traded outside the country in

whose currency its value is stated (originally US dollars held in Europe).

Eu•ro•dol•lar ▸ n. a US dollar deposit held in Europe or elsewhere outside the US.

Eu•ro•mar•ket ▸ n. a financial market that deals with Eurocurrencies. ■ the European Union regarded as a single commercial or financial market.

ex an•te ▸ adj. & adv. based on forecasts rather than actual results.

ex•change ▸ n. the giving of money for its equivalent in the money of another country.

■ the fee or percentage charged for converting the currency of one country into that of another. ■ a system or market in which commercial transactions involving currency, shares, commodities, etc., can be carried out within or between countries. ■ a building or institution used for the trading of a particular commodity or commodities: *the New York Stock Exchange*.

ex•change con•trol ▸ n. a governmental restriction on the movement of currency between countries.

ex•change rate ▸ n. (also **rate of exchange**) the value of one currency for the purpose of conversion to another.

ex•cise ▸ n. a tax levied on certain goods and commodities produced or sold within a country and on licenses granted for certain activities.

ex•clu•sive ec•o•nom•ic zone ▸ n. an area of coastal water and seabed within a certain distance of a country's coastline, to which the country claims exclusive rights for fishing, drilling, and other economic activities.

ex div. ▸ abbr. ex dividend.

ex div•i•dend ▸ adj. & adv. (of stocks or shares) not including the next dividend.

ex•ec ▸ n. informal an executive: *top execs*.

ex•ec•u•tive ▸ n. a person with senior managerial responsibility in a business organization.

■ an executive committee or other body within an organization: *the union executive*.

ex•emp•tion ▸ n. (also **personal exemption**) the process of exempting a person from paying taxes on a speci-

fied amount of income for themselves and their dependents.

■ a dependent exempted in this way.

ex•er•cise price ▸ n. the price per share at which the owner of a traded option is entitled to buy or sell the underlying security.

ex•pense ▸ n. the cost required for something; the money spent on something.

■ (**expenses**) the costs incurred in the performance of one's job or a specific task, esp. one undertaken for another person.

▸v. (usu. **be expensed**) offset (an item of expenditure) as an expense against taxable income.

ex•pense ac•count ▸ n. an arrangement under which sums of money spent in the course of business by an employee are later reimbursed by their employer.

ex•pi•ra•tion ▸ n. the ending of the fixed period for which a contract is valid.

ex•po•nen•tial growth ▸ n. growth whose rate becomes ever more rapid in proportion to the growing total number or size.

ex•port ▸ v. send (goods or services) to another country for sale: *we exported $16 million worth of mussels to Japan*.

▸n. (usu. **exports**) a commodity, article, or service sold abroad.

■ (**exports**) sales of goods or services to other countries, or the revenue from such sales: *meat exports*. ■ the selling and sending out of goods or services to other countries: *the export of Western technology*. ■ of a high standard suitable for export: *high-grade export coal*.

ex•port sur•plus ▸ n. the amount by which the value of a country's exports exceeds that of its imports.

ex post ▸ adj. & adv. based on actual results rather than forecasts.

ex•po•sure ▸ n. the action of placing oneself at risk of financial losses, e.g., through making loans, granting credit, or underwriting insurance.

ex•ter•nal•i•ty ▸ n. (pl. **-ies**) a side effect or consequence of an industrial or commercial activity that affects other parties without this being reflected in the cost of the goods or services involved, such as the pollination of surrounding crops by bees kept for honey.

ex•tinc•tion ▸ n. the wiping out of a debt.

ex•tin•guish ▸ v. (often **be extinguished**) cancel (a debt) by full payment.

ex•traor•di•nar•y ▸ n. (usu. **extraordinaries**) an item in a company's accounts not arising from its normal activities.

face val•ue ▸ n. the value printed or depicted on a coin, banknote, postage stamp, ticket, etc., esp. when less than the actual or intrinsic value.

fac•tor ▸ n. a business agent; a merchant buying and selling on commission.
■ a company that buys a manufacturer's invoices at a discount and takes responsibility for collecting the payments due on them.
▸v. sell (one's receivable debts) to a factor.

fac•tor•age ▸ n. the commission or charges payable to a factor.

fac•tor cost ▸ n. the cost of an item or a service in terms of the various factors that have played a part in its production or availability, and exclusive of tax costs.

Fan•nie Mae ▸ n. informal the Federal National Mortgage Association, a corporation (now privately owned) that trades in mortgages.

farm ▸ n. an area of land and its buildings used for growing crops and rearing animals, typically under the control of one owner or manager.
■ an establishment at which something is produced or processed: *an energy farm.*
▸v. (**farm someone/something out**) send out or subcontract work to others.

FDIC ▸ abbr. Federal Deposit Insurance Corporation, a body that underwrites most private bank deposits.

feath•er•bed ▸ v. (also **feather-bed**) provide (someone) with advantageous economic or working conditions.
■ (**featherbedding**) deliberately limit

production or retain excess staff in (a business) in order to create jobs or prevent unemployment, typically as a result of a union contract.

Fed•er•al Re•serve the federal banking authority in the US that performs the functions of a central bank and is used to implement the country's monetary policy, providing a national system of reserve cash available to banks. Created in 1913, the Federal Reserve System consists of twelve Federal Reserve Districts, each having a Federal Reserve Bank. These are controlled from Washington, DC by the Federal Reserve Board consisting of governors appointed by the US president with Senate approval.

fi•at mon•ey ▸ n. inconvertible paper money made legal tender by a government decree.

fi•du•ci•ar•y ▸ adj. involving trust, esp. with regard to the relationship between a trustee and a beneficiary.
■ (of a paper currency) depending for its value on securities (as opposed to gold) or the reputation of the issuer.
▸n. (pl. **-ies**) a trustee.

FIFO ▸ abbr. first in, first out (chiefly with reference to methods of stock valuation and data storage).

fi•nance ▸ n. the management of large amounts of money, esp. by governments or large companies.
■ monetary support for an enterprise: *housing finance.* ■ (**finances**) the monetary resources and affairs of a country, organization, or person.
▸v. provide funding for (a person or enterprise).

fi•nance com•pa•ny ▸ n. a company concerned primarily with providing money, e.g., for short-term loans.

fi•nan•cial ▸ adj. of or relating to finance: *an independent financial adviser.*

Fi•nan•cial Times in•dex another term for FTSE INDEX.

fin•an•cier ▸ n. a person concerned with the management of large amounts of money on behalf of governments or other large organizations.

firm[1] ▸ adj. (of a currency, a commodity, or shares) having a steady value or price that is more likely to rise than fall: *the dollar was **firm against** the yen.*

▸v. (of a price) rise slightly to reach a level considered secure: *he believed house prices would firm by the end of the year.*

firm² ▸ n. a business concern, esp. one involving a partnership of two or more people: *a law firm.*

fis•cal ▸ adj. of or relating to government revenue, esp. taxes: *monetary and fiscal policy.*
■ of or relating to financial matters: *the domestic fiscal crisis.* ■ used to denote a fiscal year: *the budget deficit for fiscal 1996.*

fis•cal year ▸ n. a year as reckoned for taxing or accounting purposes.

fixed as•sets ▸ plural n. assets that are purchased for long-term use and are not likely to be converted quickly into cash, such as land, buildings, and equipment.

fixed cap•i•tal ▸ n. capital invested in fixed assets.

fixed charge ▸ n. a liability to a creditor that relates to specific assets of a company.

fixed costs ▸ plural n. business costs, such as rent, that are constant whatever the amount of goods produced.

flat ▸ adj. (**flatter, flattest**) (of a market, prices, etc.) not showing much activity; sluggish: *cash flow was flat at $214 million | flat sales in the drinks industry.* (of a fee, wage, or price) the same in all cases, not varying with changed conditions or in particular cases: *a $30 flat fare.*

fli•er (also **flyer**) ▸ n. a small handbill advertising an event or product. a speculative investment.

flight cap•i•tal ▸ n. money transferred abroad to avoid taxes or inflation, achieve better investment returns, or to provide for possible emigration.

float ▸ v. offer the shares of (a company) for sale on the stock market for the first time. ■ (of a currency) fluctuate freely in value in accordance with supply and demand in the financial markets.
■ allow (a currency) to fluctuate in such a way.

float•er ▸ n. a worker who is required to

do a variety of tasks as the need for each arises. an insurance policy covering loss of articles without specifying a location.

float•ing debt ▸ n. a debt that is repayable in the short term.

floor ▸ n. figurative the minimum level of prices or wages: *the dollar's floor against the yen.* ■ (of the stock exchange) the large central hall where trading takes place.

flo•ta•tion (also **floatation**) ▸ n. the process of offering a company's shares for sale on the stock market for the first time.

f.o.b. ▸ abbr. free on board.

Foot•sie ▸ n. Brit. informal term for FTSE INDEX.

f.o.r. ▸ abbr. free on rail.

fore•clo•sure ▸ n. the process of taking possession of a mortgaged property as a result of someone's failure to keep up mortgage payments.

for•eign ex•change ▸ n. the currency of other countries.
■ an institution or system for dealing in such currency.

fran•chise ▸ n. an authorization granted by a government or company to an individual or group enabling them to carry out specified commercial activities, e.g., providing a broadcasting service or acting as an agent for a company's products.
■ a business or service given such authorization to operate. ■ an authorization given by a league to own a sports team.
▸v. grant a franchise to (an individual or group).
■ grant a franchise for the sale of (goods) or the operation of (a service).

free ▸ adj. (**freer, freest**) given or available without charge: *free health care.*
▸adv. without cost or payment.
–PHRASES **for free** informal without cost or payment: *these professionals were giving their time for free.* **free on board** (abbr.: **f.o.b.**) including or assuming delivery without charge to the buyer's named destination.

free en•ter•prise ▸ n. an economic system in which private business operates in competition and largely free of state control.

free mar•ket ▶ n. an economic system in which prices are determined by unrestricted competition between privately owned businesses.

free trade ▶ n. international trade left to its natural course without tariffs, quotas, or other restrictions.

freeze ▶ v. (past **froze**; past part. **frozen**) prevent (assets) from being used for a period of time: *the charity's bank account has been frozen.*
▶ n. an act of holding or being held at a fixed level or in a fixed state: *workers faced a pay freeze.*

fric•tion•al un•em•ploy•ment ▶ n. the unemployment which exists in any economy due to people being in the process of moving from one job to another.

fringe ben•e•fit ▶ n. an extra benefit supplementing an employee's salary, for example, a company car, subsidized meals, health insurance, etc.

front-run•ning ▶ n. the practice by market makers of dealing on advance information provided by their brokers and investment analysts, before their clients have been given the information.

FRS ▶ abbr. ◼ Federal Reserve System.

FTA ▶ abbr. Free Trade Agreement, used to refer to that signed in 1988 between the US and Canada.

FTC ▶ abbr. Federal Trade Commission.

FT in•dex ▶ another term for **FTSE INDEX**.

FTSE in•dex a figure (published by the *Financial Times*) indicating the relative prices of shares on the London Stock Exchange, esp. (also **FTSE 100 index**) one calculated on the basis of Britain's one hundred largest public companies.

fund ▶ n. a sum of money saved or made available for a particular purpose.
◼ (**funds**) financial resources: *the misuse of public funds.* ◼ an organization set up for the administration and management of a monetary fund.
▶ v. provide with money for a particular purpose.

fund•ed debt ▶ n. debt in the form of

securities with long-term or indefinite redemption.

fund man•ag•er ▶ n. an employee of a large institution (such as a pension fund or an insurance company) who manages the investment of money on its behalf.

fun•gi•ble ▶ adj. (of goods contracted for without an individual specimen being specified) able to replace or be replaced by another identical item; mutually interchangeable.

fu•ture ▶ n. (**futures**) short for **FUTURES CONTRACT**.

FY ▶ abbr. fiscal year.

GDP ▶ abbr. gross domestic product.

gilt-edged ▶ adj. relating to or denoting stocks or securities that are regarded as extremely reliable investments.

GNP ▶ abbr. gross national product.

gold card ▶ n. a charge card or credit card issued to people with a high credit rating and giving benefits not available with the standard card.

gold•en par•a•chute ▶ n. informal a large payment or other financial compensation guaranteed to a company executive should the executive be dismissed as a result of a merger or takeover.

gold re•serve ▶ n. a quantity of gold held by a central bank to support the issue of currency.

good•will (also **good will**) ▶ n. the established reputation of a business regarded as a quantifiable asset, e.g., as represented by the excess of the price paid at a takeover for a company over its fair market value.

gov•ern•ment se•cu•ri•ties ▶ plural n. bonds or other promissory certificates issued by the government.

gray mar•ket ▶ n. an unofficial market or trade in something, esp. unissued shares or controlled or scarce goods.

green•field ▶ adj. relating to or denoting previously undeveloped sites for commercial development or exploitation.
▶ n. an undeveloped site, esp. one being evaluated and considered for commercial development or exploitation.

green•mail ▶ n. the practice of buying enough shares in a company to threaten a takeover, forcing the owners to buy them back at a higher price in order to retain control.

Gresh•am's law the tendency for money of lower intrinsic value to circulate more freely than money of higher intrinsic and equal nominal value (often expressed as "Bad money drives out good").

gross ▸ adj. (of income, profit, or interest) without deduction of tax or other contributions; total.Often contrasted with NET.

▸ adv. without tax or other contributions having been deducted.

▸ v. produce or earn (an amount of money) as gross profit or income.

▸ n. (pl. **grosses**) a gross profit or income.

gross do•mes•tic prod•uct (abbr.: GDP) ▸ n. the total value of goods produced and services provided in a country during one year.Compare with GROSS NATIONAL PRODUCT.

gross na•tion•al prod•uct (abbr.: GNP) ▸ n. the total value of goods produced and services provided by a country during one year, equal to the gross domestic product plus the net income from foreign investments.

group ▸ n. a commercial organization consisting of several companies under common ownership.

growth in•dus•try ▸ n. an industry that is developing particularly rapidly.

growth stock ▸ n. a company stock that tends to increase in capital value rather than yield high income.

guar•an•tee fund ▸ n. a sum of money pledged as a contingent indemnity for loss.

guar•an•ty (also **guarantee**) ▸ n. (pl. -ies) a formal pledge to pay another person's debt or to perform another person's obligation in the case of default.

■ a thing serving as security for a such a pledge.

han•dler ▸ n. Informal a publicity agent.

Hang Seng in•dex a figure indicating the relative price of shares on the Hong Kong Stock Exchange.

hard ▸ adj. (of prices of stock, commodities, etc.) stable or firm in value.

hard cash ▸ n. negotiable coins and

paper money as opposed to other forms of payment.

hard cur•ren•cy ▸ n. currency that is not likely to depreciate suddenly or to fluctuate greatly in value.

hard•en ▸ v. (of prices of stocks, commodities, etc.) rise and remain steady at a higher level.

hard sell ▸ n. a policy or technique of aggressive salesmanship or advertising.

haul•age ▸ n. the commercial transport of goods.

■ a charge for such transport.

head count ▸ n. a total number of people, esp. the number of people employed in a particular organization.

head•hunt•er ▸ n. a person who identifies and approaches suitable candidates employed elsewhere to fill business positions.

heav•y in•dus•try ▸ n. the manufacture of large, heavy articles and materials in bulk.

hedge ▸ n. a contract entered into or asset held as a protection against possible financial loss.

▸ v. protect (one's investment or an investor) against loss by making balancing or compensating contracts or transactions.

hid•den re•serves ▸ plural n. a company's funds that are not declared on its balance sheet.

high-end ▸ adj. denoting the most expensive of a range of products.

high fi•nance ▸ n. financial transactions involving large amounts of money.

hire ▸ v. employ (someone) for wages.

■ employ for a short time to do a particular job. ■ (**hire oneself out**) make oneself available for temporary employment.

▸ n. the action of hiring someone or something. a recently recruited employee.

hold•back ▸ n. a sum of money withheld under certain conditions.

hold•ing ▸ n. (**holdings**) stocks, property, and other financial assets in someone's possession.

hold•ing com•pa•ny ▸ n. a company created to buy and possess the shares of other companies, which it then controls.

hon•or ▸ v. accept (a bill) or pay (a check) when due.

hon•o•rar•i•um ▸ n. (pl. **honorariums** or **honoraria**) a payment given for professional services that are rendered nominally without charge.

hos•tile ▸ adj. (of a takeover bid) opposed by the company to be bought.

hot-desk•ing ▸ n. the practice in an office of allocating desks to workers when they are required or on a rotating system, rather than giving each worker their own desk.

hot mon•ey ▸ n. capital that is frequently transferred between financial institutions in an attempt to maximize interest or capital gain.

house ▸ n. a business or institution.

hu•man cap•i•tal ▸ n. the skills, knowledge, and experience possessed by an individual or population, viewed in terms of their value or cost to an organization or country.

hy•poth•e•cate ▸ v. pledge (money) by law to a specific purpose.

i•dle ▸ adj. (**idler**, **idlest**) (esp. of a machine or factory) not active or in use. ▪ (of a person) not working; unemployed. ▪ (of money) held in cash or in accounts paying no interest.
▸v. take out of use or employment: *he will close the newspaper, idling 2,200 workers.*

il•liq•uid ▸ adj. (of assets) not easily converted into cash: *illiquid assets.* ▪ (of a market) with few participants and a low volume of activity.

im•age-mak•er ▸ n. a person employed to identify and create a favorable public image for a person, organization, or product.

IMF ▸ abbr. International Monetary Fund.

im•per•fect com•pe•ti•tion ▸ n. the situation prevailing in a market in which elements of monopoly allow individual producers or consumers to exercise some control over market prices.

im•port ▸ v. bring (goods or services) into a country from abroad for sale.
▸n. (usu. **imports**) a commodity, article, or service brought in from abroad for sale.
▪ (**imports**) sales of goods or services brought in from abroad, or the revenue from such sales: *this surplus pushes up the yen, which ought to boost imports.* ▪ the action or process of importing goods or services.

im•po•si•tion ▸ n. a thing that is imposed, especially a tax or duty.

im•post ▸ n. a tax or similar compulsory payment.

im•prest ▸ n. a fund used by a business for small items of expenditure and restored to a fixed amount periodically.
▪ an advance of money made to someone engaged in some business with the state, enabling them to carry out the business. ▪ a sum of money advanced to a person for a particular purpose.

im•pute ▸ v. assign (a value) to something by inference from the value of the products or processes to which it contributes.

Inc. ▸ abbr. incorporated.

in•come ▸ n. money received, esp. on a regular basis, for work or through investments.

in•come tax ▸ n. tax levied directly on personal income.

in•con•vert•i•ble ▸ adj. (of currency) not able to be converted into another form on demand.

in•cor•po•rate ▸ v. (often **be incorporated**) constitute (a company, city, or other organization) as a legal corporation.

in•cor•po•rat•ed ▸ adj. (of a company or other organization) formed into a legal corporation.

in•dem•ni•ty ▸ n. (pl. **-ies**) security or protection against a loss or other financial burden.

in•dex ▸ n. (pl. **indexes** or esp. in technical use **indices**) a figure in a system or scale representing the average value of specified prices, shares, or other items as compared with some reference figure.
▸v. link the value of (prices, wages, or other payments) automatically to the value of a price index.

in•dif•fer•ence curve ▶ n. a curve on a graph (the axes of which represent quantities of two commodities) linking those combinations of quantities that the consumer regards as of equal value.

in•di•rect ▶ adj. (of costs) deriving from overhead charges or subsidiary work. ■ (of taxation) levied on goods and services rather than income or profits.

in•di•rect tax ▶ n. a tax levied on goods and services and not on income or profits.

in•dul•gence ▶ n. an extension of the time in which a bill or debt has to be paid.

in•dus•tri•al ▶ n. (industrials) shares in industrial companies.

in•dus•tri•al es•pi•o•nage ▶ n. spying directed toward discovering the secrets of a rival manufacturer or other industrial company.

in•fla•tion ▶ n. a general increase in prices and fall in the purchasing value of money.

in•fla•tion•ar•y ▶ adj. of, characterized by, or tending to cause monetary inflation.

in•fo•mer•cial ▶ n. a television program that promotes a product in an informative and supposedly objective way.

in•i•tial pub•lic of•fer•ing ▶ n. a company's flotation on the stock exchange.

in-serv•ice ▶ adj. (of training) intended for those actively engaged in the profession or activity concerned.

in•sid•er trad•ing ▶ n. the illegal practice of trading on the stock exchange to one's own advantage through having access to confidential information.

in•sol•vent ▶ adj. unable to pay debts owed.

in•stall•ment ▶ n. a sum of money due as one of several equal payments for something, spread over an agreed period of time.

in•stall•ment plan ▶ n. an arrangement for payment by installments.

in•sti•tu•tion•al ▶ adj. (of advertising) intended to create prestige rather than immediate sales.

in•sti•tu•tion•al in•ves•tor ▶ n. a large organization such as a bank, pension fund, labor union, or insurance company, that makes substantial investments on the stock exchange.

in•sur•ance ▶ n. a practice or arrangement by which a company or government agency provides a guarantee of compensation for specified loss, damage, illness, or death in return for payment of a premium.

in•sur•ance a•gent ▶ n. a person employed to sell insurance policies.

in•sur•ance car•ri•er ▶ n. an insurer; an insurance company.

in•sur•ance pol•i•cy ▶ n. a document detailing the terms and conditions of a contract of insurance.

in•sure ▶ v. arrange for compensation in the event of damage to or loss of (property), or injury to or the death of (someone), in exchange for regular advance payments to a company or government agency. ■ provide insurance coverage with respect to.

in•sured ▶ adj. covered by insurance. ▶ n. (the insured) (pl. same) a person or organization covered by insurance.

in•sur•er ▶ n. a person or company that underwrites an insurance risk; the party in an insurance contract undertaking to pay compensation.

in•tan•gi•ble ▶ adj. (of an asset or benefit) not constituting or represented by a physical object and of a value not precisely measurable.

in•ter•bank ▶ adj. agreed, arranged, or operating between banks.

in•ter•est ▶ n. money paid regularly at a particular rate for the use of money lent, or for delaying the repayment of a debt. a stake, share, or involvement in an undertaking, esp. a financial one. – PHRASES **declare an (or one's) interest** make known one's financial interests in an undertaking before it is discussed. **with interest** with interest charged or paid.

in•tra•pre•neur ▶ n. a manager within a company who promotes innovative product development and marketing.

in•ven•to•ry ▶ n. (pl. -ies) a complete list of items such as property, goods in stock, or the contents of a building.

■ a quantity of goods held in stock. ■ (in accounting) the entire stock of a business, including materials, components, work in progress, and finished products.

in•vest ▸ v. expend money with the expectation of achieving a profit or material result by putting it into financial schemes, shares, or property, or by using it to develop a commercial venture.

in•vest•ment ▸ n. the action or process of investing money for profit or material result.
■ a thing that is worth buying because it may be profitable or useful in the future.

in•vest•ment bank ▸ n. a bank that purchases large holdings of newly issued shares and resells them to investors.

in•vest•ment grade ▸ n. a level of credit rating for stocks regarded as carrying a minimal risk to investors.

in•vest•ment trust ▸ n. a limited company whose business is the investment of shareholders' funds, the shares being traded like those of any other public company.

in•voice ▸ n. a list of goods sent or services provided, with a statement of the sum due for these; a bill.
▸v. send an invoice to (someone).
■ send an invoice for (goods or services provided).

IPO ▸ abbr. initial public offering.

IRA ▸ abbr. individual retirement account.

ir•re•deem•a•ble ▸ adj. (of paper currency) for which the issuing authority does not undertake ever to pay coin.

Jay•cee ▸ n. a member of a Junior Chamber of Commerce, a civic organization for business and community leaders.

JIT ▸ abbr. (of manufacturing systems) just-in-time.

job ▸ n. a paid position of regular employment. a task or piece of work, esp. one that is paid.
▸v. (jobbed, jobbing) buy and sell (stocks) as a broker-dealer, esp. on a small scale.
–PHRASES on the job while working; at work. out of a job unemployed.

job an•a•lyst ▸ n. a person employed to assess the essential factors of particular jobs and the qualifications needed to carry them out.

job•ber ▸ n. a wholesaler. ■ a person who does casual or occasional work.

job ro•ta•tion ▸ n. the practice of moving employees between different tasks to promote experience and variety.

joint ac•count ▸ n. a bank account held by more than one person, each individual having the right to deposit and withdraw funds.

joint stock ▸ n. a portion of capital held jointly; a common fund.

joint-stock com•pa•ny ▸ n. a company whose stock is owned jointly by the shareholders.

joint ven•ture ▸ n. a commercial enterprise undertaken jointly by two or more parties that otherwise retain their distinct identities.

jour•nal ▸ n. (in bookkeeping) a daily record of business transactions with a statement of the accounts to which each is to be debited and credited.

junk bond ▸ n. a high-yield, high-risk security, typically issued by a company seeking to raise capital quickly in order to finance a takeover.

just-in-time ▸ adj. denoting a manufacturing system in which materials or components are delivered immediately before they are required in order to minimize inventory costs.

kai•zen ▸ n. a Japanese business philosophy of continuous improvement of working practices, personal efficiency, etc.

kan•ban ▸ n. (also kanban system) a Japanese manufacturing system in which the supply of components is regulated through the use of a card displaying a sequence of specifications and instructions, sent along the production line.
■ a card of this type.

kei•ret•su ▸ n. (pl. same) (in Japan) a conglomeration of businesses linked together by crossshareholdings to form a robust corporate structure.

la•bor mar•ket ▸ n. the supply of available workers with reference to the demand for them.

Laf•fer curve ▸ n. a supposed relationship between economic activity and the rate of taxation that suggests the existence of an optimum tax rate that maximizes tax revenue.

lais•sez-faire ▸ n. abstention by governments from interfering in the workings of the free market.

land bank ▸ n. a bank whose main function is to provide loans for land purchase, esp. by farmers.

laun•der ▸ v. conceal the origins of (money obtained illegally) by transfers involving foreign banks or legitimate businesses.

lay•off ▸ n. a discharge, esp. temporary, of a worker or workers.
■ a period when this is in force.

LBO ▸ abbr. leveraged buyout.

l.c. ▸ abbr. letter of credit.

lead time ▸ n. the time between the initiation and completion of a production process.

leak•age ▸ n. deliberate disclosure of confidential information.

ledg•er ▸ n. a book or other collection of financial accounts of a particular type.

lend ▸ v. (past and past part. **lent**) allow (a person or organization) the use of (a sum of money) under an agreement to pay it back later, typically with interest.

lend•er ▸ n. an organization or person that lends money.

let•ter of cred•it ▸ n. a letter issued by a bank to another bank (typically in a different country) to serve as a guarantee for payments made to a specified person under specified conditions.

lev•er•age ▸ n. the ratio of a company's loan capital (debt) to the value of its ordinary shares (equity).
▸ v. (**leveraged**) use borrowed capital for (an investment), expecting the profits made to be greater than the interest payable.

lev•er•aged buy•out ▸ n. the purchase of a controlling share in a company by its management, using outside capital.

li•a•bil•i•ty ▸ n. (pl. **-ies**) (usu. **liabilities**) a thing for which someone is responsible, esp. a debt or financial obligation.

life in•sur•ance ▸ n. insurance that pays out a sum of money either on the death of the insured person or after a set period.

life ta•ble ▸ n. a table of statistics relating to life expectancy and mortality for a given category of people.

LIFO ▸ abbr. last in, first out (chiefly with reference to methods of stock valuation and data storage). Compare with **FIFO**.

light in•dus•try ▸ n. the manufacture of small or light articles.

lim•it•ed ▸ adj. (**Limited**) Brit. denoting a company whose owners are legally responsible for its debts only to the extent of the amount of capital they invested (used after a company name).

lim•it•ed part•ner ▸ n. a partner in a company or venture who receives limited profits from the business and whose liability toward its debts is legally limited to the extent of his or her investment.

line ▸ n. a company that provides ships, aircraft, or buses on particular routes on a regular basis. a range of commercial goods.
–PHRASES **above the line** denoting or relating to money spent on items of current expenditure. **below the line** denoting or relating to money spent on items of capital expenditure. **line of credit** an amount of credit extended to a borrower.

liq•uid ▸ adj. (of assets) held in cash or easily converted into cash.
■ having ready cash or liquid assets. ■ (of a market) having a high volume of activity.

liq•ui•date ▸ v. wind up the affairs of (a company or firm) by ascertaining liabilities and apportioning assets.
■ (of a company) undergo such a process. ■ convert (assets) into cash. ■ pay off (a debt).

liq•ui•da•tion ▸ n. the process of liquidating a company or firm.
■ the conversion of assets into cash (i.e., by selling them). ■ the clearing of a debt.
–PHRASES **go into liquidation** (of a company or firm) be closed and have its assets apportioned.

liq•ui•da•tor ▸ n. a person appointed to wind up the affairs of a company or firm.

liq•uid•i•ty ▸ n. the availability of liquid assets to a market or company. ■ liquid assets; cash. ■ a high volume of activity in a market.

li•quid•i•ty ra•tio ▸ n. the ratio between the liquid assets and the liabilities of a bank or other institution.

list•ed ▸ adj. admitted for trading on a stock exchange.

list price ▸ n. the price of an article as shown in a list issued by the manufacturer or by the general body of manufacturers of the particular class of goods.

liv•er•y ▸ n. (pl. -ies) a special design and color scheme used on the vehicles, aircraft, or products of a particular company.

liv•ing wage ▸ n. [in sing.] a wage that is high enough to maintain a normal standard of living.

load ▸ v. add an extra charge to (an insurance premium) in the case of a poorer risk.

load•ing ▸ n. an increase in an insurance premium due to a factor increasing the risk involved.

loan ▸ n. a thing that is borrowed, esp. a sum of money that is expected to be paid back with interest. ■ an act of lending something to someone.
▸ v. (often **be loaned**) borrow (a sum of money or item of property).

lock-in ▸ n. an arrangement according to which a person or company is obliged to negotiate or trade only with a specific company.

lock•up ▸ n. an investment in assets that cannot readily be realized or sold on in the short term.

lodg•ment (also **lodgement**) ▸ n. the depositing of money in a particular bank, account, etc.

lo•go ▸ n. (pl. -os) a symbol or other small design adopted by an organization to identify its products, uniform, vehicles, etc.

long ▸ adj. (**longer, longest**) (of shares, bonds, or other assets) bought in advance, with the expectation of a rise in price.
■ (of a broker or their position in the market) buying or based on long stocks. ■ (of a security) maturing at a distant date.
▸ n. (**longs**) long-dated securities, esp. gilt-edged securities.
■ assets held in a long position.

loss-lead•er ▸ n. a product sold at a loss to attract customers.

loss-mak•ing ▸ adj. (esp. of a business) losing money, rather than making a profit.

low-ball ▸ adj. informal (of an estimate, bid, etc.) deceptively or unrealistically low.
▸ v. offer a deceptively or unrealistically low estimate, bid, etc.

Ltd. Brit. ▸ abbr. (after a company name) Limited.

lump sum ▸ n. a single payment made at a particular time, as opposed to a number of smaller payments or installments.

mac•ro•ec•o•nom•ics ▸ plural n. [treated as sing.] the part of economics concerned with large-scale or general economic factors, such as interest rates and national productivity.

mac•ro•e•con•o•my ▸ n. a large-scale economic system.

mail or•der ▸ n. the selling of goods to customers by mail, generally involving selection from a special catalog.

mall ▸ n. (also **shopping mall**) a large building or series of connected buildings containing a variety of retail stores and typically also restaurants.

man•aged cur•ren•cy ▸ n. a currency whose exchange rate is regulated or controlled by the government.

man•aged fund ▸ n. an investment fund run on behalf of an investor by an agent (typically an insurance company).

man•age•ment ac•count•ing ▸ n. the provision of financial data and advice to a company for use in the organization and development of its business.

man•age•ment com•pa•ny ▸ n. a company that is set up to manage a group of properties, a mutual fund, an investment fund, etc.

mar•gin ▸ n. a profit margin.
■ a sum deposited with a broker to

cover the risk of loss on a transaction or account.

▸v. (margined, margining) deposit an amount of money with a broker as security for (an account or transaction).

mar•gin•al ▸ adj. (chiefly of costs or benefits) relating to or resulting from small or unit changes.

■ (of taxation) relating to increases in income. ■ close to the limit of profitability, esp. through difficulty of exploitation.

mar•gin•al cost ▸ n. the cost added by producing one extra item of a product.

mar•gin call ▸ n. a demand by a broker that an investor deposit further cash or securities to cover possible losses.

mark•down ▸ n. a reduction in price.

mar•ket ▸ n. an area or arena in which commercial dealings are conducted: *the labor market.*

■ a demand for a particular commodity or service. ■ the state of trade at a particular time or in a particular context. ■ the free market; the operation of supply and demand. ■ a stock market.

▸v. (marketed, marketing) advertise or promote (something).

■ offer for sale. ■ buy or sell provisions in a market.

–PHRASES make a market take part in active dealing in particular shares or other assets.

mar•ket forc•es ▸ plural n. the economic factors affecting the price, demand, and availability of a commodity.

mar•ket•ing ▸ n. the action or business of promoting and selling products or services, including market research and advertising.

mar•ket•ing mix ▸ n. a combination of factors that can be controlled by a company to influence consumers to purchase its products.

mar•ket•iza•tion ▸ n. the exposure of an industry or service to market forces.

■ the conversion of a national economy from a planned to a market economy.

mar•ket mak•er (also market-maker) ▸ n. a dealer in securities or other assets who undertakes to buy or sell at specified prices at all times.

mar•ket pen•e•tra•tion ▸ n. the action of entering a market with a new product or brand.

■ a measure of the success with which a product or brand has entered a market.

mar•ket price ▸ n. the price of a commodity when sold in a given market.

mar•ket re•search ▸ n. the action or activity of gathering information about consumers' needs and preferences.

mar•ket share ▸ n. the portion of a market controlled by a particular company or product.

mar•ket val•ue ▸ n. the amount for which something can be sold on a given market.

mark-to-mar•ket ▸ adj. denoting or relating to a system of valuing assets by the most recent market price.

mark•up ▸ n. the amount added to the cost price of goods to cover overhead and profit.

mart ▸ n. a trade center or market.

mass mar•ket ▸ n. the market for goods that are produced in large quantities.

▸v. (mass-market) market (a product) on a large scale.

ma•trix ▸ n. (pl. matrices or matrixes) an organizational structure in which two or more lines of command, responsibility, or communication may run through the same individual.

ma•ture ▸ adj. (maturer, maturest) denoting an economy, industry, or market that has developed to a point where substantial expansion and investment no longer takes place. ■ (of a bill) due for payment.

▸v. (of an insurance policy, security, etc.) reach the end of its term and hence become payable.

ma•tur•i•ty ▸ n. the time when an insurance policy, security, etc., matures.

MBA ▸ abbr. Master of Business Administration.

meg•a•store ▸ n. a very large store, typically one specializing in a particular type of product.

mel•on ▸ n. figurative a large profit, esp. a

stock dividend, to be divided among a number of people.

melt•down ▸ n. figurative a disastrous event, esp. a rapid fall in share prices.

merg•er ▸ n. a combination of two things, esp. companies, into one.

met•age ▸ n. the official weighing of loads of coal, grain, or other material. ■ the duty paid for this.

mez•za•nine ▸ adj. relating to or denoting unsecured, higher-yielding loans that are subordinate to bank loans and secured loans but rank above equity.

MFN ▸ abbr. most favored nation.

mi•cro•ec•o•nom•ics ▸plural n. [treated as sing.] the part of economics concerned with single factors and the effects of individual decisions.

mid•dle•man ▸ n. (pl. -men) a person who buys goods from producers and sells them to retailers or consumers. ■ a person who arranges business or political deals between other people.

mid•dle man•age•ment ▸ n. the level in an organization just below that of senior administrators. ■ the managers at this level regarded collectively.

mid•dling ▸ n. (middlings) bulk goods of medium grade, esp. flour of medium fineness.

mill ▸ n. a monetary unit used only in calculations, worth one thousandth of a dollar.

min•i-mall ▸ n. a shopping mall containing a relatively small number of retail outlets and with access to each shop from the outside rather than from an interior hallway.

mint par (also **mint parity**) ▸ n. the ratio between the gold equivalents of currency in two countries. ■ their rate of exchange based on such a ratio.

mixed e•con•o•my ▸ n. an economic system combining private and public enterprise.

MLR ▸ abbr. minimum lending rate.

mon•e•ta•rism ▸ n. the theory or practice of controlling the supply of money as the chief method of stabilizing the economy.

mon•e•tar•y ▸ adj. of or relating to money or currency.

mon•e•tize ▸ v. convert into or express in the form of currency.

mon•ey•chang•er (also **money-changer**) ▸ n. a person whose business is the exchanging of one currency for another.

mon•ey•lend•er (also **money-lender**) ▸ n. a person whose business is lending money to others who pay interest.

mon•ey market ▸ n. the trade in short-term loans between banks and other financial institutions.

mon•ey of ac•count ▸ n. a denomination of money used in reckoning, but not issued as actual coins or paper money.

mon•ey or•der ▸ n. a printed order for payment of a specified sum, issued by a bank or post office.

mon•ey sup•ply ▸ n. the total amount of money in circulation or in existence in a country.

mon•ey wag•es ▸ plural n. income expressed in terms of its monetary value, with no account taken of its purchasing power.

mo•nop•o•list ▸ n. a person or business that has a monopoly.

mo•nop•o•ly ▸ n. (pl. -ies) the exclusive possession or control of the supply or trade in a commodity or service. ■ a company or group having exclusive control over a commodity or service. ■ a commodity or service controlled in this way: *electricity, gas, and water were considered to be natural monopolies.*

mo•nop•so•ny ▸ n. (pl -ies) a market situation in which there is only one buyer.

mort•gage ▸ n. the charging of real (or personal) property by a debtor to a creditor as security for a debt (esp. one incurred by the purchase of the property), on the condition that it shall be returned on payment of the debt within a certain period. ■ a deed effecting such a transaction. ■ a loan obtained through the conveyance of property as security. ▸v. (often **be mortgaged**) convey (a property) to a creditor as security on a loan.

mort•ga•gee ▸ n. the lender in a mortgage, typically a bank.

mort•gage rate ▸ n. the rate of interest charged by a mortgage lender.

mort•ga•gor ▸ n. the borrower in a mortgage, typically a homeowner.

most fa•vored na•tion ▸ n. a country that has been granted the most favorable trading terms available by another country.

moun•tain ▸ n. a large surplus stock of a commodity.

move ▸ v. (of merchandise) be sold: *despite the high prices, goods are moving.* ▣ sell (merchandise).
▸n. a change of job, career, or business direction.

mul•ti•pli•er ▸ n. a factor by which an increment of income exceeds the resulting increment of savings or investment.

mu•ni ▸ n. (pl. **munis**) short for MUNICIPAL BOND.

mu•nic•i•pal bond ▸ n. a security issued by or on behalf of a local authority.

mu•tu•al ▸ adj. denoting an insurance company or other corporate organization owned by its members and dividing some or all of its profits between them.

mu•tu•al fund ▸ n. an investment program funded by shareholders that trades in diversified holdings and is professionally managed.

mu•tu•al in•sur•ance ▸ n. insurance in which some or all of the profits are divided among the policyholders.

mu•tu•al•ize ▸ v. organize (a company or business) on mutual principles.
▣ divide (something, esp. insurance losses) between involved parties.

nar•row mon•ey ▸ n. money in forms that can be used as a medium of exchange, generally banknotes, coins, and certain balances held by banks.

NASDAQ ▸ abbr. National Association of Securities Dealers Automated Quotations, a computerized system for trading in securities.

na•tion•al bank ▸ n. a commercial bank that is chartered under the federal government and is a member of the Federal Reserve System.

na•tion•al debt ▸ n. the total amount of money that a country's government has borrowed, by various means.

na•tion•al in•come ▸ n. the total amount of money earned within a country.

NAV ▸ abbr. net asset value.

near mon•ey ▸ n. assets that can readily be converted into cash, such as government bonds.

neg•a•tive eq•ui•ty ▸ n. potential indebtedness arising when the market value of a property falls below the outstanding amount of a mortgage secured on it.

neg•a•tive in•come tax ▸ n. money credited as allowances to a taxed income, and paid as a benefit when it exceeds debited tax.

ne•go•ti•ate ▸ v. transfer (a check, bill, or other document) to the legal ownership of another person.
▣ convert (a check) into cash.

ne•go•ti•a•tion ▸ n. (also **negotiations**) the action or process of transferring ownership of a document.

net ▸ adj. (of an amount, value, or price) remaining after a deduction, such as tax or a discount, has been made: *net earnings per share rose.* Often contrasted with GROSS.
▣ (of a price) to be paid in full; not reducible.
▸v. (**netted, netting**) acquire or obtain (a sum of money) as clear profit.
▣ return (profit or income) for (someone). ▣ (**net something down/off/out**) exclude a nonnet amount, such as tax, when making a calculation, in order to reduce the amount left to a net sum.

net book val•ue ▸ n. the value of an asset as recorded in the accounts of its owner.

net na•tion•al prod•uct (abbr.: **NNP**) ▸ n. the total value of goods produced and services provided in a country during one year, after depreciation of capital goods has been allowed for.

net prof•it ▸ n. the actual profit after working expenses not included in the calculation of gross profit have been paid.

NIC ▸ abbr. newly industrialized country.

niche ▸ n. a specialized but profitable corner of the market.

Nik•kei in•dex a figure indicating the relative price of representative shares on the Tokyo Stock Exchange. Also called **Nikkei average**.

NNP ▸ abbr. net national product.

no-fault ▸ adj. denoting an insurance policy that is valid regardless of whether the policyholder was at fault.

no-load ▸ adj. (of shares in a mutual fund) sold without a commission being charged at the time of sale.

nom•i•nal ▸ adj. (of a price or amount of money) very small; far below the real value or cost: *some firms charge only a nominal fee for the service.* ■ (of a quantity or dimension, esp. of manufactured articles) stated or expressed but not necessarily corresponding exactly to the real value.

■ (of a rate or other figure) expressed in terms of a certain amount, without making allowance for changes in real value over time: *the nominal exchange rate.*

nom•i•nal ac•count ▸ n. an account recording the financial transactions of a business in a particular category, rather than with a person or other organization.

nom•i•nal ledg•er ▸ n. a ledger containing nominal accounts, or one containing both nominal and real accounts.

nom•i•nal val•ue ▸ n. the value that is stated on currency; face value. ■ the price of a share, bond, or security when it was issued, rather than its current market value.

nom•i•nee ▸ n. a person or company whose name is given as having title to a stock, real estate, etc., but who is not the actual owner.

non•con•trib•u•to•ry ▸ adj. (of a pension or pension plan) funded by regular payments by the employer, not the employee.

non•earn•ing ▸ adj. (esp. of a person or an investment) not earning a regular income.

non•ne•go•ti•a•ble ▸ adj. (of a document) not able to be transferred or assigned to the legal ownership of another person.

non•par•tic•i•pat•ing ▸ adj. (of an insurance policy) not allowing the holder a share of the profits, typically in the form of a bonus, made by the company.

non•pay•ment ▸ n. failure to pay an amount of money that is owed.

North A•mer•i•can Free Trade A•gree•ment (abbr.: **NAFTA**) an agreement that came into effect in January 1994 between the US, Canada, and Mexico to remove barriers to trade between the three countries over a ten-year period.

NPV ▸ abbr. net present value. See PRESENT VALUE.

num•bered ac•count ▸ n. a bank account, esp. in a Swiss bank, identified only by a number and not bearing the owner's name.

nu•me•raire ▸ n. an item or commodity acting as a measure of value or as a standard for currency exchange.

NYSE ▸ abbr. New York Stock Exchange.

oc•troi ▸ n. a tax levied in some countries on various goods entering a town or city.

odd lot ▸ n. a transaction involving less than the usual round number of shares.

OECD ▸ abbr. Organization for Economic Cooperation and Development.

OEM ▸ abbr. original equipment manufacturer (an organization that makes devices from component parts bought from other organizations).

off-brand ▸ adj. denoting or relating to an item of retail goods of an unknown, unpopular, or inferior brand.
▸ n. an unknown, unpopular, or inferior brand.

of•fer ▸ v. (usu. **be offered**) make available for sale: *the product is offered at a very competitive price.*
▸ n. an amount of money that someone is willing to pay for something: *the prospective purchaser who made the highest offer.* ■ a specially reduced price or terms for something on sale: *the offer runs right up until Christmas Eve.*

– PHRASES **on offer** available: *the number of permanent jobs on offer is relatively small.* **open to offers** willing to sell something or do a job for a reasonable price.

of•fer doc•u•ment ▸ n. a document containing details of a takeover bid that is sent to the shareholders of the target company.

of•fer•ing price ▸ n. the price at which a dealer or institution is prepared to sell securities or other assets.

of•fice ▸ n. a room, set of rooms, or building used as a place for commercial, professional, or bureaucratic work. ▪ the local center of a large business. ▪ a room, department, or building used to provide a particular service: *a ticket office | a post office.* ▪ the consulting room of a professional person.

of•fi•cer ▸ n. a holder of a post in a society, company, or other organization, esp. one who is involved at a senior level in its management: *a chief executive officer.*

off-price ▸ n. a method of retailing in which brand-name goods (esp. clothing) are sold for less than the usual retail price.
▸adv. using this method: *selling goods off-price.*

off•set ▸ n. a consideration or amount that diminishes or balances the effect of a contrary one: *an offset against taxable profits.*

off•shore ▸ adj. & adv. of or relating to the business of extracting oil or gas from the seabed: *offshore drilling.* ▪ made, situated, or conducting business abroad, esp. in order to take advantage of lower costs or less stringent regulation: *deposits in offshore accounts.*

ol•i•gop•o•ly ▸ n. (pl. **-ies**) a state of limited competition, in which a market is shared by a small number of producers or sellers.

ol•i•gop•so•ny ▸ n. (pl. **-ies**) a state of the market in which only a small number of buyers exists for a product.

OPEC ▸ abbr. Organization of the Petroleum Exporting Countries.

o•pen ▸ adj. (of a store, place of entertainment, etc.) officially admitting customers or visitors; available for business.
▪ (of a bank account) available for transactions.

o•pen en•roll•ment ▸ n. a period during which employees may change, add, or drop benefits coverage.

o•pen in•ter•est ▸ n. the number of contracts or commitments outstanding in futures and options that are trading on an official exchange at any one time.

o•pen mar•ket ▸ n. (often **the open market**) an unrestricted market with free access by and competition of buyers and sellers.

o•pen out•cry ▸ n. a system of financial trading in which dealers shout their bids and contracts aloud.

op•er•at•ing prof•it ▸ n. profit from business operations (gross profit less operating expenses) before deduction of fixed costs.

op•er•a•tions re•search ▸ n. the application of scientific principles to business management, providing a quantitative basis for complex decisions.

op•por•tu•ni•ty cost ▸ n. the loss of potential gain from other alternatives when one alternative is chosen: *idle cash balances represent an opportunity cost in terms of lost interest.*

op•tion ▸ n. a right to buy or sell a particular thing at a specified price within a set time: *Columbia Pictures has an option on the script.*
▸v. buy or sell an option on (something): *his script will have been optioned by the time you read this.*

Or•gan•i•za•tion of the Pe•tro•le•um Ex•port•ing Coun•tries (abbr.: **OPEC**) an association of eleven major oil-producing countries, founded in 1960 to coordinate policies and prices and headquartered in Vienna. Members are Algeria, Gabon, Indonesia, Iran, Iraq, Kuwait, Libya, Nigeria, Qatar, Saudi Arabia, the United Arab Emirates, and Venezuela.

o•rig•i•na•tion fee ▸ n. a fee charged by a lender on entering into a loan agreement to cover the cost of processing the loan.

out•let ▸ n. a place from which goods are sold or distributed. ▪ a retail store that sells the goods of a specific manufacturer or brand. ■ a retail store offering discounted merchandise, esp. overstocked or irregular items. ■ a market for goods.

out•place•ment ▸ n. the provision of assistance to laid-off employees in finding new employment, either as a benefit provided by the employer directly, or through a specialist service.

out•sert ▸ n. a piece of promotional material that is placed on the outside of a package, publication, or other product.

out•side ▸ adj. (of an estimate) the greatest or highest possible: *new monthly charges that, according to outside estimates, may total $8 per line.*

out•side di•rec•tor ▸ n. a director of a company who is not employed by that company, typically an employee of an associated company.

out•side mon•ey ▸ n. money held in a form such as gold that is an asset for the holder and does not represent a corresponding liability for someone else.
■ money or investment from an independent source.

out•source ▸ v. obtain (goods or a service) from an outside supplier, esp. in place of an internal source.
■ contract (work) out: *you may choose to outsource this function to another company or do it yourself.*

out•turn ▸ n. the amount of something produced, esp. money; output: *the financial outturn.*

o•ver•age ▸ n. an excess or surplus, esp. the amount by which a sum of money is greater than a previous estimate.

o•ver•buy ▸ v. (past and past part. -bought) buy more of (something) than one needs.

o•ver•ca•pac•i•ty ▸ n. the situation in which an industry or factory cannot sell as much as it can produce.

o•ver•cap•i•tal•ize ▸ v. (overcapitalized) provide (a company) with more capital than is advisable or necessary.
■ estimate or set the capital value of (a company) at too high an amount.

o•ver•draft ▸ n. a deficit in a bank account caused by drawing more money than the account holds.

o•ver•draw ▸ v. (past -drew; past part. -drawn) (usu. be overdrawn) draw money from (one's bank account) in excess of what the account holds: *you only pay interest if your account is overdrawn.*
■ (be overdrawn) (of a person) have taken money out of an account in excess of what it holds.

o•ver•ful•fill (Brit. -fulfil) ▸ v. (-fulfilled, -fulfilling) fulfill (a contract or quota) earlier or in greater quantity than required: *he overfulfilled the quota by forty percent.*

o•ver•head ▸ adj. (of a cost or expense) incurred in the general upkeep or running of a plant, premises, or business, and not attributable to specific products or items.
▸ n. overhead cost or expense.

o•ver•heat ▸ v. (of a country's economy) show marked inflation when increased demand results in rising prices rather than increased output.

o•ver•in•sured ▸ adj. having insurance coverage beyond what is necessary.

o•ver•is•sue ▸ v. (-issues, -issued, -issuing) issue (bonds, shares of stock, etc.) beyond the authorized amount or the issuer's ability to pay them on demand.
▸ n. the action of overissuing bonds, shares of stock, etc.

o•ver•pro•duce ▸ v. produce more of (a product or commodity) than is wanted or needed.

o•ver•sell ▸ v. (past and past part. -sold) sell more of (something) than exists or can be delivered: *a surge in airlines overselling flights.*

o•ver•stock ▸ n. (esp. in a manufacturing or retailing context) a supply or quantity in excess of demand or requirements: *factory overstock | publishers' overstocks and remainders.*

o•ver•sub•scribed ▸ adj. applied for in greater quantities than are available or expected: *those bonds were said to be 12 to 14 times oversubscribed.*

o•ver•trade ▸ v. engage in more business than can be supported by the market or by the funds or resources available.

o•ver•val•ue ▸ v. (-values, -valued, -valuing) fix the value of (something, esp. a currency) at too high a level.

pack•ag•ing ▸ n. materials used to wrap or protect goods.
■ the business or process of packing goods.

pack•er ▸ n. a person or machine that packs something, esp. someone who prepares and packs food for transportation and sale.

paid-up ▸ adj. denoting the part of the subscribed capital of an undertaking that has actually been paid: *paid-up capital.*
■ denoting an endowment policy in which the policyholder has stopped paying premiums, resulting in the surrender value being used to purchase single-premium whole-life insurance.

P & L ▸ abbr. profit and loss account.

par ▸ n. the face value of a stock or other security, as distinct from its market value.
■ (also **par of exchange**) the recognized value of one country's currency in terms of another's.

par•cel ▸ n. a quantity or amount of something, in particular:
■ a piece of land, esp. one considered as part of an estate. ■ a quantity dealt with in one commercial transaction: *a parcel of shares.*

par•i•ty ▸ n. the value of one currency in terms of another at an established exchange rate.

part•ner ▸ n. a person who takes part in an undertaking with another or others, esp. in a business or company with shared risks and profits.

part•ner•ship ▸ n. the state of being a partner or partners: *we should go on working together in partnership.*
■ an association of two or more people as partners: *an increase in partnerships with housing associations.* ■ a business or firm owned and run by two or more partners. ■ a position as one of the partners in a business or firm.

pass ▸ v. (of a company) not declare or pay (a dividend).

pass•book ▸ n. a booklet issued by a bank to an account holder for recording sums deposited and withdrawn.

pat•ent ▸ n. a government authority to an individual or organization conferring a right or title, esp. the sole right to make, use, or sell some invention: *he took out a patent for an improved steam hammer.*
▸ adj. made and marketed under a patent; proprietary: *patent milk powder.*
▸ v. obtain a patent for (an invention).

pat•ent•ee ▸ n. a person or organization that obtains or holds a patent for something.

pay•a•ble ▸ adj. (of money) required to be paid; due: *interest is payable on the money owing.* ■ able to be paid: *it costs just $195, payable in five monthly installments.*
▸ n. (**payables**) debts owed by a business; liabilities.

pay-as-you-go ▸ adj. relating to a system of paying debts or meeting costs as they arise.

pay•back ▸ n. financial return or reward, esp. profit equal to the initial outlay of an investment: *a long time lag between investment and payback.*

pay•back pe•ri•od ▸ n. the length of time required for an investment to recover its initial outlay in terms of profits or savings.

pay•ee ▸ n. a person to whom money is paid or is to be paid, esp. the person to whom a check is made payable.

pay•roll ▸ n. a list of a company's employees and the amount of money they are to be paid: *there are just three employees on the payroll.*
■ the total amount of wages and salaries paid by a company to its employees: *small employers with a payroll of less than $45,000.*

peg ▸ n. a point or limit on a scale, esp. of exchange rates. informal a strong throw, esp. in baseball.
▸ v. (**pegged, pegging**) fix (a price, rate, or amount) at a particular level.

pen•e•tra•tion ▸ n. the successful selling of a company's or country's products in a particular market or area: *Japanese import penetration.* ■ the extent to which a product is recognized and bought by customers in a particular market.

pen•ny stock ▸ n. a common stock valued at less than one dollar, and therefore highly speculative.

pen•sion ▸ n. a regular payment made during a person's retirement from an investment fund to which that person or their employer has contributed during their working life.
■ a regular payment made by the government to people of or above the official retirement age and to some widows and disabled people.
▸v. (**pension someone off**) dismiss someone from employment, typically because of age or ill health, and pay them a pension.

pen•sion•a•ble ▸ adj. entitling to or qualifying for a pension.

pen•sion•ar•y ▸ adj. of or concerning a pension.

pen•sion fund ▸ n. a fund from which pensions are paid, accumulated from contributions from employers, employees, or both.

per an•num ▸ adv. for each year (used in financial contexts): *an average growth rate of around 2 percent per annum.*

p/e ra•tio ▸ abbr. price–earnings ratio.

per con•tra ▸ n. the opposite side of an account or an assessment.

per di•em ▸ adv. & adj. for each day (used in financial contexts).
▸n. an allowance or payment made for each day.

per•fect com•pe•ti•tion ▸ n. the situation prevailing in a market in which buyers and sellers are so numerous and well informed that all elements of monopoly are absent and the market price of a commodity is beyond the control of individual buyers and sellers.

per•form ▸ v. (of an investment) yield a profitable return.

per•for•mance ▸ n. the extent to which an investment is profitable, esp. in relation to other investments.

per•for•mance bond ▸ n. a bond issued by a bank or other financial institution, guaranteeing the fulfillment of a particular contract.

per•pet•u•al ▸ adj. (of an investment) having no fixed maturity date; irredeemable.

per•pe•tu•i•ty ▸ n. (pl. **-ies**) a bond or other security with no fixed maturity date.

per•son•al i•den•ti•fi•ca•tion num•ber (abbr.: **PIN**) ▸ n. a number allocated to an individual and used to validate electronic transactions.

per•son•al shop•per ▸ n. an individual who is paid to help another to purchase goods, either by accompanying them while shopping or by shopping on their behalf.

per•son•nel de•part•ment ▸ n. the part of an organization concerned with the appointment, training, and welfare of employees.

pet•ro•dol•lar ▸ n. a notional unit of currency earned by a country from the export of petroleum: *petrodollars were pouring into the kingdom.*

pet•ty cash ▸ n. an accessible store of money kept by an organization for expenditure on small items.

phan•tom ▸ n. denoting a financial arrangement or transaction that has been invented for fraudulent purposes but that does not really exist.

phar•ma•ceu•ti•cal ▸ n. (usu. **pharmaceuticals**) (**pharmaceuticals**) companies manufacturing medicinal drugs.

Phil•lips curve ▸ n. a supposed inverse relationship between the level of unemployment and the rate of inflation.

piece rate ▸ n. a rate of payment for piecework.

piece•work ▸ n. work paid for according to the amount produced.

PIN (also **PIN number**) ▸ abbr. personal identification number.

pi•rate ▸ n. a person who appropriates or reproduces the work of another for profit without permission, usually in contravention of patent or copyright.
▸v. (**pirated**) use or reproduce (another's work) for profit without permission, usually in contravention of patent or copyright: *he sold pirated tapes of Hollywood blockbusters.*

pit ▸ n. an area reserved or enclosed for a specific activity, in particular:
■ a part of the floor of an exchange in which a particular stock or commodity is traded, typically by open outcry.

place ▸ v. dispose of (something, esp. shares) by selling to a customer.

planned ob•so•les•cence ▸ n. a policy of producing consumer goods that rapidly become obsolete and so require replacing, achieved by frequent changes in design, termination of the supply of spare parts, and the use of nondurable materials.

plas•tic ▸ n. informal credit cards or other types of plastic card that can be used as money: *he pays with cash instead of with plastic.*

plc (also **PLC**) Brit. ▸ abbr. public limited company.

PO ▸ abbr. purchase order.

point ▸ n. a percentage of the profits from a movie or recording offered to certain people involved in its production.
■ a unit of varying value, used in quoting the price of stocks, bonds, or futures.

point of sale (abbr.: **POS**) ▸ n. the place at which goods are retailed.

poi•son pill ▸ n. a tactic used by a company threatened with an unwelcome takeover bid to make itself unattractive to the bidder.

pol•i•cy ▸ n. (pl. **-ies**) a contract of insurance: *they took out a joint policy.*

pool ▸ n. a group of people available for work when required: *the typing pool.*
■ a group of people considered as a resource: *a nationwide pool of promising high-school students.* ■ an arrangement, illegal in many countries, between competing parties to fix prices or rates and share business in order to eliminate competition. ■ a common fund into which all contributors pay and from which financial backing is provided: *big public investment pools.* ■ a source of common funding for speculative operations on financial markets.
▸ v. (of two or more people or organizations) put (money or other assets) into a common fund.

port•fo•li•o ▸ n. (pl. **-os**) a range of investments held by a person or organization: *better returns on its investment portfolio.*
■ a range of products or services offered by an organization, esp.

when considered as a business asset: *an unrivaled portfolio of quality brands.*

POS ▸ abbr. point of sale.

po•si•tion ▸ n. an investor's net holdings in one or more markets at a particular time; the status of an individual or institutional trader's open contracts: *traders were covering short positions.*
▸ v. promote (a product, service, or business) within a particular sector of a market, or as the fulfillment of that sector's specific requirements.

post[1] ▸ v. (often **be posted**) announce or publish (something, esp. a financial result): *the company posted a $460,000 loss.*

post[2] ▸ v. (in bookkeeping) enter (an item) in a ledger: *post the transaction in the second column.*
■ complete (a ledger) in this way.

post[3] ▸ n. a position of paid employment; a job.

post•in•dus•tri•al ▸ adj. of or relating to an economy that no longer relies on heavy industry.

post-tax ▸ adj. (of income or profits) remaining after the deduction of taxes.

pov•er•ty line ▸ n. the estimated minimum level of income needed to secure the necessities of life.

PPP ▸ abbr. purchasing power parity (a way of measuring what an amount of money will buy in different countries).

PR ▸ abbr. press release.
■ public relations.

pred•a•to•ry pric•ing ▸ n. the pricing of goods or services at such a low level that other suppliers cannot compete and are forced to leave the market.

pre•emp•tive ▸ adj. relating to the purchase of goods or shares by one person or party before the opportunity is offered to others: *preemptive rights.*

pref. ▸ abbr. preference (with reference to preference shares).
■ preferred (with reference to a preferred stock).

pref•er•en•tial ▸ adj. (of a union shop) giving employment preference to union members.
■ (of a creditor) having a claim on the receipt of payment from a debtor

that will be met before those of other creditors.

pre•ferred stock ▸ n. stock that entitles the holder to a fixed dividend, whose payment takes priority over that of common-stock dividends.

pre•mi•um ▸ n. (pl. **premiums**) an amount to be paid for an insurance policy. a sum added to an ordinary price or charge.
■ a sum added to interest or wages; a bonus. ■ relating to or denoting a commodity or product of superior quality and therefore a higher price: *premium beers.* ■ the amount by which the price of a share or other security exceeds its issue price, its nominal value, or the value of the assets it represents: *the fund has traded at a premium of 12%.*

pre•need ▸ adj. denoting a scheme in which one pays in advance for a service or facility: *preneed funeral sales.*

pres•ent val•ue (also **net present value**) ▸ n. the value in the present of a sum of money, in contrast to some future value it will have when it has been invested at compound interest.

pres•tige pric•ing ▸ n. the practice of pricing goods at a high level in order to give the appearance of quality.

pre•tax ▸ adj. (of income or profits) considered or calculated before the deduction of taxes.

price con•trol ▸ n. a government regulation establishing a maximum price to be charged for specified goods and services, esp. during periods of war or inflation.

price dis•crim•i•na•tion ▸ n. the action of selling the same product at different prices to different buyers, in order to maximize sales and profits.

price-earn•ings ra•tio (also **price-earnings multiple**) ▸ n. the current market price of a company share divided by the earnings per share of the company.

price-fix•ing (also **price fixing**) ▸ n. the maintaining of prices at a certain level by agreement between competing sellers.

price list ▸ n. a list of current prices of items on sale.

price point ▸ n. a point on a scale of possible prices at which something might be marketed.

price-sen•si•tive ▸ adj. denoting a product whose sales are greatly influenced by the price.
■ (of information) likely to affect share prices if it were made public.

price sup•port ▸ n. government assistance in maintaining the levels of market prices regardless of supply or demand.

price tag ▸ n. the label on an item for sale, showing its price.
■ figurative the cost of a company, enterprise, or undertaking: *a $400 billion price tag was put on the venture.*

price-tak•er ▸ n. a company that must accept the prevailing prices in the market of its products, its own transactions being unable to affect the market price.

price war ▸ n. a fierce competition in which retailers cut prices in an attempt to increase their share of the market.

pri•ma•ry in•dus•try ▸ n. industry, such as mining, agriculture, or forestry, that is concerned with obtaining or providing natural raw materials for conversion into commodities and products for the consumer.

prime ▸ n. short for PRIME RATE.

prime cost ▸ n. the direct cost of a commodity in terms of the materials and labor involved in its production, excluding fixed costs.

prime rate ▸ n. the lowest rate of interest at which money may be borrowed commercially.

prin•ci•pal ▸ adj. (of money) denoting an original sum invested or lent.
▸ n. a sum of money lent or invested on which interest is paid: *the winners are paid from the interest without even touching the principal.* ■ a person for whom another acts as an agent or representative: *stockbrokers in Tokyo act as agents rather than as principals.*

pri•vate en•ter•prise ▸ n. business or industry that is managed by independent companies or private individuals rather than by the state.

pri•vate sec•tor ▸ n. the part of the national economy that is not under direct government control.

pri•vate trea•ty ▸ n. the agreement for the sale of a property at a price negotiated directly between the vendor and purchaser or their agents.

pri•va•tize ▸ v. transfer (a business, industry, or service) from public to private ownership and control: *a plan for privatizing education.*

pro•duc•er ▸ n. a person, company, or country that makes, grows, or supplies goods or commodities for sale: *an oil producer.* ■ a person responsible for the financial and managerial aspects of making of a movie or broadcast or for staging a play, opera, etc.
■ a person who supervises the making of a musical recording, esp. by determining the overall sound.

pro•duc•tion line ▸ n. an arrangement in a factory in which a thing being manufactured is passed through a set linear sequence of mechanical or manual operations.

pro•duc•tiv•i•ty ▸ n. the state or quality of producing something, esp. crops: *the long-term productivity of land | agricultural productivity.*
■ the effectiveness of productive effort, esp. in industry, as measured in terms of the rate of output per unit of input.

prod•uct li•a•bil•i•ty ▸ n. the legal liability a manufacturer or trader incurs for producing or selling a faulty product.

prod•uct life-cy•cle ▸ n. the series of four stages (introduction, growth, maturity, and decline) through which the levels of sales of a product pass during its market life.

prod•uct mix ▸ n. the total range of products offered by a company.

prof•it ▸ n. a financial gain, esp. the difference between the amount earned and the amount spent in buying, operating, or producing something.
▸ v. (**profited, profiting**) obtain a financial advantage or benefit, esp. from an investment.
–PHRASES **at a profit** making more money than is spent buying, operating, or producing something: *fixing up houses and selling them at a profit.*

prof•it•a•ble ▸ adj. (of a business or activity) yielding profit or financial gain.

prof•it and loss ac•count (abbr.: **P & L**) ▸ n. an account in the books of an organization to which incomes and gains are credited and expenses and losses debited, so as to show the net profit or loss over a given period.
■ a financial statement showing a company's net profit or loss in a given period.

prof•it cen•ter ▸ n. a part of an organization with assignable revenues and costs and hence ascertainable profitability.

prof•it mar•gin ▸ n. the amount by which revenue from sales exceeds costs in a business.

prof•it-tak•ing (also **profit taking**) ▸ n. the sale of securities that have risen in price.

pro for•ma ▸ adj. denoting a standard document or form, esp. an invoice sent in advance of or with goods supplied.
■ (of a financial statement) showing potential or expected income, costs, assets, or liabilities, esp. in relation to some planned or expected act or situation.
▸ n. a standard document or form or financial statement of such a type.

pro•gram trad•ing ▸ n. the simultaneous purchase and sale of many different stocks, or of stocks and related futures contracts, with the use of a computer program to exploit price differences in different markets.

prom•is•so•ry note ▸ n. a signed document containing a written promise to pay a stated sum to a specified person or the bearer at a specified date or on demand.

pro•mote ▸ v. give publicity to (a product, organization, or venture) so as to increase sales or public awareness: *they are using famous personalities to promote the library nationally.* ■ (often **be promoted**) advance or raise (someone) to a higher position or rank: *she was promoted to general manager.*

pro•mot•er ▸ n. a person or thing that promotes something, in particular:
■ a person or company that finances or organizes a sporting event or theatrical production: *a boxing promoter.*

■ a person involved in setting up and funding a new company.

pro•mo•tion ▸ n. the publicization of a product, organization, or venture so as to increase sales or public awareness. ■ a publicity campaign for a particular product, organization, or venture: *the paper is reaping the rewards of a series of promotions.* ■ (**promotions**) the activity or business of organizing such publicity or campaigns: *she's the promotions manager for the museum.* ■ the action of raising someone to a higher position or rank or the fact of being so raised: *a promotion to divisional sales director.*

prop. ▸ abbr. proprietor.

prop•er•ty ▸ n. (pl. -**ies**) a building or buildings and the land belonging to it or them.

pro•pri•e•tar•y ▸ adj. of or relating to an owner or ownership: *the company has a proprietary right to the property.* ■ (of a product) marketed under and protected by a registered trade name.

pro•pri•e•tar•y name ▸ n. a name of a product or service registered by its owner as a trademark and not usable by others without permission.

pro•pri•e•tor ▸ n. the owner of a business.

pro•tect ▸ v. (often **be protected**) (of an insurance policy) promise to pay (someone) an agreed amount in the event of loss, injury, fire, theft, or other misfortune. ■ shield (a domestic industry) from competition by imposing import duties on foreign goods. ■ provide funds to meet (a bill of exchange or commercial draft).

pro•tec•tion•ism ▸ n. the theory or practice of shielding a country's domestic industries from foreign competition by taxing imports.

pro•tec•tive ▸ adj. of or relating to the protection of domestic industries from foreign competition: *protective tariffs.*

pro•vi•sion ▸ n. (**provision for/against**) financial or other arrangements for future eventualities or requirements: *farmers have been slow to make provision for their retirement.* ■ an amount set aside out of profits in the accounts of an organization for a known liability, esp. a bad debt or the diminution in value of an asset. ▸ v. set aside an amount in an organization's accounts for a known liability.

psy•chic in•come ▸ n. the nonmonetary or nonmaterial satisfactions that accompany an occupation or economic activity.

pub•lic ▸ adj. of or provided by the government rather than an independent, commercial company: *public spending.* –PHRASES **go public** become a public company.

pub•lic com•pa•ny ▸ n. a company whose shares are traded freely on a stock exchange.

pub•lic good ▸ n. a commodity or service that is provided without profit to all members of a society, either by the government or a private individual or organization: *a conviction that library informational services are a public good, not a commercial commodity.*

pub•lic•i•ty ▸ n. the giving out of information about a product, person, or company for advertising or promotional purposes. ■ material or information used for such a purpose.

pub•lic re•la•tions ▸ plural n. [also treated as sing.] the professional maintenance of a favorable public image by a company or other organization or a famous person. ■ the state of the relationship between the public and a company or other organization or a famous person.

pub•lic sec•tor ▸ n. the part of an economy that is controlled by the government.

pull•back ▸ n. a reduction in price or demand: *there is no sign of a consumer pullback.*

pump-prim•ing ▸ n. the stimulation of economic activity by investment.

pur•chase ▸ v. acquire (something) by paying for it; buy. ▸ n. the action of buying something. ■ a thing that has been bought.

put ▸ n. short for PUT OPTION.

put op•tion ▸ n. an option to sell assets at an agreed price on or before a particular date.

Pvt. (also **PVT**) ▸ abbr. (in company names) private.

pyr•a•mid ▸ n. a system of financial growth achieved by a small initial investment, with subsequent investments being funded by using unrealized profits as collateral.
▸v. achieve a substantial return on (money or property) after making a small initial investment.

pyr•a•mid scheme ▸ n. a system of selling goods in which agency rights are sold to an increasing number of distributors at successively lower levels.

Q ▸ abbr. quarter (used to refer to a specified quarter of the fiscal year): *we expect to have an exceptional Q4.*

qual•i•ty as•sur•ance ▸ n. the maintenance of a desired level of quality in a service or product, esp. by means of attention to every stage of the process of delivery or production.

qual•i•ty cir•cle ▸ n. a group of employees that meets regularly to consider ways of resolving problems and improving production in their organization.

quant ▸ n. informal a quantity analyst.

quan•ti•ty the•o•ry (also **the quantity theory of money**) ▸ n. the hypothesis that changes in prices correspond to changes in the monetary supply.

quo•ta ▸ n. a limited quantity of a particular product that under official controls can be produced, exported, or imported.

quo•ta•tion ▸ n. a price offered by a broker for the sale or purchase of a stock or other security.
■ a registration granted to a company enabling their shares to be officially listed and traded.

quote ▸ v. give someone (the estimated price of a job or service).
■ (usu. **be quoted**) give (a company) a quotation or listing on a stock exchange.
▸n. a price offered by a broker for the sale or purchase of a stock or other security.
■ a quotation or listing of a company on a stock exchange.

R ▸ abbr. (also ®) registered as a trademark.

rack rent ▸ n. an extortionate or very high rent, esp. an annual rent equivalent to the full value of the property to which it relates.
▸v. (**rack-rent**) exact an excessive or extortionate rent from (a tenant) or for (a property).

raid ▸ n. a hostile attempt to buy a major or controlling interest in the shares of a company.

raise ▸ n. an increase in salary: *he wants a raise and some perks.*

ral•ly ▸ v. (**-ies, -ied**) (of share, currency, or commodity prices) increase after a fall: *prices of metals such as aluminum and copper have rallied.*

rate ▸ n. a fixed price paid or charged for something, esp. goods or services: *the basic rate of pay.*
■ the amount of a charge or payment expressed as a percentage of some other amount, or as a basis of calculation.

rate of ex•change ▸ n. another term for EXCHANGE RATE.

rate of re•turn ▸ n. the annual income from an investment expressed as a proportion (usually a percentage) of the original investment.

rat•ing ▸ n. a classification or ranking of someone or something based on a comparative assessment of their quality, standard, or performance: *the hotel regained its five-star rating.*
■ (**ratings**) the estimated audience size of a particular television or radio program: *the soap's ratings have recently picked up.* ■ the value of a property or condition that is claimed to be standard, optimal, or limiting for a substance, material, or item of equipment: *fuel with a low octane rating.*

ra•tio ▸ n. (pl. **-os**) the relative value of silver and gold in a bimetallic system of currency.

ra•tion•al ex•pec•ta•tions hy•poth•e•sis ▸ n. the hypothesis that an economic agent will make full use of all available information when forming expectations, esp. with regard to inflation, and not just past values of a particular variable.

re•act ▸ v. (of stock prices) fall after rising.

read•y mon•ey (also **ready cash**) ▸ n. money in the form of cash that is immediately available.

re•al ▸ adj. adjusted for changes in the value of money; assessed by purchasing power.

real es•tate a•gent ▸ n. a person who sells and rents out buildings and land for clients.

re•al•i•za•ble ▸ adj. in or able to be converted into cash: *10 percent of realizable assets.*

re•al•i•za•tion ▸ n. the action of converting an asset into cash.
■ a sale of goods: *auction realizations.*

re•al•ize ▸ v. make (money or a profit) from a transaction: *she realized a profit of $100,000.*
■ (of goods) be sold for (a specified price); fetch. ■ convert (an asset) into cash.

re•al•tor ▸ n. a person who acts as an agent for the sale and purchase of buildings and land; a real estate agent.

re•badge ▸ v. relaunch (a product) under a new name or logo.

re•base ▸ v. establish a new base level for (a tax level, price index, etc.).

re•bate ▸ n. a partial refund to someone who has paid too much money for tax, rent, or a utility.
■ a deduction or discount on a sum of money due.
▸ v. pay back (such a sum of money).

re•brand ▸ v. change the corporate image of (a company or organization).

re•cap•i•tal•ize ▸ v. provide (a business) with more capital, esp. by replacing debt with stock.

re•ceipt ▸ n. a written or printed statement acknowledging that something has been paid for or that goods have been received.
■ (**receipts**) an amount of money received during a particular period by an organization or business: *box-office receipts.*
▸ v. mark (a bill) as paid: *the receipted hotel bill.*
■ write a receipt for (goods or money).

re•ceiv•a•ble ▸ plural n. (**receivables**) amounts owed to a business, regarded as assets.

re•ceiv•er ▸ n. a person or company appointed by a court to manage the financial affairs of a business or person that has gone bankrupt.

re•ceiv•er•ship ▸ n. the state of being dealt with by an official receiver.

re•ces•sion ▸ n. a period of temporary economic decline during which trade and industrial activity are reduced, generally identified by a fall in GDP in two successive quarters.

re•ces•sive ▸ adj. undergoing an economic recession: *the recessive housing market.*

rec•on•cile ▸ v. (often **be reconciled**) make (one account) consistent with another, esp. by allowing for transactions begun but not yet completed.

rec•on•cil•i•a•tion state•ment ▸ n. a statement of account in which discrepancies are adjusted so that different accounts balance.

re•coup ▸ v. regain (money spent or lost), esp. through subsequent profits: *oil companies are keen to recoup their investment.*
■ reimburse or compensate (someone) for money spent or lost. ■ deduct or keep back (part of a sum due).

re•course ▸ n. [in sing.] the legal right to demand compensation or payment.
–PHRASES **without recourse** a formula used to disclaim responsibility for future nonpayment, esp. of a negotiable financial instrument.

re•cov•er•y stock ▸ n. a stock that has fallen in price but is thought to have the potential of climbing back to its original level.

re•deem ▸ v. gain or regain possession of (something) in exchange for payment.
■ repay (a stock, bond, or other instrument) at the maturity date. ■ exchange (a coupon, voucher, or trading stamp) for merchandise, a discount, or money. ■ pay the necessary money to clear (a debt): *owners were unable to redeem their mortgages.*
■ exchange (paper money) for gold or silver.

re•demp•tion ▸ n. the action of regaining or gaining possession of something in exchange for payment, or clearing a debt.

re•demp•tion yield ▸ n. the yield of a stock calculated as a percentage of the redemption price with an adjustment made for any capital gain or loss the price represents relative to the current price.

re•dis•count ▸ v. (of a central bank) discount (a bill of exchange or similar instrument) that has already been discounted by a commercial bank.

re•em•ploy ▸ v. employ (someone, typically a former employee) again.

re•en•gi•neer ▸ v. restructure (a company or part of its operations), esp. by exploiting information technology.

re•ex•port ▸ v. export (imported goods), typically after they have undergone further processing or manufacture.

re•fi•nance ▸ v. finance (something) again, typically with a new loan at a lower rate of interest.

re•flate ▸ v. expand the level of output of (an economy) by government stimulus, using either fiscal or monetary policy.

reg•u•late ▸ v. control or supervise (something, esp. a company or business activity) by means of rules and regulations.

reg•u•la•tor ▸ n. a person or body that supervises a particular industry or business activity.

re•im•port ▸ v. import (goods processed or made from exported materials).

re•in•sure ▸ v. (of an insurer) transfer (all or part of a risk) to another insurer to provide protection against the risk of the first insurance.

re•in•vest ▸ v. put (the profit on a previous investment) back into the same place.

re•mit ▸ v. (**remitted, remitting**) send (money) in payment or as a gift.

re•mort•gage ▸ v. take out another or a different kind of mortgage on (a property).
▸ n. a different or additional mortgage.

re•mu•ner•ate ▸ v. pay (someone) for services rendered or work done.

re•na•tion•al•ize ▸ v. transfer (a privatized industry) back into state ownership or control.

rent ▸ n. a tenant's regular payment to a landlord for the use of property or land.
■ a sum paid for the hire of equipment.
▸ v. pay someone for the use of (something, typically property, land, or a car).
■ (of an owner) let someone use (something) in return for payment: *he purchased a large tract of land and rented out most of it to local farmers.*
■ be let or hired out at a specified rate: *skis or snowboards rent for $60–80 for six days.*
–PHRASES **for rent** available to be rented.

rent•a•ble ▸ adj. available or suitable for renting.

ren•tal ▸ n. an amount paid or received as rent.
■ the action of renting something: *the office was on weekly rental.* ■ a rented house or car.
▸ adj. of, relating to, or available for rent: *rental properties.*

re•or•der ▸ n. a renewed or repeated order for goods.

rep informal ▸ n. a representative: *a union rep.*
■ a sales representative.
▸ v. (**repped, repping**) act as a sales representative for a company or product: *at eighteen she was working for her dad, repping on the road.*

re•pa•tri•ate ▸ v. send or bring (money) back to one's own country: *foreign firms would be permitted to repatriate all profits.*

re•po informal ▸ n. (pl. **-os**) a car or other item that has been repossessed.
▸ v. (**repo's, repo'd**) repossess (a car or other item) when a buyer defaults on payments.

re•pos•sess ▸ v. retake possession of (something) when a buyer defaults on payments.

re•pos•ses•sor ▸ n. a person hired by a credit company to repossess an item when the buyer defaults on payments.

re•pre•sent ▸ v. present (a check or bill) again for payment.

re•price ▸ v. put a different price on (a product or commodity).

re•pur•chase ▸ v. buy (something) back.

▸n. the action of buying something back.

re•pur•chase a•gree•ment ▸ n. a contract in which the vendor of a security agrees to repurchase it from the buyer at an agreed price.

re•sale ▸ n. the sale of a thing previously bought.

re•sell ▸ v. (past and past part. **resold**) sell (something one has bought) to someone else.

re•serve ▸ n. (often **reserves**) a supply of a commodity not needed for immediate use but available if required.
■ funds kept available by a bank, company, or government: *the foreign exchange reserves.* ■ a part of a company's profits added to capital rather than paid as a dividend. ■ short for RESERVE PRICE.

re•serve bank ▸ n. a regional bank operating under and implementing the policies of the US Federal Reserve.

re•serve price ▸ n. the price stipulated as the lowest acceptable by the seller for an item sold at auction.

re•sid•u•al ▸ n. a royalty paid to a performer, writer, etc., for a repeat of a play, television show, etc. the resale value of a new car or other item at a specified time after purchase, expressed as a percentage of its purchase price.

re•source ▸ n. (usu. **resources**) a stock or supply of money, materials, staff, and other assets that can be drawn on by a person or organization in order to function effectively.
■ (**resources**) a country's collective means of supporting itself or becoming wealthier, as represented by its reserves of minerals, land, and other assets. ■ (**resources**) available assets.
▸v. provide (a person or organization) with materials, money, staff, and other assets necessary for effective operation.

re•stock ▸ v. replenish (a store) with fresh stock or supplies.

re•straint of trade ▸ n. action that interferes with free competition in a market.

re•struc•ture ▸ v. convert (the debt of a business in difficulty) into another

kind of debt, typically one that is repayable at a later time.

re•tail ▸ n. the sale of goods to the public in relatively small quantities for use or consumption rather than for resale.
▸adv. being sold in such a way: *it is not yet available retail.*
▸v. sell (goods) to the public in such a way: *the difficulties in retailing the new products.*
■ (**retail at/for**) (of goods) be sold in this way (at a specified price): *the product retails for around $20.*

re•tire ▸ v. leave one's job and cease to work, typically upon reaching the normal age for leaving employment: *he retired from the navy in 1966.*
■ withdraw (a bill or note) from circulation or currency. ■ pay off or cancel (a debt).

re•trench ▸ v. (of a company, government, or individual) reduce costs or spending in response to economic difficulty: *as a result of the recession the company retrenched.*

re•turn ▸ v. yield or make (a profit).
▸n. (often **returns**) a profit from an investment.
■ a good rate of return.

re•val•ue ▸ v. (**revalues, revalued, revaluing**) assess the value of (something) again.
■ adjust the value of (a currency) in relation to other currencies.

rev•e•nue ▸ n. income, esp. when of a company or organization and of a substantial nature.

rev•e•nue tar•iff ▸ n. a tariff imposed principally to raise government revenue rather than to protect domestic industries.

re•verse en•gi•neer•ing ▸ n. the reproduction of another manufacturer's product following detailed examination of its construction or composition.

re•verse take•o•ver ▸ n. a takeover of a public company by a smaller company.

re•volv•ing cred•it ▸ n. credit that is automatically renewed as debts are paid off.

re•volv•ing fund ▸ n. a fund that is continually replenished as withdrawals are made.

RFP ▸abbr. request for proposal, a detailed specification of goods or services required by an organization, sent to potential contractors or suppliers.

rig ▸v. (**rigged, rigging**) cause an artificial rise or fall in prices in (a market, esp. the stock market) with a view to personal profit.

rights is•sue ▸n. an issue of shares offered at a special price by a company to its existing shareholders in proportion to their holding of old shares.

risk ▸n. the possibility of financial loss.

risk cap•i•tal ▸n. another term for VENTURE CAPITAL.

ROCE ▸abbr. return on capital employed.

ROI ▸abbr. return on investment.

roll•out (also **roll-out**) ▸n. the official launch of a new product or service.

roll•o•ver ▸n. the extension or transfer of a debt or other financial arrangement.

run ▸n. (**a run on**) a widespread and sudden or continuous demand for (a particular currency or commodity): *there's been a big run on nostalgia toys this year.*
■ a sudden demand for repayment from a bank made by a large number of lenders.

run-up ▸n. a marked rise in the value or level of something.

sales tax ▸n. a tax on sales or on the receipts from sales.

sat•u•rate ▸v. (usu. **be saturated**) supply (a market) beyond the point at which the demand for a product is satisfied.

sav•ings ac•count ▸n. a bank account that earns interest.

sav•ings and loan (also **savings and loan association**) ▸n. an institution that accepts savings at interest and lends money to savers chiefly for home mortgage loans and may offer checking accounts and other services.

sav•ings bank ▸n. a financial institution that receives savings accounts and pays interest to depositors.

sav•ings bond ▸n. a bond issued by the government and sold to the general public.

Say's law a law stating that supply creates its own demand.

SBA ▸abbr. (in the US) Small Business Administration.

sci•en•tif•ic man•age•ment ▸n. management of a business, industry, or economy, according to principles of efficiency derived from experiments in methods of work and production, esp. from time-and-motion studies.

scrip ▸n. a provisional certificate of money subscribed to a bank or company, entitling the holder to a formal certificate and dividends.
■ such certificates collectively. ■ (also **scrip issue** or **dividend**) an issue of additional shares to shareholders in proportion to the shares already held. ■ (also **land scrip**) a certificate entitling the holder to acquire possession of certain portions of public land.

SDR ▸abbr. special drawing right (from the International Monetary Fund).

SEAQ ▸abbr. (in the UK) Stock Exchange Automated Quotations (the computer system on which dealers trade shares and seek or provide price quotations on the London Stock Exchange).

SEC ▸abbr. Securities and Exchange Commission, a US governmental agency that monitors trading in securities and company takeovers.

sec•ond mort•gage ▸n. a mortgage taken out on a property that is already mortgaged.

se•cure ▸v. seek to guarantee repayment of (a loan) by having a right to take possession of an asset in the event of nonpayment.

se•cu•ri•tize ▸v. convert (an asset, esp. a loan) into marketable securities, typically for the purpose of raising cash by selling them to other investors.

se•cu•ri•ty ▸n. (pl. **-ies**) (often **securities**) a certificate attesting credit, the ownership of stocks or bonds, or the right to ownership connected with tradable derivatives.

seign•ior•age (also **seignorage**) ▸n. profit made by a government by issuing currency, esp. the difference between the face value of coins and their production costs.

self-as•sess•ment ▸ n. assessment or evaluation of oneself or one's actions and attitudes, in particular, of one's performance at a job or learning task considered in relation to an objective standard.

self-fi•nanc•ing ▸ adj. (of an organization or enterprise) having or generating enough income to finance itself.

self-in•sur•ance ▸ n. insurance of oneself or one's interests by maintaining a fund to cover possible losses rather than by purchasing an insurance policy.

self-liq•ui•dat•ing ▸ adj. denoting an asset that earns back its original cost out of income over a fixed period.
  ■ denoting a loan used to finance a project that will bring a sufficient return to pay back the loan and its interest and leave a profit. ■ denoting a sales promotion offer that pays for itself by generating increased sales.

sell ▸ v. (past and past part. **sold**) give or hand over (something) in exchange for money.
  ■ have a stock of (something) available for sale: *the store sells hi-fis, TVs, videos, and other electrical goods.* ■ (of a thing) be purchased: *this magazine of yours won't sell.* ■ (of a publication or recording) attain sales of (a specified number of copies): *the album sold 6 million copies in the United States.* ■ (**sell for/at**) be available for sale at (a specified price): *these antiques sell for about $375.* ■ (**sell out**) sell all of one's stock of something: *they had nearly sold out of the initial run of 75,000 copies.* ■ (**sell out**) be all sold: *it was clear that the performances would not sell out.* ■ (**sell through**) (of a product) be purchased by a customer from a retail outlet. ■ (**sell up**) sell all of one's property, possessions, or assets.

sell•er ▸ n. a person who sells something.
  ■ (**the seller**) the party in a legal transaction who is selling: *the seller may accept the buyer's offer.* ■ a product that sells in some specified way: *the game will undoubtedly be the biggest seller of the year.*

–PHRASES **seller's (or sellers') mar-**ket an economic situation in which goods or shares are scarce and sellers can keep prices high.

sell-in ▸ n. the sale of goods to retail traders prior to public retailing.

sell•ing point ▸ n. a feature of a product for sale that makes it attractive to customers.

sell-off ▸ n. a sale of assets, typically at a low price, carried out in order to dispose of them rather than as normal trade.
  ■ a sale of shares, bonds, or commodities, esp. one that causes a fall in price.

sell•out ▸ n. the selling of an entire stock of something, esp. tickets for an entertainment or sports event.
  ■ an event for which all tickets are sold. ■ a sale of a business or company.

sell-through ▸ n. the ratio of the quantity of goods sold by a retail outlet to the quantity distributed to it wholesale.
  ■ the retail sale of something, typically a prerecorded videocassette, as opposed to its rental.

sen•si•tive ▸ adj. (of a market) unstable and liable to quick changes of price because of outside influences.

serv•ice ▸ n. assistance or advice given to customers during and after the sale of goods.
  ■ short for SERVICE INDUSTRY: *a private security service.* ■ work done for a customer other than manufacturing. ■ the action or process of serving food and drinks to customers: *they complained of poor bar service.* ■ short for SERVICE CHARGE: *service is included in the final bill.* ■ a period of employment with a company or organization: *he retired after 40 years' service.* ■ employment as a servant.
  ■ pay interest on (a debt): *taxpayers are paying $250 million just to service that debt.*

serv•ice charge (also **service fee**) ▸ n. an extra charge assessed for a service.

serv•ice con•tract ▸ n. a business agreement between a contractor and customer covering the maintenance and servicing of equipment over a specified period.

serv•ice in•dus•try ▸ n. a business that does work for a customer, and occasionally provides goods, but is not involved in manufacturing.

serv•ice mark ▸ n. a legally registered name or designation used in the manner of a trademark to distinguish an organization's services from those of its competitors.

set-off ▸ n. an item or amount that is or may be set off against another in the settlement of accounts.

set•tle•ment ▸ n. the action or process of settling an account.

sev•er•ance ▸ n. dismissal or discharge from employment.
■ short for SEVERANCE PAY.

sev•er•ance pay ▸ n. an amount paid to an employee upon dismissal or discharge from employment.

shade ▸ v. make a slight reduction in the amount, rate, or price of: *banks may shade the margin over base rate they charge customers.*

shad•ow price ▸ n. the estimated price of a good or service for which no market price exists.

share ▸ n. a part or portion of a larger amount that is divided among a number of people, or to which a number of people contribute.
■ one of the equal parts into which a company's capital is divided, entitling the holder to a proportion of the profits: *bought 33 shares of American Standard.* ■ part proprietorship of property held by joint owners.

share•hold•er ▸ n. an owner of shares in a company.

shelf life ▸ n. the length of time for which an item remains usable, fit for consumption, or saleable.

shell com•pa•ny ▸ n. an inactive company used as a vehicle for various financial maneuvers or kept dormant for future use in some other capacity.

shel•ter ▸ v. protect (income) from taxation.

shift ▸ n. one of two or more recurring periods in which different groups of workers do the same jobs in relay: *the night shift.*
■ a group of workers who work in this way.

shift work ▸ n. work comprising recurring periods in which different groups of workers do the same jobs in rotation.

ship ▸ v. (**shipped, shipping**) (often **be shipped**) transport (goods or people) on a ship.
■ transport by some other means: *the freight would be shipped by rail.* ■ send (a package) somewhere via the mail service or a private company ■ make (a product) available for purchase.

ship•ment ▸ n. the action of shipping goods: *logs waiting for shipment | shipments begin this month.*
■ a quantity of goods shipped; a consignment.

ship•ping ▸ n. ships considered collectively, esp. those in a particular area or belonging to a particular country.
■ the transport of goods by sea or some other means. ■ a charge imposed by a retail company to send merchandise to a customer.

shock ▸ n. a disturbance causing instability in an economy.

short ▸ adj. (of stocks or other securities or commodities) sold in advance of being acquired, with reliance on the price falling so that a profit can be made.
■ (of a broker, position in the market, etc.) buying or based on such stocks or other securities or commodities. ■ denoting or having a relatively early date for the maturing of a bill of exchange.
▸ n. a person who sells short.
■ (**shorts**) short-dated stocks.

short cov•er•ing ▸ n. the buying in of stocks or other securities or commodities that have been sold short, typically to avoid loss when prices move upward.

short-dat•ed ▸ adj. (of a stock or bond) due for early payment or redemption.

short-term•ism ▸ n. concentration on short-term projects or objectives for immediate profit at the expense of long-term security.

shrink•age ▸ n. an allowance made for reduction in the earnings of a business due to wastage or theft.

siege e•con•o•my ▸ n. an economy in which import controls are imposed and the export of capital is curtailed.

sight de•pos•it ▸ n. a bank deposit that can be withdrawn immediately without notice or penalty.

si•lent part•ner ▸ n. a partner not sharing in the actual work of a firm.

sim•ple ▸ adj. (**simpler, simplest**) (of interest) payable on the sum loaned only.

sin•gle-en•try ▸ adj. denoting a system of bookkeeping in which each transaction is entered in one account only.

sin•gle mar•ket ▸ n. an association of countries trading with each other without restrictions or tariffs.

sin•gle-source ▸ v. give a franchise to a single supplier for (a particular product).

sink•ing fund ▸ n. a fund formed by periodically setting aside money for the gradual repayment of a debt or replacement of a wasting asset.

sin tax ▸ n. informal a tax on items considered undesirable or harmful, such as alcohol or tobacco.

skim ▸ v. (**skimmed, skimming**) informal steal or embezzle (money), esp. in small amounts over a period of time.

skunk•works (also **skunk works**) ▸ plural n. [usu. treated as sing.] informal an experimental laboratory or department of a company or institution, typically smaller than and independent of its main research division.

slack ▸ adj. (of business) characterized by a lack of work or activity; quiet: *business was rather slack.*

slid•ing scale ▸ n. a scale of fees, taxes, wages, etc., that varies in accordance with variation of some standard.

slo•gan ▸ n. a short and striking or memorable phrase used in advertising.

slow•down ▸ n. a decline in economic activity.

slump ▸ v. undergo a sudden severe or prolonged fall in price, value, or amount: *land prices slumped.*
▸ n. a sudden severe or prolonged fall in the price, value, or amount of something.
  ■ a prolonged period of abnormally low economic activity, typically bringing widespread unemployment.

small-cap ▸ adj. denoting or relating to the stock of a company with a small capitalization.

smart card ▸ n. a plastic card with a built-in microprocessor, used typically to perform financial transactions.

so•cial cred•it ▸ n. the economic theory that consumer purchasing power should be increased either by subsidizing producers so that they can lower prices or by distributing the profits of industry to consumers.

so•cial mar•ket e•con•o•my (also **social market**) ▸ n. an economic system based on a free market operated in conjunction with state provision for those unable to sell their labor, such as the elderly or unemployed.

so•cial se•cu•ri•ty ▸ n. any government system that provides monetary assistance to people with an inadequate or no income.
  ■ (**Social Security**) (in the US) a federal insurance program that provides benefits to retired persons, the unemployed, and the disabled.

soft ▸ adj. (of a market, currency, or commodity) falling or likely to fall in value.

soft loan ▸ n. a loan, typically one to a developing country, made on terms very favorable to the borrower.

so•go sho•sha ▸ n. (pl. same) a very large Japanese company that trades internationally in a wide range of goods and services.

sol•vent ▸ adj. having assets in excess of liabilities; able to pay one's debts.

spe•cial draw•ing rights (abbr.: **SDR**) ▸ plural n. a form of international money, created by the International Monetary Fund, and defined as a weighted average of various convertible currencies.

spe•cie ▸ n. money in the form of coins rather than notes.
– PHRASES in specie in coin.

spe•cif•ic ▸ adj. (of a duty or a tax) levied at a fixed rate per physical unit of the thing taxed, regardless of its price.

spec•u•late ▸ v. invest in stocks, property, or other ventures in the hope of gain but with the risk of loss.

spec•u•la•tive ▸ adj. (of an investment) involving a high risk of loss.

◼ (of a business venture) undertaken on the chance of success, without a preexisting contract.

split ▸ v. (**splitting**; past and past part. **split**) issue new shares of (stock) to existing stockholders in proportion to their current holdings.
▸n. short for STOCK SPLIT.

split shift ▸ n. a working shift comprising two or more separate periods of duty in a day.

spot ▸ n. denoting a system of trading in which commodities or currencies are delivered and paid for immediately after a sale.

spread ▸ n. the difference between two rates or prices.

squeeze ▸ n. a strong financial demand or pressure, typically a restriction on borrowing, spending, or investment in a financial crisis.

sta•bi•liz•er ▸ n. a financial mechanism that prevents unsettling fluctuation in an economic system.

stag ▸ n. a person who applies for shares in a new issue with a view to selling at once for a profit.

stag•fla•tion ▸ n. persistent high inflation combined with high unemployment and stagnant demand in a country's economy.

stake•hold•er ▸ n. a person with an interest or concern in something, esp. a business.
◼ denoting a type of organization or system in which all the members or participants are seen as having an interest in its success.

stale ▸ adj. (of a check or legal claim) invalid because out of date.

stand•ard ▸ n. a system by which the value of a currency is defined in terms of gold or silver or both.

stand•ard of liv•ing ▸ n. the degree of wealth and material comfort available to a person or community.

stand•ing or•der ▸ n. an order for goods that remains in effect until cancelled.

stand•still a•gree•ment ▸ n. an agreement between two countries in which a debt owed by one to the other is held in abeyance for a specified period.
◼ an agreement between a company and a bidder for the company in

which the bidder agrees to buy no more shares for a specified period.

state•ment ▸ n. a document setting out items of debit and credit between a bank or other organization and a customer.

ster•ling ▸ n. British money: *prices in sterling are shown.*

stock ▸ n. the goods or merchandise kept on the premises of a business or warehouse and available for sale or distribution. ◼ farm animals such as cattle, pigs, and sheep, bred and kept for their meat or milk; livestock. ◼ the capital raised by a business or corporation through the issue and subscription of shares: *between 1982 and 1986, the value of the company's stock rose by 86%.*
◼ (also **stocks**) a portion of this as held by an individual or group as an investment: *she owned $3000 worth of stock.* ◼ (also **stocks**) the shares of a particular company, type of company, or industry: *blue-chip stocks.* ◼ securities issued by the government in fixed units with a fixed rate of interest: *government gilt-edged stock.*
▸adj. (of a product or type of product) usually kept in stock and thus regularly available for sale.
▸v. have or keep a supply of (a particular product or type or product) available for sale.
–PHRASES **in (or out of) stock** (of goods) available (or unavailable) for immediate sale in a store.

stock ex•change ▸ n. a market in which securities are bought and sold: *the company was floated on the Stock Exchange.*
◼ (**the Stock Exchange**) the level of prices in such a market.

stock•hold•er ▸ n. a shareholder.

stock in•dex fu•tures ▸ plural n. contracts to buy a range of shares at an agreed price but delivered and paid for later.

stock-in-trade ▸ n. the typical subject or commodity a person, company, or profession uses or deals in: *information is our stock-in-trade.*
◼ the goods kept on hand by a business for the purposes of its trade.

stock mar•ket ▸ n. (usu. **the stock market**) a stock exchange.

stock op•tion ▸ n. a benefit in the form of an option given by a company to an employee to buy stock in the company at a discount or at a stated fixed price.

stock•out ▸ n. a situation in which an item is out of stock.

stock split ▸ n. an issue of new shares in a company to existing shareholders in proportion to their current holdings.

stop ▸ v. (**stopped, stopping**) instruct a bank to withhold payment on (a check).
–PHRASES **stop payment** instruct a bank to withhold payment on a check.

stop-loss ▸ adj. denoting or relating to an order to sell a security or commodity at a specified price in order to limit a loss.

strad•dle ▸ n. a simultaneous purchase of options to buy and to sell a security or commodity at a fixed price, allowing the purchaser to make a profit whether the price of the security or commodity goes up or down.

straight-line ▸ adj. of or relating to a method of depreciation allocating a given percentage of the cost of an asset each year for a fixed period.

straight time ▸ n. normal working hours, paid at a regular rate.

street ▸ n. (**the street**) used to refer to the financial markets and activities on Wall Street.

street name ▸ n. the name of a brokerage firm, bank, or dealer in which stock is held on behalf of a purchaser.

strike ▸ v. (past and past part. **struck**) (of employees) refuse to work as a form of organized protest, typically in an attempt to obtain a particular concession or concessions from their employer.
■ undertake such action against (an employer). (in financial contexts) reach (a figure) by balancing an account:
▸n. a refusal to work organized by a body of employees as a form of protest, typically in an attempt to gain a concession or concessions from their employer.

strike pay ▸ n. money paid to strikers by their trade union.

strip ▸ v. (**stripped, stripping**) sell off (the assets of a company) for profit.
■ divest (a bond) of its interest coupons so that it and they may be sold separately.

strip mall ▸ n. a shopping mall consisting of stores and restaurants typically in one-story buildings located on a busy main road.

strong ▸ adj. (**stronger, strongest**) in a secure financial position.
■ (of a market) having steadily high or rising prices.

struc•tur•al un•em•ploy•ment ▸ n. unemployment resulting from industrial reorganization, typically due to technological change, rather than fluctuations in supply or demand.

sub•con•tract ▸ v. employ a business or person outside one's company to do (work) as part of a larger project.
■ (of a business or person) carry out work for a company as part of a larger project.
▸n. a contract for a company or person to do work for another company as part of a larger project.

sub•con•trac•tor ▸ n. a business or person that carries out work for a company as part of a larger project.

sub•or•di•nat•ed debt ▸ n. a debt owed to an unsecured creditor that can only be paid, in the event of a liquidation, after the claims of secured creditors have been met.

sub•scribe ▸ v. apply for or undertake to pay for an offering of shares of stock.

sub•sid•i•ar•y ▸ adj. (of a company) controlled by a holding or parent company.
▸n. (pl. **-ies**) a company controlled by a holding company.

sub•ten•ant ▸ n. a person who leases property from a tenant.

sun•rise in•dus•try ▸ n. a new and growing industry, esp. in electronics or telecommunications.

sun•set in•dus•try ▸ n. an old and declining industry.

su•per•an•nu•a•tion ▸ n. regular payment made into a fund by an employee toward a future pension.

■ a pension of this type paid to a retired person. ■ the process of superannuating an employee.

su•per•store ▸ n. a retail store, as a grocery store or bookstore, with more than the average amount of space and variety of stock.

su•per•tax ▸ n. an additional tax on something already taxed.

sup•ply ▸ n. (pl. -ies) the amount of a good or service offered for sale.
–PHRASES **supply and demand** the amount of a good or service available and the desire of buyers for it, considered as factors regulating its price.

sup•ply chain ▸ n. the sequence of processes involved in the production and distribution of a commodity.

sup•ply-side ▸ adj. denoting or relating to a policy designed to increase output and employment by changing the conditions under which goods and services are supplied, esp. by measures that reduce government involvement in the economy and allow the free market to operate.

sur•charge ▸ n. an additional charge or payment.
■ a charge made by assessors as a penalty for false returns of taxable property. ■ the showing of an omission in an account for which credit should have been given.
▸ v. exact an additional charge or payment from.

sur•plus ▸ n. an amount of something left over when requirements have been met; an excess of production or supply over demand.
■ an excess of income or assets over expenditure or liabilities in a given period, typically a fiscal year: *a trade surplus of $1.4 billion.* ■ the excess value of a company's assets over the face value of its stock.

sur•ren•der ▸ v. (of an insured person) cancel (a life insurance policy) and receive back a proportion of the premiums paid.

sur•ren•der val•ue ▸ n. the amount payable to a person who surrenders a life insurance policy.

sur•tax ▸ n. an additional tax on something already taxed, such as a higher rate of tax on incomes above a certain level.

sus•pense ac•count ▸ n. an account in the books of an organization in which items are entered temporarily before allocation to the correct or final account.

swap (also **swop**) ▸ n. an exchange of liabilities between two borrowers, either so that each acquires access to funds in a currency they need or so that a fixed interest rate is exchanged for a floating rate.

swap•tion ▸ n. an option giving the right but not the obligation to engage in a swap.

sweat eq•ui•ty ▸ n. informal an interest or increased value in a property earned from labor toward upkeep or restoration.

sweat•shop ▸ n. a factory or workshop, esp. in the clothing industry, where manual workers are employed at very low wages for long hours and under poor conditions.

swipe card ▸ n. a plastic card such as a credit card or ID card bearing magnetically encoded information that is read when the edge of the card is slid through an electronic device.

SWOT a•nal•y•sis ▸ n. a study undertaken by an organization to identify its internal strengths and weaknesses, as well as its external opportunities and threats.

syn•di•cate ▸ n. a group of individuals or organizations combined to promote some common interest.
▸ v. (usu. **be syndicated**) control or manage by a syndicate.

syn•er•gy (also **synergism**) ▸ n. the interaction or cooperation of two or more organizations, substances, or other agents to produce a combined effect greater than the sum of their separate effects: *the synergy between artist and record company.*

tai•pan ▸ n. a foreigner who is head of a business in China or Hong Kong.

tare ▸ n. an allowance made for the weight of the packaging in order to determine the net weight of goods.

tar•iff ▸ n. a tax or duty to be paid on a particular class of imports or exports.
■ a list of these taxes. ■ a table of the

fixed charges made by a business, esp. in a hotel or restaurant.

▸v. fix the price of (something) according to a tariff: *these services are tariffed by volume.*

tax ▸ n. a compulsory contribution to state revenue, levied by the government on workers' income and business profits or added to the cost of some goods, services, and transactions.

▸v. impose a tax on (someone or something).

tax•a•tion ▸ n. the levying of tax. ■ money paid as tax.

tax a•void•ance ▸ n. the arrangement of one's financial affairs to minimize tax liability within the law.

tax brack•et ▸ n. a range of incomes taxed at a given rate.

tax break ▸ n. informal a tax concession or advantage allowed by a government.

tax cred•it ▸ n. an amount of money that can be offset against a tax liability.

tax-de•duct•i•ble ▸ adj. able to be deducted from taxable income or the amount of tax to be paid.

tax e•va•sion ▸ n. the illegal nonpayment or underpayment of tax.

tax ex•ile ▸ n. a person with a high income or considerable wealth who chooses to live in a country or area with low rates of tax.

tax ha•ven ▸ n. a country or independent area where taxes are levied at a low rate.

tax loss ▸ n. a loss that can be offset against taxable profit earned elsewhere or in a different period.

tax•pay•er ▸ n. a person who pays taxes.

tax re•turn ▸ n. a form on which a taxpayer makes an annual statement of income and personal circumstances, used by the tax authorities to assess liability for tax.

tax shel•ter ▸ n. a financial arrangement made to avoid or minimize taxes.

tech•no•struc•ture ▸ n. [treated as sing. or pl.] a group of technologists or technical experts having considerable control over the workings of industry or government.

tel•e•mar•ket•ing ▸ n. the marketing of goods or services by means of telephone calls, typically unsolicited, to potential customers.

tel•e•phone bank•ing ▸ n. a method of banking in which the customer conducts transactions by telephone, typically by means of a computerized system using touch-tone dialing or voice-recognition technology.

tel•e•sales ▸ plural n. the selling of goods or services over the telephone.

tell•er ▸ n. a person employed to deal with customers' transactions in a bank. ■ an automated teller machine.

temp informal ▸ n. a temporary employee, typically an office worker who finds employment through an agency.

▸v. work as a temporary employee.

ten•der ▸ v. offer (money) as payment. ■ make a formal written offer to carry out work, supply goods, or buy land, shares, or another asset for a stated fixed price. ■ make such an offer giving (a stated fixed price).

▸n. an offer to carry out work, supply goods, or buy land, shares, or another asset at a stated fixed price.

– PHRASES **put something out to tender** seek offers to carry out work or supply goods at a stated fixed price.

ten•or ▸ n. the time that must elapse before a bill of exchange or promissory note becomes due for payment.

terms of trade ▸ plural n. the ratio of an index of a country's export prices to an index of its import prices.

think tank ▸ n. a body of experts providing advice and ideas on specific political or economic problems.

third mar•ket ▸ n. used to refer to over-the-counter trading in listed stocks outside the stock exchange.

third par•ty ▸ adj. of or relating to a person or group besides the two primarily involved in a situation: *third-party suppliers.*

thrift ▸ n. another term for SAVINGS AND LOAN.

tick ▸ n. the smallest recognized amount by which a price of the security or future may fluctuate.

tie-in ▸ n. denoting sales made conditional on the purchase of an additional item or items from the same supplier.

ti•ger ▸ n. (also **tiger economy**) a dynamic economy of one of the smaller eastern Asian countries, esp. that of Singapore, Taiwan, or South Korea.

tight mon•ey ▸ n. money or finance that is available only at high rates of interest.

till ▸ n. a cash register or drawer for money in a store, bank, or restaurant. –PHRASES **have (or with) one's fingers (or hand) in the till** used in reference to theft from one's place of work.

time-and-mo•tion stud•y ▸ n. a procedure in which the efficiency of an industrial or other operation is evaluated.

time de•pos•it ▸ n. a deposit in a bank account that cannot be withdrawn before a set date or for which notice of withdrawal is required.

tomb•stone ▸ n. (also **tombstone advertisement** or **tombstone ad**) an advertisement listing the underwriters or firms associated with a new issue of securities.

ton-mile ▸ n. one ton of freight carried one mile, as a unit of traffic.

ton•nage ▸ n. shipping considered in terms of total carrying capacity: *the port's total tonnage.*

ton•tine ▸ n. an annuity shared by subscribers to a loan or common fund, the shares increasing as subscribers die until the last survivor enjoys the whole income.

top-heav•y ▸ adj. (of an organization) having a disproportionately large number of people in senior administrative positions.

trade ▸ n. the action of buying and selling goods and services. ■ a skilled job, typically one requiring manual skills and special training.

■ (**the trade**) [treated as sing. or pl.] the people engaged in a particular area of business.

▸v. buy and sell goods and services.

■ buy or sell (a particular item or product). ■ (esp. of shares or currency) be bought and sold at a specified price. ■ exchange (something) for something else, typically as a commercial transaction.

trade def•i•cit ▸ n. the amount by which the cost of a country's imports exceeds the value of its exports.

trade dis•count ▸ n. a discount on the retail price of something allowed or agreed between traders or to a retailer by a wholesaler.

trad•ed op•tion ▸ n. an option on a stock exchange or futures exchange which can itself be bought and sold.

trade•mark ▸ n. a symbol, word, or words legally registered or established by use as representing a company or product.

▸v. (**trademarked**) provide with a trademark.

trade name ▸ n. a name that has the status of a trademark. a name by which something is known in a particular trade or profession.

trade sur•plus ▸ n. the amount by which the value of a country's exports exceeds the cost of its imports.

trade-up ▸ n. a sale of an article in order to buy something similar but more expensive and of higher quality.

trade war ▸ n. a situation in which countries try to damage each other's trade, typically by the imposition of tariffs or quota restrictions.

trad•ing floor ▸ n. an area within an exchange or a bank or securities house where dealers trade in stocks or other securities.

trad•ing post ▸ n. a store or small settlement established for trading, typically in a remote place.

trad•ing stamp ▸ n. a stamp given by some stores to a customer according to the amount spent, and exchangeable in the appropriate number for various articles.

tranche ▸ n. a portion of something, esp. money: *they released the first tranche of the loan.*

trans•fer pay•ment ▸ n. a payment made or income received in which no goods or services are being paid for, such as a benefit payment or subsidy.

trans•na•tion•al ▸ n. a large company operating internationally; a multinational.

trav•el•er's check ▸ n. a check for a fixed amount that can be cashed or used in payment after endorsement with the holder's signature.

treas•ur•er ▸ n. a person appointed to administer or manage the financial assets and liabilities of a society, company, local authority, or other body.

treas•ur•y ▸ n. (pl. **-ies**) the funds or revenue of a government, corporation, or institution.
- ◾ (**Treasury**) (in some countries) the government department responsible for budgeting for and controlling public expenditure, management of the national debt, and the overall management of the economy.

Treas•ur•y bill ▸ n. a short-dated government security, yielding no interest but issued at a discount on its redemption price.

Treas•ur•y bond ▸ n. a government bond issued by the US Treasury.

tri•al bal•ance ▸ n. a statement of all debits and credits in a double-entry account book, with any disagreement indicating an error.

tri•ple A (also **AAA**) ▸ n. the highest grading available from credit rating agencies.

trough ▸ n. a low level of economic activity.

trust ▸ n. a body of trustees.
- ◾ an organization or company managed by trustees. ◾ dated a large company that has or attempts to gain monopolistic control of a market.

trust•bust•er ▸ n. informal a person or agency employed to enforce antitrust legislation.

trust com•pa•ny ▸ n. a company formed to act as a trustee or to deal with trusts.

trust fund ▸ n. a fund consisting of assets belonging to a trust, held by the trustees for the beneficiaries.

turn•a•round ▸ n. the process of completing or the time needed to complete a task, esp. one involving receiving something, processing it, and sending it out again: *a seven-day turnaround*.
- ◾ the process of or time taken for unloading and reloading a ship, aircraft, or vehicle.

turn•key ▸ adj. of or involving the provision of a complete product or service that is ready for immediate use.

turn•o•ver ▸ n. the amount of money taken by a business in a particular period.
- ◾ the volume of shares traded during a particular period, as a percentage of total shares listed. the rate at which employees leave a workforce and are replaced.
- ◾ the rate at which goods are sold and replaced in a shop.

un•au•dit•ed ▸ adj. (of financial accounts) not having been officially examined.

un•brand•ed ▸ adj. (of a product) not bearing a brand name: *unbranded computer systems*.

un•bun•dle ▸ v. market or charge for (items or services) separately rather than as part of a package. split (a company or conglomerate) into its constituent businesses, esp. before selling them off.

un•cap ▸ v. (**uncapped, uncapping**) remove a limit or restriction on (a price, rate, or amount).

un•cashed ▸ adj. (of a check or money order) not yet cashed.

un•charged ▸ adj. not charged to a particular account: *an uncharged fixed cost*.

un•cleared ▸ adj. (of a check) not having passed through a clearinghouse and been paid into the payee's account.

un•com•mer•cial ▸ adj. not making, intended to make, or allowing a profit.

un•com•pet•i•tive ▸ adj. (with reference to business or commerce) not competitive.

UNCTAD ▸ abbr. United Nations Conference on Trade and Development.

un•der•cap•i•tal•ize ▸ v. provide (a company) with insufficient capital to achieve desired results.

un•der•charge ▸ v. charge (someone) a price or amount that is too low.

un•der•con•sump•tion ▸ n. purchase of goods and services at a level lower than that of their supply.

un•der•cut ▸ v. (**-cutting**; past and past part. **-cut**) offer goods or services at a lower price than (a competitor).

un•der•de•vel•oped ▸ adj. (of a country or region) not advanced economically.

un•der•ground e•con•o•my ▸ n. the part of a country's economic activity that is unrecorded and untaxed by its government.

un•der•in•sured ▸ adj. (of a person) having inadequate insurance coverage.

un•der•per•form ▸ v. increase in value less than.

un•der•price ▸ v. sell or offer something at a lower price than (the competition).
  ■ sell or offer (something) at too low a price.

un•der•sell ▸ v. (past and past part. **-sold**) sell something at a lower price than (a competitor).

un•der•spend ▸ v. (past and past part. **-spent**) spend less than (a specified or allocated amount).

un•der•val•ue ▸ v. (**-values, -valued, -valuing**) underestimate the financial value of (something).

un•der•weight ▸ adj. (also **underweighted**) having less investment in a particular area than is considered desirable or appropriate.

un•der•write ▸ v. (past **-wrote**; past part. **-written**) sign and accept liability under (an insurance policy), thus guaranteeing payment in case loss or damage occurs.
  ■ accept (a liability or risk) in this way. (of a bank or other financial institution) engage to buy all the unsold shares in (an issue of new securities).
  ■ undertake to finance or otherwise support or guarantee (something).

un•earned in•come ▸ n. income from investments rather than from work.

un•earned in•cre•ment ▸ n. an increase in the value of land or property without labor or expenditure on the part of the owner.

un•ec•o•nom•ic ▸ adj. unprofitable.
  ■ constituting an inefficient use of money or other resources.

un•ec•o•nom•i•cal ▸ adj. wasteful of money or other resources; not economical.

un•em•ploy•a•ble ▸ adj. (of a person) not able or likely to get paid employment, esp. because of a lack of skills or qualifications.
  ▸ n. an unemployable person.

un•em•ployed ▸ adj. (of a person) without a paid job but available to work.

un•em•ploy•ment ▸ n. the state of being unemployed.
  ■ the number or proportion of unemployed people: *a time of high unemployment.* ■ short for UNEMPLOYMENT BENEFIT.

un•em•ploy•ment ben•e•fit (also **unemployment compensation**) ▸ n. a payment made by a government or a labor union to an unemployed person.

un•en•cum•bered ▸ adj. free of debt or other financial liability.

un•freeze ▸ v. (past **unfroze**; past part. **unfrozen**) remove restrictions on the use or transfer of (an asset).

un•fund•ed ▸ adj. not funded, in particular:
  ■ not receiving public funds. ■ (of a debt) repayable on demand rather than having been converted into a more or less permanent debt at fixed interest.

un•hedged ▸ adj. (of an investment or investor) not protected against loss by balancing or compensating contracts or transactions.

un•in•cor•po•rat•ed ▸ adj. (of a company or other organization) not formed into a legal corporation: *an unincorporated business.*

un•in•sur•a•ble ▸ adj. not eligible for insurance coverage.

un•in•sured ▸ adj. not covered by insurance.

un•is•sued ▸ adj. (esp. of shares of stock) not yet issued.

un•liq•ui•dat•ed ▸ adj. (of a debt) not cleared or paid off.

un•list•ed ▸ adj. denoting or relating to a company whose shares are not listed on a stock exchange.

un•mar•ket•a•ble ▸ adj. not marketable.

un•mer•chant•a•ble ▸ adj. not suitable for purchase or sale.

un•peg ▸ v. (**unpegged, unpegging**) cease to maintain a fixed relationship between (a currency) and another currency.

un•priced ▸ adj. having no marked or stated price.

un•quot•ed ▸ adj. not quoted or listed

on a stock exchange: *an unquoted company.*

un•se•cured ▸ adj. (of a loan) made without an asset given as security.
◼ (of a creditor) having made such a loan.

un•taxed ▸ adj. not subject to taxation.
◼ (of an item, income, etc.) not having had the required tax paid on it.

up•front informal ▸ adv. (usu. **up front**) (of a payment) in advance.
▸adj. (of a payment) made in advance.

up•mar•ket (also **up-market**) ▸ adj. & adv. upscale.

up•set price ▸ n. the lowest acceptable selling price for a property in an auction; a reserve price.

up•side ▸ n. [in sing.] an upward movement of stock prices.

u•til•i•ty ▸ n. (pl. **-ies**) a public utility.
◼ stocks and bonds in public utilities.

val•or•ize ▸ v. raise or fix the price or value of (a commodity or currency) by artificial means, esp. by government action.

val•u•a•tion ▸ n. the monetary worth of something, esp. as estimated by an appraiser.

val•ue ▸ v. (**values, valued, valuing**) (often **be valued**) estimate the monetary worth of (something).

val•ue add•ed ▸ n. the amount by which the value of an article is increased at each stage of its production, exclusive of initial costs.
▸adj. (**value-added**) (of goods) having features added to a basic line or model for which the buyer is prepared to pay extra.
◼ (of a company) offering specialized or extended services in a commercial area.

val•ue-add•ed tax (abbr.: **VAT**) ▸ n. a tax on the amount by which the value of an article has been increased at each stage of its production or distribution.

val•ue a•nal•y•sis ▸ n. the systematic and critical assessment by an organization of every feature of a product to ensure that its cost is no greater than is necessary to carry out its functions.

va•lu•ta ▸ n. the value of one currency with respect to its exchange rate with another.
◼ foreign currency.

VAR ▸ abbr. value-added reseller, a company that adds extra features to products it has bought before selling them on. ◼ value at risk, a method of quantifying the risk of holding a financial asset.

var•i•a•ble cost ▸ n. a cost that varies with the level of output.

var•i•ance ▸ n. (in accounting) the difference between expected and actual costs, profits, output, etc., in a statistical analysis.

VAT ▸ abbr. value added tax.

ve•loc•i•ty ▸ n. (pl. **-ies**) (also **velocity of circulation**) the rate at which money changes hands within an economy.

vend•ing ma•chine ▸ n. a machine that dispenses small articles such as food, drinks, or cigarettes when a coin, bill, or token is inserted.

ven•dor (also **vender**) ▸ n. a person or company offering something for sale, esp. a trader in the street.
◼ a person or company whose principal product lines are office supplies and equipment.

ven•dor plac•ing ▸ n. a type of placing used as a method of financing a takeover in which the purchasing company issues its own shares as payment to the company being bought, with the prearranged agreement that these shares are then placed with investors in exchange for cash.

ven•ture ▸ n. a business enterprise involving considerable risk.

ven•ture cap•i•tal ▸ n. capital invested in a project in which there is a substantial element of risk, typically a new or expanding business.

ver•ti•cal ▸ adj. involving all the stages from the production to the sale of a class of goods.

ver•ti•cal in•te•gra•tion ▸ n. the combination in one company of two or more stages of production normally operated by separate companies.

ver•ti•cal mar•ket ▸ n. a market comprising all the potential purchasers in a particular occupation or industry.

vi•at•i•cal set•tle•ment ▸ n. an arrangement whereby a person with a terminal illness sells their life insurance policy to a third party for less than its mature value, in order to benefit from the proceeds while alive.

vic•to•ry bond ▸ n. a bond issued by a government during or immediately after a major war.

vis•i•ble ▸ adj. of or relating to imports or exports of tangible commodities: *the visible trade gap.*

vouch•er ▸ n. a small printed piece of paper that entitles the holder to a discount or that may be exchanged for goods or services.
■ a receipt.

wage dif•fer•en•tial ▸ n. the difference in earnings between workers with different skills in the same industry or between workers with similar skills in different industries or localities.

wage drift ▸ n. the tendency for the average level of wages actually paid to rise above wage rates through increases in overtime and other factors.

Wal•ras' law a law stating that the total value of goods and money supplied equals that of goods and money demanded.

ware•house ▸ n. a large building where raw materials or manufactured goods may be stored before their export or distribution for sale.
■ a large wholesale or retail store.
▸v. store (goods) in a warehouse.
■ place (imported goods) in a bonded warehouse pending the payment of import duty.

ware•house club ▸ n. an organization that operates from a large store and sells goods in bulk at discounted prices to business and private customers who must first become club members.

ware•hous•ing ▸ n. the practice or process of storing goods in a warehouse.

war•rant ▸ n. a document that entitles the holder to receive goods, money, or services.
■ a negotiable security allowing the holder to buy shares at a specified price at or before some future date.

war•ran•ty ▸ n. (pl. -ies) a written guarantee, issued to the purchaser of an article by its manufacturer, promising to repair or replace it if necessary within a specified period of time.

wa•ter ▸ n. capital stock that represents a book value greater than the true assets of a company.
▸v. (usu. **be watered**) increase (a company's debt, or nominal capital) by the issue of new shares without a corresponding addition to assets.

weak ▸ adj. not in a secure financial position.
■ (of prices or a market) having a downward tendency.

weight•ing ▸ n. an allocated proportion of an investment.

when-is•sued ▸ adj. of or relating to trading in securities that have not yet been issued.

whip•saw ▸ v. (past part. **-sawn** or **-sawed**) (usu. **be whipsawed**) informal subject to a double loss, as when buying a security before the price falls and selling before the price rises.

white goods ▸ plural n. large electrical goods used domestically such as refrigerators and washing machines, typically white in color.

white knight ▸ n. a person or company making an acceptable counteroffer for a company facing a hostile takeover bid.

white sale ▸ n. a store's sale of household linens.

whole-life ▸ adj. relating to or denoting a life insurance policy that pays a specified amount only on the death of the person insured.

whole•sale ▸ n. the selling of goods in large quantities to be retailed by others.
▸adv. being sold in such a way.
▸v. sell (goods) in large quantities at low prices to be retailed by others.

whol•ly-owned ▸ adj. denoting a company all of whose shares are owned by another company.

wind•fall prof•its tax (also **windfall tax**) ▸ n. a tax levied on an unforeseen or unexpectedly large profit, esp. one regarded to be excessive or unfairly obtained.

wind•ing ▸ n. (**winding up**) the process

of closing down a company or a financial institution.

wire fraud ▸ n. financial fraud involving the use of telecommunications or information technology.

with•hold•ing tax ▸ n. the amount of an employee's pay withheld by the employer and sent directly to the government as partial payment of income tax.

work•ers' co•op•er•a•tive ▸ n. a business or industry owned and managed by those who work for it.

work•group ▸ n. a group within a workforce that normally works together.

work•ing cap•i•tal ▸ n. the capital of a business that is used in its day-to-day trading operations, calculated as the current assets minus the current liabilities.

write ▸ v. (past **wrote**; past part. **written**) underwrite (an insurance policy).

▸**write something off** cancel the record of a bad debt; acknowledge the loss of or failure to recover an asset.

write something up reduce the nominal value of stock or goods.

write-back ▸ n. the process of restoring to profit a provision for bad or doubtful debts previously made against profits and no longer required.

write-down ▸ n. a reduction in the estimated or nominal value of an asset.

write-off ▸ n. a cancellation from an account of a bad debt or worthless asset.

writ•er ▸ n. a broker who makes an option available for purchase or sells options.

write-up ▸ n. an increase in the estimated or nominal value of an asset.

xd ▸ abbr. ex dividend.

year end (also **year's end**) ▸ n. the end of the fiscal year.

yield ▸ v. (of a financial or commercial process or transaction) generate (a specified financial return).
▸ n. the amount of money brought in, e.g., interest from an investment, revenue from a tax; return.

yield curve ▸ n. a curve on a graph in which the yield of fixed-interest securities is plotted against the length of time they have to run to maturity.

yield gap ▸ n. the difference between the return on government-issued securities and that on ordinary shares.

zai•ba•tsu ▸ n. (pl. same) a large Japanese business conglomerate.

ze•ro-based ▸ adj. (of a budget or budgeting) having each item costed anew, rather than in relation to its size or status in the previous budget.

ze•ro-cou•pon bond ▸ n. a bond that is issued at a deep discount to its face value but pays no interest.

Index

BERKLEY OXFORD

THE WORLD TURNS TO OXFORD FOR ANSWERS.

THE OXFORD BUSINESS SPANISH DICTIONARY

0-425-19095-1

THE OXFORD ESSENTIAL DICTIONARY OF
ABBREVIATIONS

0-425-19704-2

THE OXFORD ESSENTIAL DICTIONARY OF
LEGAL WORDS

0-425-19706-9

THE OXFORD ESSENTIAL OFFICE HANDBOOK

0-425-19703-4